THE HIPPY GOURMET'S QUICK AND SIMPLE COOKBOOK FOR HEALTHY EATING

Bruce Brennan and James Ehrlich

with Elizabeth Butler-Witter

WELLNESS CENTRAL

NEW YORK   BOSTON

Andrew Field's Vegan Applesauce Cake, on page 260, appears courtesy of Raven's Restaurant at the Stanford Inn.

The Roasted Corn Sopes with Tomatillo Salsa, on page 157, appears courtesy of Gunnar Thompson, Raven's Restaurant at the Stanford Inn.

The Salad Olivier (page 95), Beet Salad (page 92), and vegan Borscht (page 122) recipes appear thanks to Larisa Blank of Lara's Delicious.

The Beet Tarts recipe, on page 140, appears courtesy of Martijn Kajuiter—Restaurant De Kas, Amsterdam.

Wellness Central
Hachette Book Group USA
237 Park Avenue
New York, NY 10017

Visit our Web site at www.HachetteBookGroupUSA.com.

Printed in the United States of America

First Edition: September 2007
10 9 8 7 6 5 4 3 2 1

Wellness Central is an imprint of Grand Central Publishing. The Wellness Central name and logo is a trademark of Hachette Book Group USA, Inc.

Library of Congress Cataloging-in-Publication Data

Brennan, Bruce.
    The hippy gourmet's quick and simple cookbook for healthy eating / Bruce Brennan
and James Ehrlich with Elizabeth Butler-Witter.
        p. cm.
    Includes index.
    ISBN-13: 978-0-446-69984-6
    ISBN-10: 0-446-69984-5
    1. Cookery (Natural foods) 2. Cookery, International 3. Natural foods. I. Ehrlich, James.
II. Butler-Witter, Elizabeth. III. Title.
    TX741.B64 2007
    641.5′63—dc22
                            2007004241

Book design by Anne Ricigliano.

Illustrations by Scott Buggeln; clip art from Nova Corporation.

Acknowledgments

Neither this book nor our show would be possible without the help of countless others. We'd like to give a word of thanks to these people, plus the many more who have helped us over the years.

Lena Blanc

Allen Duzak

Peter McGuigan

Natalie Kaire

Elizabeth Butler-Witter

Dennis Minnick

Gary Dominguez

Pam Brennan

Stan Marvin, KRCB

Luca Centoni and Phoenix Media

Mel and Dolores Ehrlich

Larisa Blank at Lara's Delicious

Boris Kapilev

Dano and the gang at Transcendental Hayride

Chris Cochran

Jamie Judd

Steven Fabing and Bay Area Recorders

Doron Amiron—Solar Living Institute

Jeffrey Weissman

Gayle Loeber, NETA

Neil Connan, TOTN

Alina Polyakova

Rick Tucker, NPAT

Buck Stoval

Ellen Abrams

Donna and Kevin Compton

David Dominguez

Manny the Hippie

Denise Olson

Jihyun Kim

Chet Helms

Allen Cohen

Steve Jobs and Apple Computer for all their support

Pat Derby and Ed Stewart at PAWSweb.org

St. Lawrence String Quartet

Dave Stoelk CBS TV
Hank Donat—Mr. San Francisco
Mr. Natural
M.E. Woodside
Peter Furlotte
Chef Doi, Doug and Jasmine Arrison
Paul and Julie, our Youthful Hippie Hosts
Teddy Witherington, SFLGBT
Chef Dorsey Manogue—Sanford House,
    Ukiah, CA
Scot Medbury—San Francisco, Conservatory
    of Flowers
Ray Kochevar and Robert Mazurek
    Monterey Bay Aquarium
Dennis and Nancy Freeze and Chef Rhonda
    Gollihar—Agate Cove Inn, Mendocino, CA
JCX Expendables, San Francisco, CA
Swiss Airlines
Chef Walter Alfare—Gate Gourmet, Zurich,
    Switzerland
Holland.com and the Netherlands Board
    of Tourism
Gert-Jan Haggeman, Chef Martijn Kajuiter,
    and Walter Abma—Restaurant De Kas,
    Amsterdam
Charles Vos—NH Barbizon Hotel
Katwouder Molen
Irene Hoeve
Janneke Weiss, Robert, and Ronald on
    Basisrust.nl

Rembert Vonk and Chef Andrew Gaskell—
    Grand Sofitel, Amsterdam
Ulpho Van Der Zalm—Djava, Den Hague
Chef Sander and Eric, It Rains Fishes, Den
    Hague
Albert Veerman and Chef Martijn Van
    Zwieten, Five Flies, Amsterdam
Chef Joop Braakeheke, En Pluche, and
    Le Garage, Amsterdam
Carmine and Chef Massimo at Cinema
    Paradiso, Amsterdam
Carlo Riccardi, Cowboy Guest Ranch, Italy
Chef Vittonio Siegheiri, Siegheiri Pizza, and
    Torta, Livorno, Italy
Chef Giuseppe at Locanda Lorena, Cinque
    Terra, Italy
Ivio and Tony Paperini at La Grotta, La
    Sassa, Italy
Walter Alfeo at Ceralti Vineyards
Michele Satta at Satta Vineyards
Giuseppina Grasso and Chef Maria
    Capaccioli at Lucumone in Papalonia,
    Italy
David and Bruno Gastildin at Osteria del
    Contadino in Italy
Roberto Volpi at Mira Mare, Livorno, Italy
G. Fuso Carmignani, Lucca, Italy
Joan and Jeff Stanford, Chef Gunner
    Thompson, and Chef Andrew Field,
    Stanford Inn, Medocino

Hawaiian Airlines

McNeil Wilson Public Relations

Chef Beverly Gannon at Hali'I Maile on Maui, HI

Chef James MacDonald at O'O Farms and I'O and Pacifco'O, Maui, HI

Drew and Oceana Castellini

Thomas and Eva Kofsack, Surfing Goat Dairy, Maui, HI

Kathy Nobriga at Roselani Ice Cream, Maui, HI

Lani Medina at Ali'I Kula Lavender Farm, Maui, HI

Chef Greg Gaspar and Kirk Nelson, Maui Prince Hotel

Chef Kirk Lowe and Gana Maheshwaran at Plantation Gardens, Kauai, HI

Stephanie Reid, Chef Todd Oldham, and Phil Davies, Princeville Resort, Kauai, HI

Chef Glen Chu at Indigo Restaurant, Oahu, HI

David Orr, Waimea Audubon Society

Stryker, Weiner, and Yokota PR

Chef Goran Streng at Waikiki Prince Hotel, Oahu, HI

Bernd Schmitt and Joachim Splichal

Susanne Mannion

Lufthansa Airlines, Jennifer Urbaniak, Thomas Stets, and Frank Hahn

Federica Damiani—STB Toscana

Antonio Niccoli, Chef Fabio Fanti, Andre Balleri, and Pasquale Lapore, Grotto Giusti, Italy

Roberto Tommasoni and Ivano Busciantella, Bagni di Pisa

Mauro Bonacini, Chef Franco Sanna, and Chef Daniele Turco at Gritti Palace, Venice, Italy

Chef Mauro Stoppa, Antonio Fiorentini, and Stefano Scutari, on Eolo in Venice, Italy

Orinda and Maria at Locande a la Porte

Minchio family, Paula, Paolo, Christian, and Chef Massimilan at Villa Goetzen in Dolo, Italy

Maurizio Martin Bonifacio Brass at Locande Cipriani

Chef Antonio Bufi, Pastry Chef Francesca Luri, and Sergio Fragiacomo at Bistro di Venise, Venice, Italy

Chef Corrado Corti and Chef Roberto Villa at Hotel Splendido, Portofino, Italy

Massimo D'Onofrio and Chef Nardi Marco at Calidario, Toscana, Italy

Marcello Cicalo—Delphina Resorts

Luca Cagliari, Chef Rosso Fernando Augusto, and Claudio Romanini at Capo d'Orso, Sardinia, Italy

Allesandro Fumagali and Chef Gianfranco Riccobono at La Marinedda Resort, Sardinia, Italy

Lorenzo Giannuzzi, Cristina Cesario, Chef
   Antonello Arruz, and Chef Roberto
   Chergia
Doctor Stefano Lampati at La Foce village
   and camping
Doctor Patrizia Fanni at Capo Ferrato,
   Sardinia, Italy
Gianfilillo Bellini and Chef Marco Battista
   at des Pecheurs on Corsica, France
Dr. Emiliano Marrucchi-Locatelli and
   Daniela Marrucchi-Locatelli at Pieve di
   Caminino, Italy
Michael Funk and Jason Ramey, Wild and
   Scenic Film Festival, Nevada City, CA
Farmer John Peterson and Lesley Littlefield,
   The Real Dirt on Farmer John
Jan Mettler, Boss Dog Marketing
Paul Dolan, Tom, Tim, and Roselle Thornhill
   at Mendocino Wine Co., Mendocino, CA
Mika Ryan, Cindy Burr, Kate Colley Lo, and
   Rick Graham, BC Tourism
Annabel Hawksworth and Kate Rogers
Katharine Carol—Granville Island, BC
Brian Hopkins and Chef David Hawksworth
   at West Restaurant, Vancouver, BC

Jeff VanGeest, Heidi Noble, and Michael
   Dinn at Aurora Bistro, Vancouver, BC
Stephanie Yuen
Hidekazu Tojo at Tojo's in Vancouver, BC
Vikram Vij at Vij's in Vancouver, BC
Alice Spurrell at les amid u Fromage,
   Vancouver, BC
Jason Boyce, Vancouver Aquarium
Harinder Toor at Punjab Food Center,
   Vancouver, BC
Chef Ray Henry, Jeremy Roncoroni, and
   Nicole Folino at Diva, Vancouver, BC
Frederique and Dr. Sinclair Philip and
   Chef Edward Tuson at Sooke Harbor
   House, Vancouver Island, BC
Hotel Grand Pacific, Victoria, BC
Bob Schneeveis
Lesley Nagy TV 20
Kevin Danaher Global Exchange, and
   the Green Festivals
Thu Tam
Medicine Mike
Pirate's Booty

Contents

Introduction
THE HIPPY WAY

Move from the great, swirling mass of stars that we call the Milky Way, to the big blue marble that is planet Earth, to a city perched by the edge of a great ocean ringed with fire, to a kitchen and a table and a bowl. There it is, dude . . . cosmic oatmeal. Maybe that's a dramatic introduction for a breakfast cereal, but when you're hungry, food really does seem to be the most important thing in the universe.

Maybe we have a strange way of viewing breakfast, but *The Hippy Gourmet* is happy to be strange. Eating a simple bowl of cereal touches countless lives, from the farmers who grow the grain, to the workers who harvest it, to our hearts and our bodies. Each of us is a part of something much bigger than ourselves, and so our little PBS cooking show is part of something much bigger, too.

Our show has been a journey, and what a long, strange trip it's been. *The Hippy Gourmet TV Show* began with a vision and a grainy high-eight video camera, and it's grown to a PBS show broadcast all over the country. We've filmed in locations as exotic as the middle of the Amazon, as luxurious as poolside at an Italian resort, and as simple as a kitchen back home in the Haight-Ashbury. We've cooked dishes as simple and homey as a big pot of chili and as wild and out there as gourmet ratatouille in a solar oven.

No matter where we film, or what we're cooking, the show's essential vision has stayed the same. We began as a show dedicated to peace, love, and good eats, and that's the spirit we've maintained. Our host, Bruce Brennan, began as the same man with a grand vision for the planet and an eye for dinner—even if he does try to connect the cosmic dots together all the time. Our producer, James Ehrlich, remains dedicated to making the show into a power for good, from using hemp plastic for our DVD containers to attracting the most dedicated organic farmers and chefs as our guests. Bruce brings his free-spirited and sometimes just plain wild vision, and James brings his producing talents and good sense. Both are still peaceful warriors fighting to change the world for the better, one meal at a time. These two men, our yin and yang, our id and ego, our Martin and Lewis, somehow balance their talents and work in synchronicity to produce something that everyone who touches our show can be proud of.

The *Hippy* in *Hippy Gourmet*

Bruce Brennan came of age during the heyday of the flower children. The show is about one hippy and his vision, not the entire hippie movement; that's why the show is spelled *Hippy* rather than *Hippie*. Bruce was always socially responsible—his participation in anti-Vietnam protests helped to get

him moved from a high school in New York to a free school in California—but it was changing the world through food that became his passion. Reading Euell Gibbons's *Stalking the Wild Asparagus* helped him realize that what we eat really is part of who we are. He started cooking natural and delicious foods for his friends and family.

After finishing Pacific High School in California, Bruce returned to New York, where he worked his way up through the ranks from dishwasher and ultimately became a line chef at the IBM Executive Training Center in Sands Point, New York. He cooked for the upper management and executives in the elegant Mediterranean-style dining room and catered all their events.

Bruce then escaped from the beast that is corporate America and hitchhiked his way around the country, trading his talents with his pots and pans for rides and tickets to shows. At both Woodstock and Altamont, Bruce prepared food for wayward travelers.

Eventually, Bruce and his sister Pam picked up everything and moved to the heart of the Haight-Ashbury. Bruce quickly found himself cooking for literally hundreds of people a day. He "served his country" not by feeding the military-industrial complex but by feeding hungry hippies as they danced and twirled up to his soup pots.

During this time, Bruce continued on his personal path of learning about sustainable agriculture and wild food sources. He foraged for ingredients in the forests of Northern California, then shared his knowledge with others. He taught folks how to live off the land and nourish themselves with delicious, all-natural food. His travels took him far, from building geodesic domes in Nova Scotia, Canada, to hitchhiking the highways of the United States, and, always, journeying and learning. He even saw a UFO or two, but those were the 1960s, and it's hard to know for sure.

Bruce eventually returned to California, where he cooked professionally. He catered for everyone from Stevie Nicks to Francis Ford Coppola. Even Ronald Reagan sampled the wares. Bruce soon became adept at serving large-scale events, and he knew how to please every palate and taste.

In 1988, Bruce's sister Pam opened The Herb'n Inn and realized her vision of establishing a bed-and-breakfast that was more than a place to crash. She built a revolving international family. Pam understood that Bruce's culinary expertise, familiarity with commercial kitchens, and love of herb and vegetable gardening had a place in this family. Together, they were soon serving breakfast to hungry travelers from around the world. The business flourished and word about the "cool and cozy little inn in the heart of the Haight" spread around the globe.

If You're Going to San Francisco . . .

Bruce was back in his spiritual home, and, no matter how far abroad we travel, it is the place that will always be the spiritual home of *The Hippy Gourmet TV Show* as well. In the 1960s, young people hungered for something more than some corrupt, consumerist dream, and they found it in California. The Haight-Ashbury was the center of psychedelic music, of underground art and comics, of love and peace. And thanks to Bruce and those like him, it was also home to a new way of eating. A lot has changed about the Haight over the years, but its heart and soul, and the heart and soul of those who stayed and made it a home, have remained unchanged.

Bruce stayed in the Haight, and he might have cooked for a relatively small audience if a man with a media background hadn't noticed him. James Ehrlich realized that others shared Bruce's love of food that was both hippy and gourmet, and he came along and put *The Hippy Gourmet* on the screen. The show succeeded because it never went far from the Haight, either physically or spiritually. Even in episodes when we jet around the globe, we still take time to interview the people passing through the streets.

James never sought to make Bruce into a big-shot TV host—though he did convince him to trim the beard . . . just a little. He didn't turn him into some cookie-cutter "personality" who baked with a certain brand of flour just because its maker happened to be the sponsor that day. Instead, he let Bruce be the free spirit he always was, let him cook how he always cooked, and left him and the show to blossom naturally.

The Hippy Way

Looking at our country today, you might suspect that the 1960s never happened. Even the Haight is home to chain stores and expensive condos. But that's not the whole picture. Everything from the Clean Water Act to hybrid vehicles and solar power are manifestations of the hippie movement. There are tiny acts of charity and big acts of rebellion everywhere you look. Our show has a following of people of all ages and backgrounds who share the same vision of

good times and togetherness while living on a clean and peaceful planet.

We're not going to give some manifesto of what we believe. The hippy way, after all, is about making your own way, not following some other guy's rule book. Still, these are the beliefs that our show stands for, the things that put the *hippy* in *Hippy Gourmet*. It doesn't mean going out and joining a commune. It just means living, and eating, in a sensible, life-affirming way.

- **Sustainability.** In the food we buy, and how we cook it, we want to leave as little impact on Mother Earth as possible. That means buying food produced without antibiotics and with no pesticides and herbicides. We buy and cook organically or sustainably grown food on the show, and we feature where it comes from whenever possible.

- **Eliminating Waste.** We don't leave any garbage behind. We try to use every bit of what we buy or grow, and recycle or compost what we can't. We use reusable or biodegradable serving utensils and plates. Eating this way can be a lot of fun; look at the people in Southeast Asia eating out of banana leaves, and you see how a culture can eliminate waste in a convenient, and delicious, way.

* **Exploration.** We travel the world on the show. We explore new cultures, foods, and ideas. We also like to explore inside ourselves. It's a big, beautiful world out there, even in terms of experiencing new tastes and flavors. Every day, we try something new, and every day we learn a new pleasure.

* **Vegan, Vegetarian, and Pescatarian Food.** The lower we eat on the food chain, the less impact we make on the world. Vegans generally try to avoid any food that comes from an animal. Vegetarians eat no meat, but they may eat eggs or dairy products. Pescatarians are vegetarians who will also eat fish and seafood. We're not into labels. If you want to be an omnivore and eat meat occasionally, we're not going to come down on you. Although if you do make the choice of eating meat, it sure does make more sense to buy free-range and hormone-free products. And the Hippy Gourmet does his best to feature and stand behind the vegan and vegetarian lifestyle.

* **Caring.** Life is about more than being focused on your immediate friends and family. It is way too easy for us to get caught up in a pod-like lifestyle that sequesters us from the community at large. We highlight worthy organizations such as the Monterey Bay Aquarium, CARE, Red Cross, GlobalExchange.org, GreenFestivals.org, Co-Op America, and PAWSweb.org. These brave people are changing the world one heart at a time. Finding a worthy nonprofit to donate your time and energy to is one of the most rewarding parts about being human.

* **Celebrating Every Instant.** Our show is infused with the joy of good eating, good living, and good music. Transcendental Hayride, a local San Francisco jam band, provides our music. It's the spirit of freedom, of loving, of letting loose and being ourselves. Edible flowers and decorative fruits and vegetables on the plate aren't just garnishes. They add beauty and joy to what we're doing, and whatever spreads the love spreads the peace.

Cooking the Hippy Way

Whatever else we stand for, the show's main goal is to help spread the joy of hippy gourmet cooking. Cooking the hippy way is as simple as following your pleasure. Pull a perfectly ripe peach from a sun-speckled branch.

Its rich, sweet scent is stronger in the sunlight. It's heavy, solid, yet giving. Its down is soft in your hand. Bite into it. Feel the skin grow taut beneath your teeth, then burst in a rush of sweet juice. That's how eating should feel. It should be a joy for you, and it should be a joy to share with those you love.

How do you get that pleasure every time you eat? Simple. Pick the freshest, most natural ingredients you can find. No, biting into a perfect brussels sprout won't have all the rich, decadent pleasure of the perfect peach, but it will thrill in its own way. Eating good food makes you feel good, inside and out. It's not just a matter of what your cholesterol count or blood pressure numbers are—though becoming healthy will naturally follow if you eat healthy food; eating well is about finding pleasure and joy in every day.

It isn't always easy to find the perfect anything, especially if you're shopping in a conventional supermarket. You can't touch and smell and enjoy produce when everything is wrapped in layers of plastic.

So how do you find great food?

* **Grow it yourself.** Bruce made our own oasis from the big city here in San Francisco. Even if you don't have a yard, you can grow a few herbs. Try experimenting with plants that grow in small containers; there's even a variety of tomato called "patio" for those who don't have more than a couple of square feet of concrete to call their own. Get out there and get your hands dirty. Even if all you succeed in raising is a big clump of soil, you'll feel better and more relaxed for making the effort.

* **Participate in a community garden.** Many cities and towns have communal areas to garden. These are great both for those who live in cramped apartments and for those who have more space but want to grow alongside their neighbors. Some provide separate plots to each family, and some pool the labor and the harvest. Check out community bulletin boards, ask your neighbors, and phone your local representatives to find if there's one in your community—or to ask that your community start one.

* **Go to local farmers' markets.** In one of our episodes, we traveled to an Italian market; it's the heart and soul of local culture. Here in the United States, farmers' markets are full of the spirit of dedicated growers and buyers. You'll find the freshest food available, and you'll dis-

cover a lot of unusual produce you might never have known about otherwise. When was the last time you saw cardoons or rainbow chard at the big-box store down the road? At the farmers' market, you'll not only find these things, you'll find out what on earth to do with them. Take some time to talk to the farmers, and you'll learn what's best when, and how to cook your finds. If you don't know where a farmers' market is, check your local newspapers, cruise the Internet, or ask the best source available—the neighbor down the street whose kitchen always smells so good.

* **Get involved with CSA.** That's an acronym for "Community Supported Agriculture." In CSA, people get together and support one or more local farms by paying a lump sum at the beginning of the growing season, then picking up whatever has just been harvested (always a surprise!) on a weekly basis. It's a great way to feel involved in the process of raising food, and you'll get some fine produce in the bargain, much of which you've probably never heard of before. Knowing where your food comes from is a whole lot of fun, and getting

that box can feel like Christmas. We did a wonderful episode featuring Farmer John Peterson and his movie *The Real Dirt on Farmer John*. It's about a struggling Midwestern farmer who, in connection with a CSA, converts his family farm to 100 percent organic and ends up resurrecting an entire community. To find out more, you can visit Farmer John at www.angelicorganics.com and also www.localharvest.org.

* **Shop at a natural or health food store**. There are a number of local and national natural food stores today with a good selection of produce, though often at much higher prices than you'll find at the farmers' market or a CSA. Food labeled "organic" at these stores will have been grown according to standards set by the US Department of Agriculture (USDA). If you buy organic, you know that the food was grown without synthetic pesticides and fertilizers, without sewer sludge, and without genetic engineering. "Natural" food, on the other hand, can mean just about anything, but generally refers to minimally processed food. Natural food stores aren't always as fresh as the farmers'

In the Mood for Something Wild?

There are more fruits and vegetables out there than we could ever list, and we learn about new ones almost every day. You may not find the following in your corner store, or in all parts of the country, but keep an eye out for them at farmers' markets and specialty produce stores. As your mother always said, the only way to know if you like it is to try it. Here are just a few of many interesting ones.

Jerusalem Artichokes

Description: This edible tuber looks a lot like a sunflower growing in the wild and can grow upward of seven feet tall! The plant is beautiful, but the beauty for eaters is at the base of the Jerusalem artichoke. If you grab the stalks and uproot the entire plant, you'll discover a bunch of potato-like tubers clinging to the roots.

What Do I Do with This Thing? Wash them carefully, making sure to get all the soil and dirt off. Then you can slice them up and steam them, fry them, pan-sauté them, or even make a wonderful dip!

Calabaza

Description: This thing looks like a monstrously big green pumpkin. It has bright orange flesh similar to more familiar winter squashes. It's a well-loved food all over the Caribbean—and its nutritional value may be why all those islanders look so good in their bathing suits.

What Do I Do with This Thing? Cut away the hard outer shell, and scrape out the seeds and strings. You can substitute it in a recipe calling for winter squashes such as butternut or kabocha. One delicious way of preparing it is to cut it into chunks and steam or boil until tender. Then toss with a bit of olive oil, lime juice, minced garlic, and salt.

Fiddlehead Ferns

Description: These little beauties pop up in the spring in parts of the United States and Canada. If you've ever seen newly budded ferns on a walk in the woods, you've seen plants that look a whole lot like the scroll at the end of a fiddle. If you know what you're doing, you can go right out and harvest them yourself, especially in the woods of Appalachia or southeastern Canada, or look for them in gourmet markets and some farmers' markets. Fiddleheads are mild and fresh tasting, sort of like a tender asparagus.

What Do I Do with This Thing? Cut off any brown on the stem end, and rinse them well. Carefully rub off any hairs while you wash them. Sauté or stir-fry them briefly in a tiny bit of oil, season them with salt and pepper, and they're ready to eat.

Kohlrabi

Description: In German, *kohlrabi* means "cabbage turnip," and it's one funky-looking vegetable. It looks a little bit like a turnip with strange appendages jutting out from the side, and it can be light green or even purple.

What Do I Do with This Thing? The whole thing, including the leaves, is edible, though the outer layer is tough and hard. The best thing to do is cut away the outer layer, revealing the more tender, white inside, which should be sliced. It can be eaten raw—try adding thin strips to salad or coleslaw—or cooked. Throw it in with some mixed root vegetables next time you're cooking up a pan of braised or roasted vegetables. It's always fun to have your friends and family try to pick out what the different roasted vegetables are and maybe discover a new favorite.

What's Ripe

The following chart provides a general idea of what's seasonal in most of the United States and Canada. If you live in the extreme South or North, your food will be ripe earlier or later, and if you live in California, anything goes. People who live in moderate, fertile climates like the Pacific Northwest are going to have an easier time of it, but we can all find delicious, locally grown treasures. Some fruits and vegetables span a couple of seasons; some grape and pear varieties, for instance, start in the summer, and others are best in the fall. This is just meant to give you a general idea of what's best and when.

Autumn

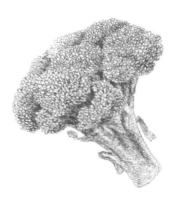

Hard squashes such as acorn, butternut, or spaghetti
Apples
Pears
Hearty greens (such as Swiss chard and kale)
Beets
Broccoli
Brussels sprouts and cabbages

Winter

Citrus such as grapefruit and oranges
Pineapples

Many vegetables are still good in the winter, even if they were harvested other times of year: cabbage, celeriac, potatoes, hard squashes, onions, carrots, turnips, and rutabagas. Think of things that old-timers would have stored in root cellars and then cooked up in hearty stews, and you have a pretty good idea of what makes good winter eating.

Spring

Asparagus
Artichokes (look for those tiny ones that are entirely edible)
English peas
Rhubarb (late spring to late summer)
Salad greens
Mangoes (depending on your variety, through late summer)
Green garlic and ramps

Summer

Apricots
Berries (though you'll find these as early
   as February and March in Texas
   and Florida)
Plums
Figs
Peaches and nectarines

Melons
Corn
Summer squashes
Peppers
Tomatoes
Okra

market, but unlike the case at the conventional grocery store, at least you'll know what you're getting.

❧ **If a supermarket is your only option, buy what's in season and try to buy organic whenever possible.** We're all busy, so don't beat yourself up if you don't have the time and the money to raise your own corn and tomatoes—you need good food, not a load of guilt. Do the best you can and look for what's freshest, what's seasonal, and you'll get the best for yourself and your family.

Thinking Globally, Buying Locally

The best way to ensure that you're eating only the best produce, and creating the least impact on the planet (since more travel time means more gas and more pesticides and preservatives), is to eat seasonally and locally. It doesn't take a lot of sleuthing to discover that the apricot you're eating in Minnesota in January probably wasn't raised down the road.

Does that mean that you always have to eat locally? Of course not. People in the Pacific Northwest want to eat a juicy mango now and then, just like people in Florida

want to bite into a crisp apple. It simply means that, for the bulk of our food buying, we should try to buy ingredients that come from closer to home. How? Buy what's in season in your area, and if your grocer doesn't label where the food comes from—and even large conventional grocers are doing this nowadays—ask.

Many people have no idea what seasonal means anymore. You can buy uniform asparagus, tomatoes, and cherries any time of year in most supermarkets. All of it's mostly uniformly tasteless, too; following the natural rhythms of the soil means you won't get all foods all of the time, but it does mean the food will be at its peak when you do get it.

Nature doesn't run on our calendar; temperatures and moisture vary, and so do the foods that depend on them to grow. The best way to know what's ripe is sticking your nose out and seeing what's best in your garden or local market.

Buying in Bulk

Not so long ago, when you bought dried food from the grocer a clerk would scoop it out of a bin, put it in a sack, and you'd take it home. There were no brand names, no fancy printed boxes, and no layers upon layers of plastic wrap. Man, it was a hippy dream world. Yet somehow we were taught that if it's not in a shiny package, it must be hard to prepare and eat.

So manufacturers put their food in boxes, slapped on a label, and charged higher prices. And consumers started paying a lot more for the same old cereals and grains.

Do you really want to pay more for a fancy label and lots of wasteful packaging? To get the highest-quality food at the best prices, the most sensible way to shop is buying in bulk. This doesn't mean picking up the economy pack of highly processed cookies; it means purchasing the quantities you want of the foods you need.

Bulk food is available at health food markets, food co-ops, and certain national natural food stores. You'll find bin upon bin of cereals, grains, and legumes. At most stores, you either scoop the food from a barrel or pour it from a dispenser into a bag yourself, label it, and pay at the cashier. It's not much more work than picking a box off the shelf; you'll save money because you buy only what you're actually going to use, and you aren't paying for extra packaging. Plus, it's a lot of fun to look at all the colors and shapes of the grains and beans. If you want

to save resources, most stores will let you bring your own bags, and they'll subtract the weight at the cashier.

So what do you buy in bulk? Cereals such as granola and wheat flakes are fairly self-explanatory, as are nuts. Familiar grains such as barley, cornmeal, and rice, as well as less well-known grains, including quinoa, are available in bulk. You can also buy pastas, including couscous, at most stores. Dried legumes—for example, black beans, kidney beans, and adzuki beans—are among the many protein-packed choices you might find. Some stores carry other foods, like dried fruit and candy.

Buying in bulk gets rid of one more level of consumerism and puts you right back where you want to be, in front of a steaming hot bowl of delicious good eating.

Using This Book

This book is divided into chapters on breakfast, munchies (appetizers and snacks), salads, soups and stews, vegetarian and vegan main dishes, pescatarian main dishes, bean and grain side dishes, vegetable side dishes, and desserts.

Because this is hippy cooking, however, don't limit yourself when it comes to deciding what's a "main" dish. A grain and a legume together from the bean and grain "side dish" chapter make a full and satisfying meal. Don't get boxed in by the idea that a meal must include meat, potatoes, and sides. Instead, try new combinations, eat what tastes good and satisfies your body, and don't worry about labels.

Many of our dishes are vegan (no animal products) friendly, and all are either vegetarian (no meat) or pescatarian (no meat except fish and seafood) friendly. While we don't specify this in the recipes, it's always better to go with organic ingredients if they're available to you. These dishes run the gamut from those so simple you could cook them in a dorm room on a hot plate to elaborate dinner-party fare. While some recipes are not as healthy as others—Bruce's training is as a French chef, after all—all are satisfying and use minimally processed ingredients.

We hope you explore this book with an open mind and an open heart. Try something you've never tasted. If you don't like it, at least you've learned something new and had an experience. We want to open up our readers to new things and share some of the fun we've had making the show. *The Hippy Gourmet* is about growing and sharing, and we hope you do a little of your own.

Peace, love, and good eats.

1. Breakfast

When Australian television comes to call, what do you cook them for breakfast? A few years ago, when we became known outside the United States, *Sunrise*—the Aussie version of *Good Morning America*—traveled across the world to visit us, and we wanted to make our friends from Down Under welcome. You can't throw another shrimp on the barbie first thing in the morning. These people have traveled from the other side of the world. They're jet-lagged. They're rumpled. They're surrounded by folks who speak in funny accents. You want to give them something as all-American as apple pie and as comforting as Grandma's hugs. They need a big, hippy-style welcome.

Pancakes and maple syrup were the answer. America didn't invent the pancake; from the crepe to the blini to the roti to the tortilla, everybody the world over seems to have some version of the cooked, flat cake. All you need is a fire and a flat pan, or even a stone. Even if flat bread is universal, though, pancakes are something that America has taken and made its own. Ours are sweet, soft, and fluffy. Sure, Americans eat too much sugar, but who worries about that when they've got a fresh homemade pancake hot off the griddle? So we decided to whip up a big batch of Blueberry Pecan Pancakes.

We brought our best organic stuff to impress our fellow colonials. Organic maple syrup, that is. Pancakes wouldn't be pancakes without the real thing; it would be like the Fourth of July without fireworks. Maple syrup is one of the products our country can truly be proud of. It's all-natural, it's environmentally responsible, and nothing tastes quite so rich and complex.

Those pancakes went down faster than you can say "G'day, mate." The Australians seemed to be impressed with us, even if we were Americans. Pancakes once again did their magic in spreading peace and love.

As Bruce learned in his years co-hosting The Herb'n Inn, nothing makes friends so fast as sharing breakfast. You've just started the day, and you're fresh, open, unguarded, and ready for anything. You're sharing a table, sharing something that we all need and love. Breaking bread—or Blueberry Pecan Pancakes—is the universal way to open your heart. Maybe what our leaders need isn't more protests and angry letters but to sit down together to a good old-fashioned pancake breakfast.

Breakfast gives energy and warmth to take with you throughout the day. *The Hippy Gourmet* has always encouraged an honest-to-goodness meal of real food, whatever food you choose. We've eaten breakfasts off fine china in some of the finest hotels in Europe, and we've picked whatever we could find near the side of the road. Breakfast doesn't have to be bacon and eggs.

The more we see of the world, the less we're sure that it even has to be limited to the cereals, pancakes and waffles, and scrambles—and cold pizza, of course—that Americans understand as breakfast food. Whatever makes you feel happy and comfortable for the rest of the day is the best breakfast food for you to eat.

On the show, we've watched our guests cook some meals that could make the biggest slugabed jump up and say "Pancakes." We visited the Sanford House in Ukiah, California, for the kind of all-organic breakfast that the lucky guests eat every morning, and we watched guest chef Dorsey Manogue cook an awesome breakfast feast, including fresh fruit smoothies and whole wheat bagels topped with olive tapenade, rosemary, and poached eggs. These foods were more or less traditional breakfasts, and we love them, but we're also open to new things.

Your grandparents may think that breakfast isn't breakfast if it doesn't come with a big piece of fatty meat on the side, and your little brother may have thought that the ultimate morning meal was the crunchy sugar bombs advertised on the Saturday cartoons, but you can make the hippy way your way in the morning. Rich, creamy fruit smoothies, fresh-baked muffins, and whole-grain granola not only taste a whole lot better than deep-fried processed junk, but will also give you energy and a clear head for the rest of the day. Sugary snacks and fatty meats will leave you feeling tired and unsatisfied.

If you're bored of the same old bowl of granola, look to the rest of the world for inspiration. In our travels on the show, we always like to see what locals eat and when; one thing we've learned is that "breakfast" isn't as rule-bound or repetitive as it is in this country. In parts of China, a thick rice stew called congee or jook is a creamy and satisfying background for all sorts of flavors.

Italians have a rich cup of coffee with milk and sometimes a small pastry. The Japanese might have a comforting bowl of hot miso soup and rice. In Jamaica, you might eat ackee, a fruit that looks like scrambled eggs when cooked, and salted fish.

This chapter has dishes that are, for the most part, conventional breakfast food. But go ahead and turn to the rest of the book for inspiration. Don't let the rules tell you that you have to have eggs or bagels unless that's what you really want; the hippy way is making your own way, at breakfast or anytime.

Super-Easy Breakfasts

Super-easy breakfasts don't have to come out of a box or from a drive-through. When we're filming the show, life isn't always as easygoing as we'd like it, and we find that simple recipes like this help a lot. If you want to get up at the crack of dawn to make a steaming pot of grain or warm, fresh bread for breakfast, that's great; there's nothing quite as beautiful as quietly cooking and contemplating during the first quiet hours of morning. For those of us who need to get out the door, however—or would rather snuggle in bed in the lazy morning—quick recipes can give a warming, nutritious start to the day. Here are a few options that come from nature, not the factory—and you can make them in a few minutes.

Quick Hot Cereal

Using leftover grains in a new way is hippy cooking at its best: It prevents waste, it nourishes the body, and it's delicious. Use the grains, nuts, milks, and fruits you like most. It's too early in the morning to worry about following someone else's rules.

 SERVES 1

½ cup cooked grain, such as millet, amaranth, barley, quinoa, or brown rice

½ cup milk of your choice, such as almond, soy, rice, hazelnut, or cow's

Toppings of your choice: fresh or dried fruit, nuts, cinnamon, nutmeg, honey, brown rice syrup, or maple syrup to taste

Place the grain and milk in a saucepan over medium heat. Heat until warmed through, about 5 minutes. Serve with toppings of your choice.

To increase serving sizes, just double, triple, quadruple . . . whatever you want.

Basic Smoothie

Go free, expand your mind, and riff on this however you want. Use fruit juice instead of milk, substitute another fruit for the banana, or use the extras as you want—it's your smoothie, your personality. Add or take away whatever you like; if it isn't to your taste, you can always try again tomorrow morning.

SERVES 1

¹/₂ frozen banana

¹/₂ cup milk of your choice, such as almond, rice, soy, or cow's

³/₄ cup fresh or frozen fruit, such as berries, peaches, papaya, kiwi, pear, or whatever is in season

Extras: about 1 tablespoon ground flaxseeds, sweetener of your choice to taste, about 1 tablespoon fresh herbs (such as mint or lavender), about ¹/₂ tablespoon cocoa powder, about ¹/₂ tablespoon bee pollen, about ¹/₈ teaspoon spices (such as cinnamon or nutmeg), about ¹/₂ teaspoon brewer's yeast, 1–2 tablespoons protein powder,

about ¹/₂ tablespoon lemon juice, about 1 teaspoon grated gingerroot

Place all the ingredients in a blender. Add extras of your choice for taste or nutritional value, if desired. Blend at high speed until the smoothie reaches the consistency that you like.

For more servings, double or triple the ingredients. Just keep in mind the size of your blender. Nobody wants to sponge strawberries and bananas off their walls at the crack of dawn.

Smoothies are best made right before you drink them, but if you can't face rolling out of bed 5 minutes early, make it the night before, cover it well, and refrigerate.

Tofu Smoothie

Totally vegan, totally natural, totally awesome . . . it's all about the bean, man. Tofu is as much at home in a blender as in a wok. The awesome, many-faceted soybean can take almost any form, even a sweet breakfast drink. Be sure to use some form of sweetener, since without it the legume flavor can be a bit too strong. If you're using stevia, use a very small quantity; this little plant packs quite a wallop. Add extras for taste or nutritional value if desired.

 SERVES 1

$^1/_2$ cup soy milk

4 ounces silken tofu

$^3/_4$ cup frozen fruit of your choice

1–2 teaspoons honey (substitute another sweetener, such as agave juice or stevia, if you wish)

Extras: about 1 tablespoon ground flaxseeds, sweetener of your choice to taste, about 1 tablespoon fresh herbs (such as mint or lavender), about $^1/_2$ tablespoon cocoa powder, about $^1/_2$ tablespoon bee pollen, about

$^1/_8$ teaspoon spices (such as cinnamon or nutmeg), about $^1/_2$ teaspoon brewer's yeast, 1–2 tablespoons protein powder, about $^1/_2$ tablespoon lemon juice, about 1 teaspoon grated gingerroot

Place all the ingredients in a blender. Blend at high speed until the smoothie reaches the consistency you like.

For more servings, just double or triple. When it comes to tofu, share all the love you can.

Nutritional Extras

If you eat a well-balanced diet, lots of supplements aren't necessary. If we listen to our bodies and follow the rhythms of nature when we eat, we can be perfectly healthy without a cartload of supplements that were manufactured in some factory. Sometimes, though, we feel a little under the weather, or we're not taking the time to eat perfectly. The following supplements might help. Better yet, ask a nutritionist to help you come up with your perfect smoothie blend.

Ground Flaxseeds: Flaxseeds can be found ground or whole in health food stores. They provide healthy oils that may lower your cholesterol, and they're packed with fiber. They'll add some bulk and a slightly nutty flavor to your smoothie.

Bee Pollen: This supplement is found in health food stores. It won't affect the taste of your smoothie, but it will provide a big boost in your vitamin intake. Some people believe that locally made pollen helps with allergies.

Brewer's Yeast: This form of yeast—not the kind typically used in baking—is found in health food stores. It's a great source of nutrients, including vitamin B_{12}, which vegans may find difficult to get from food sources. It's a little bitter, so add it to smoothies with a sparing hand.

Stevia: The stevia plant looks like any other herb, but put one leaf in your mouth and all you taste is pure sweetness. Liquid or powdered stevia extracts add sweetness to your food without adding calories, and they contain none of the strange chemicals found in artificial sweeteners. Be forewarned, though: Stevia is powerfully sweet, and some brands may have a bit of a bitter aftertaste.

Protein Powder: These powders are found even in many conventional grocery stores and pharmacies these days. Protein powders help vegetarians and vegans make sure that they're getting all the protein they need. They thicken a smoothie, and definitely add the taste of the powder.

Breakfast Parfait

*E*xplore the layers in this simple, beautiful breakfast dish. This is a great way to get picky children, or guests who swear that bacon is the only breakfast worth having, to eat a nutritious morning meal.

 SERVES 1

$^1/_2$ cup homemade or store-bought granola

$^3/_4$ cup favorite plain or sweetened yogurt (cow's, goat's, sheep's, or soy milk)

$^3/_4$ cup seasonal fruit

Optional layers: sweetened, flaked coconut, nuts of your choice, dried fruit, candied ginger, or whatever you think looks and tastes good

Honey to taste (optional)

Select a parfait glass or any nice-looking clear glass. Now's the time to break out those awesome finds from all your travels. Spoon layers of granola, yogurt, and fruit into the glass. Add any optional layers you like, too. For a wild and crazy parfait, you can even tilt the glass on its side when you add the ingredients for layers that are just a little off kilter, like us. If desired, drizzle a small amount of honey over the top.

Baked Goods

Baked goods are nature's magic at work. Yeast is alive. It's unpredictable. It's beautiful. Although bread takes some effort, watching the yeast turn ordinary flour and water into something delicious is a wonder of nature everyone should experience at least once.

Braided Whole Wheat Bread

Get your hands down and dirty, and feel that life-giving dough the way your ancestors did. Fresh whole wheat bread is by no means a quick breakfast, but by making some on the weekend, you can have a week's worth of homey meals.

 MAKES 2 LOAVES

2 cups stone-ground unbleached white flour

2 cups whole wheat flour

1³/₄ cups warm water, divided

3 tablespoons active dry yeast

1 tablespoon salt

¹/₄ cup brown sugar

¹/₄ cup vegetable shortening

2 tablespoons milk

Splash of olive oil

Enough butter to grease pans

1 pat butter, melted

Mix the two kinds of flours and 1¹/₄ cups of the water in a mixing bowl (or the bowl of an electric mixer).

In a separate bowl, combine the remaining ¹/₂ cup water and the yeast. Let this mixture sit until bubbles form, about 5 minutes. Add the salt, brown sugar, vegetable shortening, yeast mixture, and milk to the flour-water mixture.

To really experience bread making, mix by hand until dough pulls away from the sides of the bowl. It should be sticky and elastic. Continue kneading for several minutes. Or, if you are using an electric mixer, use the dough hook attachment on low for about 5 minutes.

Place the dough in a bowl coated with a splash of olive oil. Cover with a clean kitchen towel and let rise in a warm place for about 1 hour. Remove the dough and punch it down (push the dough to remove any large pockets of air). Slice in half. Then cut one of the halves into thirds. Roll each third out by hand (it helps to lightly coat your hands in flour first) to about 12 to 18 inches long. Braid the three strands together. Pinch the ends together to form a braided loaf. Repeat the procedure with the other half of the dough.

Butter one extra-large baking sheet (17 × 12 inches) or two regular baking sheets (15 × 12 inches)—whatever it takes to fit the loaves. Place the braided dough on the pan(s) and cover with plastic wrap. Let rise for about 1 hour.

While the loaves sit, preheat the oven to 400 degrees.

Remove the plastic wrap and place the bread in the oven for 25 minutes, or until it sounds hollow when you tap it. When it's done, place it on cooling racks and brush on the melted butter. Allow it to sit until completely cool, about an hour or so. To store, keep in an airtight container or wrap in plastic wrap.

French "Freedom" Toast

olitical winds blow this way and that, so don't let them into the kitchen to spoil a perfectly good breakfast. No matter what your political sympathies, you'll love this delicious brunch recipe. Share a little breakfast and a little peace.

🍓 SERVES 3–6

1 cup peeled and sliced papaya

6 strawberries

$\frac{1}{3}$ cup apple juice

$\frac{1}{2}$ plus $\frac{1}{8}$ teaspoon ground cinnamon, divided

6 slices whole-grain wheat bread (homemade or store-bought)

3 eggs

$\frac{1}{2}$ cup milk

1 teaspoon vanilla extract

Oil to grease skillet

Maple syrup (optional)

Sliced banana and mango (optional)

In a blender or food processor, blend the papaya, strawberries, apple juice, and $\frac{1}{2}$ teaspoon of the cinnamon. Pour the mixture into a glass bowl.

Preheat a skillet or griddle over a medium flame.

Soak each piece of whole wheat bread in the fruit mixture for a second or two on each side.

In a separate bowl, add the eggs, milk, vanilla, and remaining $\frac{1}{8}$ teaspoon cinnamon. Mix well with a fork. Soak each piece of bread for a second or two in the egg-milk bowl.

Lightly oil the hot skillet or griddle. Cook the bread for a minute or two on each side, or until golden brown. Serve with real maple syrup and slices of either banana or mango along the side.

What on Earth Is Mochi?

Mochi is a Japanese product made when steamed glutenous (sticky) rice is pounded and then made into cakes. It is eaten as a traditional New Year's food or as a snack all year round. In Japan, mochi is usually made with a variety of white rice, and it's often made into sweets. But in the United States, mochi is often made with brown rice and it's eaten more as a health food. Whatever kind of mochi you eat, it's delicious. Mochi is gooey and chewy and, if it's baked, crisp on the outside.

It's possible to make your own homemade mochi by pounding steamed, glutenous rice with a large mortar or round, flat piece of wood, but you'll need a lot of friends with strong arms to get the proper consistency. You can find mochi in the refrigerated section of most health food stores and some large conventional supermarkets. Use your imagination with American-style mochi. Try it plain or with syrup, dipped in soy sauce, alongside soups and stews, or stuffed with your favorite savory ingredients (such as scrambled tofu or bean salad).

To cook American-style mochi, cut it into small squares, place on a baking sheet, and bake in a 450-degree oven until puffy and crisp on the outside (about 10 minutes). Serve some vegan sausage and fresh fruit on the side, and you have an impressive meal.

Blueberry Pecan Pancakes

*T*hese pancakes will make you flip! Since sometimes you're feeding the whole block at a pancake breakfast, and sometimes you're feeding just a small family, this recipe offers two alternative lists of ingredients. Whichever quantity you choose, the preparation instructions remain the same.

Ingredients to Feed About 12–16 People:

4 eggs, separated

$^1/_2$ cup sugar

4 cups all-purpose flour

2 tablespoons plus 2 teaspoons baking
   powder

2 teaspoons salt

1 quart milk

2 teaspoons natural vanilla extract

$^1/_4$ cup ($^1/_2$ stick) butter, melted, plus
   additional butter for cooking pancakes

3 cups blueberries

1 cup well-chopped pecans, divided

Ingredients to Feed About 4 People:

1 egg, separated

2 tablespoons sugar

1 cup flour

2 teaspoons baking powder

$^1/_2$ teaspoon salt

1 cup milk

$^1/_2$ teaspoon natural vanilla extract

1 tablespoon butter, melted, plus
   additional butter for cooking pancakes

$^3/_4$ cup blueberries

$^1/_4$ cup well-chopped pecans, divided

Place the egg white(s) in a mixing bowl and add the sugar. Whip (or beat with an electric mixer) until stiff peaks form.

In another bowl, sift together the flour, baking powder, and salt. If you don't have a sifter, place the dry ingredients in a wire mesh strainer or colander over a bowl and shake. Add the egg yolk(s), milk, and vanilla to the flour mixture. Whisk together until smooth.

Whisk in the butter. Fold in the egg white mixture. Stir in the blueberries and half of the nuts.

If you won't be eating the pancakes the minute they come off the griddle, preheat the oven to 300 degrees.

Heat frying pan(s) over a medium flame. If you're cooking for a crowd, use two. For a smaller batch, one is enough. Add a small amount of butter to the pan(s). Let it melt, but watch carefully for burning. Preheating before adding the butter can prevent burning, and adding a small amount of oil to the pan(s) will also help.

Place small dollops of batter onto the pan to form pancakes. Use as little as a tablespoonful for mini pancakes, or a soup-ladleful for larger ones. Sprinkle some of the reserved nuts on top of each pancake. When small bubbles appear on top of the pancakes, flip them over. Continue cooking on the second side until browned.

After each round of pancakes, add a bit more butter to the pans and repeat until you use all the batter. Place the finished pancakes in the oven to keep them warm until you're ready to serve.

Currant Bran Muffins

This recipe calls for vegetable shortening. Highly processed, trans-fat-laden vegetable shortening is available in unrefrigerated cans in all conventional grocery stores. Natural food stores have trans-fat-free, healthy vegetable shortening available in the refrigerated section.

 MAKES 2 DOZEN

1⅓ cups stone-ground white flour

2 tablespoons baking powder

2 tablespoons molasses

2 tablespoons honey

Enough butter or neutral oil, such as soy or grapeseed, to grease muffin cups

½ cup sugar

2 ounces (¼ cup) vegetable shortening

1 teaspoon salt

2 large egg whites

1 tablespoon pure vanilla extract

6 ounces (¾ cup) vanilla yogurt

2 cups wheat bran

⅓ cup dried red currants or ½ apple, diced

Preheat the oven to 425 degrees.

Sift together the flour and baking powder. If you don't have a sifter, place a wire mesh strainer or colander with small holes over a small bowl and shake.

In a separate bowl, combine the molasses and honey.

Butter or oil 24 muffin cups. If you have larger- or smaller-than-average muffin cups, go ahead and use them. Just cook larger muffins a couple of extra minutes and mini muffins a few minutes less.

In a separate bowl, mix together the sugar, shortening, and salt with an electric mixer or a sturdy whisk. This process is called creaming, and though the mixture may be tough to stir for the first few seconds, as the shortening and sugar combine it will become light and fluffy.

Add 1 egg white. Mix for about 30 seconds. Then add the second egg white and mix for about $1^1/_2$ minutes, scraping down the sides of bowl while you're mixing. Add the vanilla, yogurt, and wheat bran. Mix until the consistency is fairly even, about 2 minutes. Add the molasses-honey mixture and keep mixing for about 2 more minutes.

Add the flour mixture and the currants. Mix until the consistency is fairly even, just a minute or two.

Pour the batter into the muffin cups. Bake for about 15 minutes, or until set. Let the muffins cool in the pan for about 5 minutes, then remove, transfer to a wire rack, and continue to cool for at least 15 minutes before eating.

Banana Fruit Mania Muffins

You'll be swinging from the trees! This recipe is perfect for a solar oven—a simple oven that uses reflectors to cook with nothing but the power of the sun—especially when it's a hundred degrees in your kitchen and ninety degrees outside. Why not save the climate by keeping your oven off?

 MAKES ABOUT 18 MUFFINS

1 cup dried currants
Neutral oil, such as soy or grapeseed, for greasing muffin tins
5 ripe bananas
$1/2$ cup well-chopped dried pineapple
$1/2$ cup well-chopped dried apricots
$1/2$ cup halved dried cherries
$1/2$ cup well-chopped dried papaya
$1/2$ cup finely shredded coconut (optional)
3 cups rolled oats
1 teaspoon ground cinnamon
1 tablespoon baking powder
$1/2$ cup almond butter

Soak the currants in enough warm water to cover until soft, or about 30 minutes. Grease 18 muffin tins, and preheat the oven to 350 degrees.

Mash the bananas, then add the rest of the ingredients into the bowl and mix well for about 2 minutes. The ingredients should be well combined, but a few lumps are just fine.

Pour the batter into the prepared muffin tins. Bake for 25 minutes or until golden brown. Let the muffin tins cool on a rack before gently removing each muffin.

Cinnamon Buns

Maybe some people wouldn't consider homemade cinnamon buns hippy cooking, but it's a welcoming dish that makes everyone feel like they belong. Besides, we all need a sweet treat now and then, and when we do, making it on our own, from the heart, with real ingredients, is the hippy way.

 MAKES 12–16

3 tablespoons active dry yeast

1¼ cups warm water, divided

6 tablespoons sugar, divided, plus
   1 teaspoon for yeast

4 cups all-purpose flour, plus 1 teaspoon
   for yeast

3 eggs plus 1 egg white (optional, for
   glaze)

2 tablespoons natural vanilla extract

3 teaspoons ground cinnamon

1 teaspoon salt

2 tablespoons butter, melted

Chopped dried fruits and nuts of your
   choice, about 1 cup total (optional)

2 tablespoons honey

Enough powdered sugar to form glaze
   (optional)

In a small bowl, place the yeast, ¼ cup of the warm water, and 1 teaspoon each of the sugar and flour. Stir well. When the mixture is full of bubbles, add it to a separate bowl containing the remaining flour.

Add the remaining 1 cup warm water along with the eggs, ¼ cup of the remaining sugar, the vanilla, 1 teaspoon of the cinnamon, and the salt. Mix well until a sticky dough forms. Add a bit of flour as you mix. The dough will still be sticky, but you should be able to work with it.

Cover the dough with a clean kitchen towel and put it aside in a warm place for at least 2 hours.

Roll out the dough on a lightly floured surface into a rectangle about ½ inch thick. Brush the dough with the melted butter, reserving a 1-inch-wide strip along one long top of the rectangle.

In a small bowl, combine the remaining 2 tablespoons sugar and 2 teapoons cinnamon. Sprinkle over the melted butter. If you are using the optional fruit and nuts, sprinkle them over the dough. Drizzle the honey over the dough.

Roll the dough up, starting at the long, buttered side and rolling toward the long, unbuttered side. Pinch to seal the roll. Cut into 1- to 2-inch-thick buns and lay in a lightly greased pan. The pan should be large enough for the buns to touch without being squished out of their circular shape. If you like, you can use a cookie sheet instead. Let the buns sit, covered with a kitchen towel, in a warm area to rise for at least 1 hour.

Preheat the oven to 375 degrees. Bake the buns for 12 to 15 minutes, or until lightly browned and firm to the touch.

If desired, use 1 egg white and powdered sugar to form a traditional glazed topping. Gooey is groovy, too, in moderation. When buns are cool, drizzle the glaze on top.

Buckwheat Crepes

On the show, these crepes became part of the vegetarian dessert Orange Crepes, and that recipe is included in the dessert section of this book. For breakfast, try sprinkling them with a bit of powdered sugar or some fruit compote—or lightly spread them with fruit preserves—then roll up.

SERVES 6–8

1/4 cup (1/2 stick) butter, plus a small
   amount for coating pan
1 1/2 cups white flour
3/4 cup buckwheat flour
1 tablespoon sugar
5 large eggs
2 cups milk

Melt the butter and set it aside to cool while you measure and mix the rest of the ingredients.

In a large bowl, mix together the flours and the sugar. Add the eggs to the dry ingredients and whisk. Whisk in the butter. Add the milk and whisk. The mixture should have the consistency of heavy cream. If necessary, add a bit of water to thin.

Heat a crepe pan or small skillet over a medium-high flame. Coat with a small amount of butter. Add a ladleful of batter—about 2 ounces or 1/4 cup—to the pan. Tilt the pan so that the batter will evenly coat it. When the crepe starts to brown around the edges, begin to loosen it by running a spatula under the edges. Turn and cook on the other side for a few seconds, or until firm. Remove and repeat the procedure with the rest of the crepes.

If desired, roll up before serving.

Spreads and Syrups

Homemade Nut Butter

Homemade or store-bought baked goods spread with nut butter make a quick breakfast full of healthy fats and some protein. While you can buy nut butters in the store, these often contain added fats, sugars, and "stabilizers," whatever those are. Kept in the refrigerator, homemade nut butter should last for a couple of weeks (if you can keep from eating it that long).

 MAKES ABOUT ³/₄ CUP

1 cup nuts, such as almonds, hazelnuts, or cashews

¹/₄ teaspoon salt

1 tablespoon or more neutral oil, such as soy or grapeseed

If you're going for a stronger flavor, first toast the nuts in a dry skillet over high heat until fragrant. Remove the pan from the heat.

In a food processor or blender, process the nuts until finely ground. Add the salt and oil. Continue processing until smooth. Add more oil as needed to reach your desired consistency.

Because natural nut butters contain no preservatives, they should be refrigerated. If the oils separate, stir them right back into the nut butter.

Real Maple Syrup

Getting back to nature and living off the land doesn't mean you have to forage for your own nuts and berries in the wild—though we're cool with that; it can be as simple as buying natural maple syrup. Tapping trees to make maple syrup is one of the wonders of humans working with nature. Corn syrup tinted with artificial coloring is no substitute for the rich, complex flavor of real maple syrup.

In the late winter or early spring, as warmth starts to return to the forests, maple trees wake up and their sugar sap starts to flow. Sugar farmers, as the men and women who tap trees for maple syrup are called, live by the weather, and most can feel when it's sugar season in their bones; generally it's when the days are warmer but the nights are still cold. Sugar farmers drill into sugar maples, insert a tap or small hose, and collect the sap. Then they boil it. And boil it. When the sap is collected, it's mostly water, but by the time it's concentrated, it is a thick and nourishing syrup.

Though the equipment is often more complex than it once was—modern sugar-houses contain large evaporators to make the process quicker and more efficient—it's the same basic process used a hundred years ago. In fact, the process is so simple that with a drill, a tap, a bucket, a sturdy pot, and a fire, you can make maple syrup on your own. We're not promising the best syrup you've ever tasted, but what an amazing way to feel and taste nature on your own.

When they do their work correctly, sugar farmers do no damage to the trees, which naturally replenish themselves and make more sap. The trees share a bit of life with us, and we do no harm to them. Some maple trees are known to have been tapped for 150 years. Talk about sustainable agriculture!

Breakfast Squash

 quash for breakfast may sound a little strange, but it's delicious and highly nutritious. Served with a bread, and maybe a bit of soy sausage, it's an unusual breakfast feast.

 SERVES 2–4

   1 hard winter squash, such as acorn or
      butternut (the larger the squash, the
      more you'll feed)
   A small amount of neutral oil to grease
      a cookie sheet
   ¹/₂ cup real maple syrup

Preheat the oven to 375 degrees.
   Cut the squash in half and remove the seeds and fibers. Lightly grease a baking sheet and the cut sides of the squash. Place the squash halves cut-side down on the sheet and bake for about 30 minutes.

Flip the squash over and add the maple syrup to cavity. Continue baking until tender, about 20 to 30 more minutes.
   To serve, mash up the squash a bit with a spoon to mix in the syrup. If desired, add a pinch of salt. Give one half of a smaller squash to each person, or cut each half of larger squashes in two.

Berry Syrup

You'll be berry glad you made this delicious syrup; it's like liquid summer. At breakfast, use this for pancakes or French toast. It's also great with yogurt or ice cream, pound cake, or fresh fruit.

 MAKES ABOUT 1 CUP

1½ cups fresh or frozen blackberries, raspberries, blueberries, or other seasonal berries (or a combination)
¼ cup honey
1 squeeze lemon juice
1 tablespoon cornstarch (optional)

Combine all the ingredients except the cornstarch in a blender to puree. You can eat this sauce as is.

If you'd like a finer sauce, though, force the mixture through a sieve. Use the back of a spoon to press the liquids out of the solids. Discard the solids.

To make a thicker syrup, mix the cornstarch in a small bowl with a couple of tablespoons water. Pour the syrup into a saucepan and cook over a medium flame until it's heated through. Add the cornstarch mixture and whisk well. Continue to cook until the sauce has thickened a bit.

If you'll be serving the syrup over pancakes or waffles, just before serving heat it in a saucepan over a medium flame until warmed. Keep in mind that if you've thickened the syrup with cornstarch, it will continue to thicken, so don't make it too far in advance. If you'll be serving it with fruit or as a dessert, chill thoroughly first.

Hot Cereals

Sometimes, we think that the politicians in Washington, DC, just need a good, warming bowl of hot cereal from a loving hand. Hot cereals don't simply nourish the body with their whole grains. They nourish and comfort the soul. Who wouldn't feel healthy and loved after eating one of these delicious breakfasts?

Hot Quinoa Cereal

This cereal has journeyed thousands of miles, from the mighty Andes all the way to North America, and onto your breakfast table. A grain-like plant that's packed with protein and nutrition, quinoa is as versatile as rice. Hot quinoa cereal should look like a thick cereal, similar to rolled oats.

 SERVES 3–4

1 cup quinoa

2 cups water

$\frac{1}{2}$ cup chopped apples (substitute pears or another fruit if you like)

$\frac{1}{4}$ cup raisins

$\frac{1}{8}$ teaspoon ground cinnamon

Almond, soy, or cow's milk, to taste

Honey, brown sugar, stevia, or molasses, to taste

Rinse the quinoa well in a strainer under running water. Add the rinsed quinoa and water to a saucepan or small pot. Bring to a boil over high heat. Reduce the heat to medium low, cover, and simmer for about 5 minutes. Add the fruit and cinnamon. Let the mixture cook until the liquid is absorbed. Expect it to take 10 to 15 minutes. Serve with milk and the sweetener of your choice.

Mango Nut Oatmeal

We love it when the show visits tropical paradises such as Hawaii and Dominica: beautiful people, lush scenery, and luscious fruit. A feast for every sense. This is like a little taste of the tropics in a bowl.

 SERVES 4–6

2 cups rolled oats

2 cups water

2 cups orange juice

$\frac{1}{2}$ cup unsweetened shredded coconut

$\frac{1}{8}$ teaspoon ground cinnamon

2 ripe mangoes

$\frac{1}{2}$ cup chopped walnuts or pecans

Sprig of fresh mint

Mix the oats, water, orange juice, coconut, and cinnamon in a pot. Cook over medium heat for approximately 10 to 12 minutes, or until the oats are cooked through, stirring often to prevent sticking. When the oats are cooked, add the mango and nuts. Heat through. Serve in a glass bowl with a sprig of fresh mint.

Extra-Special Oatmeal

A plain bowl of your favorite grain is fine on an ordinary day, but when you want to show folks that they're special, make the extra effort to dress it up. When cooked, this dish will have a bottom layer of oatmeal and a top layer of moist fruit and caramelized sugar.

SERVES 2

2 cups water

¹/₂ cup steel-cut oats (may also be called
    Irish oatmeal)

Enough neutral oil, such as soy or
    grapeseed, to grease a pan

1 tablespoon brown sugar

2 tablespoons chopped walnuts
    (or substitute your favorite nut)

¹/₂ cup fresh blueberries (or substitute
    seasonal fruit)

Preheat the broiler.

In a saucepan, bring the water to a boil over high heat. Add the oats. When the mixture returns to a boil, cover and reduce the heat to medium low. Cook until tender. Start checking after about 15 minutes, but it may take as long as 30 minutes.

Lightly grease an ovenproof baking or serving dish (a Pyrex pan or a small skillet with a metal handle works well). Spread out the oats in a layer about ¹/₂ inch thick. Sprinkle the brown sugar, nuts, and berries over the surface. Broil the oatmeal until the sugar is melted, the nuts are lightly browned, and the berries are just starting to burst. Watch closely—nuts burn quickly.

Rice Porridge (Congee)

Practitioners of traditional Asian medicine believe that congee, a simple rice porridge, has curative properties. Since this takes so long to cook, it's best made the day before. When cooked, congee should look like a porridge, similar to cream of wheat. It's often served with a bread that looks and tastes a lot like a cruller, but it's good on its own.

SERVES 4–6

1 cup rice of your choice (other grains, such as millet or barley, can be substituted)

7 cups water or vegetable stock

Suggested toppings: chopped scallions, tamari or other soy sauce, toasted sesame oil, chopped tofu, sautéed mushrooms, minced garlic, grated carrot, hot sauce, cilantro, chopped nuts

In a heavy pan, bring the rice and water to a boil. Reduce the heat. Cover. Simmer until the rice has the consistency of a thick porridge, about 1½ to 2 hours. Stir occasionally to keep the rice from sticking to the bottom of the pan.

Serve with your favorite toppings. Don't let the above list limit you—if you think it'll taste good, it probably will.

Variation:

To cook congee in a slow cooker, add the rice and water, turn it on low, and leave the rice to cook unattended overnight, or for about 8 hours.

Millet and Date Cereal

Millet is way more than birdseed. In parts of Asia and Africa, it's a staple food. It makes a sustaining breakfast on days when you need energy. Uncooked millet looks like small balls of off-white grain. For this recipe, expect a thick bowl of cereal similar in appearance to rolled oats.

 SERVES 4

1 cup millet

2 cups boiling water

¼ cup minced dates

¼ cup chopped walnuts (or other nut of your choice)

Sweetener of your choice

In a dry pan, toast the millet over medium-high heat. When it begins to brown, add the water. Bring to a boil, cover, reduce the heat to medium low, and cook for about 15 minutes. Stir in the dates. Continue to cook until all the water has absorbed, about 10 minutes more. Stir occasionally while cooking. Serve with walnuts and the sweetener of your choice.

Stone-Ground Grits Casserole

f all you've tasted is the highly processed white paste that passes for grits in most of the country, you might think that grits are terrible. This dish is made with stone-ground grits, a more natural, flavorful product. It's great for brunch or any time of day.

SERVES 4

3½ cups water

1 cup stone-ground grits

1 tablespoon butter, plus extra for buttering baking dish

1 clove garlic, minced

½ cup minced green onions

2 eggs

1 cup grated cheddar cheese, divided

Preheat the oven to 375 degrees.

Bring the water to a boil over medium-high heat. Gradually stir in the grits, stirring constantly. Cook, stirring often, until thick, about 10 minutes.

In a small pan, heat the butter over a medium-high flame. Add the garlic and green onions and sauté until softened but not browned, about 2 to 3 minutes.

Stir the onion mixture, eggs, and half of the cheese into the grits. Pour into a lightly buttered 2-quart baking dish. Bake for about 20 minutes. Sprinkle with the remaining cheese and bake for about 10 minutes more.

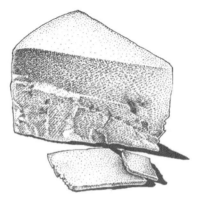

Cold Cereals

Cold cereals don't have to come out of the box. Homemade cereals taste a whole lot better than the stuff that comes from the factory. By making your own cereal, you'll be helping to save the planet, and you'll save money as well.

Fresh-Baked Granola

What could be more hippy than a big batch of granola? Eat it with milk or yogurt as a cereal, sprinkle it over fruit or ice cream, or carry it on the trail or in the car for a quick snack. You can substitute other grains and fruits to your taste. Stored in an airtight metal, glass, or plastic container, it will keep for a couple of weeks.

 SERVES 16–20

1 cup honey (light clover or mesquite)
1 cup neutral vegetable oil, such as soy
   or grapeseed, plus oil to coat pans
1 cup walnuts
1 cup almonds
1 pound rolled oats
1 tablespoon natural vanilla extract
Sprinkling of ground cinnamon
   (optional)
1/2 cup sliced dried mango

1 cup dried cranberries
1 cup raisins

Preheat the oven to 350 degrees.

Heat the honey and oil in a saucepan over a medium flame until the honey is just thinned out. Don't bring to a boil.

Roughly chop the walnuts and almonds. In a large bowl, combine the nuts and the oats. Add the oil and honey. Mix well. Add the vanilla and again mix well.

Lightly coat two baking pans with vegetable oil. Pour the oat mixture into each and spread. Dust with cinnamon, if desired. Bake for about 10 minutes. Remove the pans from the oven, stir, and return for a few minutes more. When the granola is golden brown at the edges, it's done.

Cool the granola in the pans until it's room temperature, and place in large bowl. Stir in the mango, cranberries, and raisins.

Muesli

 Unlike granola, muesli requires no cooking, and we like anything that saves fuel. It's great when you're cooking for overnight guests but have no idea when everyone will be waking up. Made with soy yogurt, it's a good vegan breakfast.

 SERVES 4–5

1 cup rolled oats

1 cup orange or apple juice

¼ cup chopped dried apricots

¼ cup chopped almonds

1 apple, cored and chopped

1 ripe banana, sliced

2 cups favorite yogurt

Honey, to taste (optional)

Mix the oats, juice, apricots, and almonds in a bowl. Cover and refrigerate overnight.

When you're ready to serve, stir in the apple. Serve with sliced banana and yogurt, drizzled with honey if you like.

Eggs, Potatoes, and Tofu

When you do want an old-fashioned egg breakfast, move beyond those greasy deep-fried things to something that will leave you and your friends truly satisfied. These dishes are great any time of day.

Zucchini Frittata

This is another one of those recipes that you can quickly personalize to make your own. Just substitute different vegetables or cheeses, or add any herbs you want. Try mushrooms and Fontina, red bell pepper and cheddar, or onions and Swiss.

 SERVES 4–6

6 large eggs

¹⁄₄ cup minced fresh basil

Salt and pepper, to taste

1 tablespoon olive oil

3 medium zucchinis, sliced

¹⁄₂ cup chopped green onions

1 cup finely grated Parmesan
   cheese

Preheat the broiler.

Whisk together the eggs, basil, and salt and pepper in a bowl.

Heat the oil in a 12-inch skillet with a metal handle over a medium flame. Cook the zucchinis until tender, about 7 to 9 minutes. Add the green onions and cook for a minute more.

Pour the eggs over the vegetables. Lift up the edges as they cook to help uncooked egg flow underneath. When the edges of the eggs are set but the top and middle are still runny (this will take 2 to 3 minutes), sprinkle with the Parmesan.

Place the frittata under the broiler. Cook until it's puffed and golden, about 3 minutes. Cut into wedges and serve.

Three-Onion Crossroads Potatoes

Your friends won't mind onion-breath kisses if you make this dish for them, so share the food and share the love! This is best prepared in a nice thick pan, such as a heavy wok or iron skillet, so that the heat cooks the potatoes evenly. Served with scrambled tofu or eggs and some fruit, this is a delicious side dish.

 SERVES 8–10

3 tablespoons olive oil

8 russet potatoes, roughly chopped

$^1\!/_2$ white onion, chopped

$^1\!/_2$ red onion, chopped

$^1\!/_2$ bunch green onions, chopped

$^1\!/_2$ clove garlic, peeled and sliced thin

$^1\!/_4$ teaspoon paprika

Heat a large frying pan or wok over a medium flame. Add the olive oil and stir-fry the potatoes for about 10 minutes, or until they're tender and beginning to brown nicely on the edges. Gently stir in the onions, garlic, and paprika. Continue cooking until the potatoes are thoroughly browned and the onions are soft and golden, about 5 minutes more. Season to taste with salt and fresh pepper. The dish is best served hot off the stove, but it's also easily reheated.

Scrambled Tofu

Mixed up, crazy, and totally out of sight. Even carnivores will love this veggie treat. Try different vegetables, experiment with the optional ingredients, or serve it on a tortilla for a quick burrito.

 SERVES 4

1 tablespoon neutral oil (such as soy or grapeseed)

1 red or yellow bell pepper, seeded and minced

2–3 green onions, minced

1 clove garlic, peeled and minced

1 package (14–16 ounces) extra-firm tofu, drained and crumbled

$\frac{1}{2}$ teaspoon ground turmeric

Salt and pepper, to taste

Extras: grated cheese, salsa, leftover cooked beans, pumpkin or sunflower seeds, minced hot peppers, minced fresh herbs (such as cilantro or Italian parsley)

Heat the oil in a skillet over a medium-high flame. Cook the bell pepper until softened, about 5 minutes. Add the green onions and garlic. Cook for about 1 minute. Add the tofu and turmeric. Stir and cook until the tofu is completely dry and warmed through. Season to taste with salt and pepper. Serve warm with any desired extras, such as grated cheddar and salsa, grated Parmesan and Italian parsley, or pumpkin seeds and hot peppers.

2. Munchies

Bruce catered for rock stars and now often cooks for crew members on the set, and he's learned that when people are working hard at being creative, they get hungry. Setting out a little or a lot between or instead of formal meals keeps the mood mellow and joyful. The same goes for any gathering: When people's bodies are satisfied, their minds are free to do other things. Munchies, appetizers, hors d'oeuvres, whatever . . . when people work or play together, they like to break a little bit of bread.

In our travels on the show, we've learned that people crave munchies the world over. In Italy, we ate from some of the brilliantly colored antipasto spreads set out before meals: mushrooms glistening with olive oil and herbs, onions soft and pink from bathing in sweet acidic vinegar, peppers lightly charred and just sweet enough. In Asia and India, street vendors sell any snack you could possibly imagine: steaming buns filled with strange and fragrant fungi, sticky rice studded with savory and sweet morsels and steamed in lotus leaves, gently chewy noodles stretched and cooked before your eyes. In the Caribbean, we tasted the hottest, most complex jerk fish you can imagine, cooked in vessels improvised from whatever is on hand and cooled with mangoes straight off the

49

trees. In Hawaii, we saw Spam sushi . . . well, maybe some of the world's munchies are better seen than tasted.

On the show, we've made appetizers that expand your mind and challenge your vision, like Jerusalem Artichoke Dip, and those that are familiar enough to be found in your corner store, like hummus. Both are great if they make you and your friends happy. It's not about making the most precious little morsel; it's about having a great time and eating great food, and most importantly about the cardinal rule of good hospitality.

Some people think of hors d'oeuvres and appetizers as 1950s cocktail food, but it's not all about stiff-haired old ladies sipping cocktails and throwing back processed wieners. You don't have to be fusty or old-fashioned or rigid at all. Just serve what you genuinely love. If all you can muster is a bowl of nuts, that's fine. But making something from the heart will just spread a little more love.

Some people think that meals with more than one dish, or small snacks between meals, are unnecessary, just another sign of consumerist decadence. If you're eating goose liver that's been fattened by force-feeding the poor animal or stuffing yourself with french fries when you aren't even

hungry, sure, that can be decadent, but if you're spending a night talking and laughing with your friends and family, what could be more natural and enjoyable?

Not only can munchies be good for us, they can do good as well. Cooking is one of the ways that Bruce is able to support the causes that mean so much to him and to us. On the show, we visited the Wild and Scenic Environmental Film Festival in Nevada City, California. This festival is an opportunity for activists to get together and feel energized by one another's work, to share in some great environmental films, and to celebrate the beauty of the natural world. The festival is a chance to gather with those who love the earth and to learn from wonderful movies ranging from political films to eco-tourism documentaries.

The South Yuba River Citizens League (SYRCL), a group dedicated to restoring and preserving the South Yuba River, is among the sponsors of the event. They've helped protect the river from damming and worked to clean its waters. Alongside indigenous people and other groups, they are helping to restore native salmon and steelhead. The festival hums with positive energy of people dedicated to making a change in the world.

We loved visiting these great folks—not that it was much of a chore in the beautiful wilderness around Nevada City. Even better was feeding all those artistic, creative, loving minds at the festival. We created stuffed mushrooms and vegan sushi, among other dishes, that were not just good to eat but a joy to look at, too.

Vegan sushi takes some time and care; it's a work of art as much as a recipe. You have to fan the rice carefully, and to make sure that all elements in the rolls are balanced. But when you're sharing that sushi with wonderful people, you know all that effort is worth it. Sharing our delicious, organic food was a way to let the activists know how grateful we are for the hard work they do.

Making a few dishes isn't going to bring back the salmon to all the rivers of the West. We don't think that a movement ever began with a vegan sushi roll. But good, lovingly made food will spread a bit of happiness and a bit of caring. And when more people do this kind of thing, the vibe spreads, the feelings grow, and soon you've got a whole lot of energy rolling along. Soon everyone's sharing their talents and working toward positive change. So maybe vegan sushi does create a movement. Regardless, it makes a good time, and what else could we hope for?

Dips

Forget sour cream and soup mix. Dips can be healthy and flavorful.

Hummus

Call this hummus no fuss! It's easy, it's delicious, and you can use it for almost anything. This is the world's most perfect dip, sandwich spread, or appetizer. Try it served with whole white pita and vegetables for dipping.

🍄 MAKES ABOUT 4 CUPS

20 ounces (about 3^1/$_2$ cups) dried
    garbanzo beans; or use 4 cans
    (16 ounces each) of cooked garbanzos,
    rinsed and drained, and skip the
    soaking and boiling steps
1 large white onion, minced
2 cloves garlic, minced
^{1}/$_2$ cup extra-virgin olive oil, divided, plus
    extra to garnish
^{1}/$_2$ cup tahini (sesame butter)
^{1}/$_4$ cup lemon juice
^{1}/$_8$ teaspoon cayenne pepper
^{1}/$_4$ teaspoon black pepper

3 tablespoons water
^{1}/$_4$ cup pitted kalamata or Greek olives

Soak the beans overnight in enough water to cover by about 2 inches. In the morning, drain the beans, add water to cover by about an inch in a large pot, and bring to a boil over medium-high heat. Reduce the heat to medium low, cover, and simmer for 45 minutes to an hour, or until tender. Drain and set aside.

In a large skillet over medium heat, sauté the onion and garlic in about a tablespoon of the olive oil until transparent. Pour the onion mixture into a blender or food processor; add the remaining ingredients, except the olives and the oil to garnish. Blend until the mixture is smooth, adding a little water if necessary to reach the consistency you like.

Spread the hummus on a plate, leaving a hole in the middle. Pour a liberal amount of olive oil into this hole. Place the olives along the outer edge of the plate.

StewBert Golden Pecan and Hemp Seed Spread

We named this spread in honor of Jon Stewart and Stephen Colbert, two men who make us laugh while working for good. We hope they like this hot, creamy dip with a nutty topping, excellent with bread, crackers, or vegetables.

 SERVES 8–10

8 ounces cream cheese, room temperature

2 tablespoons 2 percent milk

$2^1/_2$ ounces savory flavored tempeh, chopped fine (or substitute smoked or dried tofu)

2 tablespoons dried onion flakes

$^1/_4$ teaspoon garlic powder

$^1/_4$ teaspoon black pepper

$^1/_2$ cup sour cream (or substitute yogurt)

Salt, to taste

$^1/_2$ cup finely chopped pecans

$^1/_2$ cup hemp seeds

Preheat the oven to 350 degrees. Whisk together the cream cheese and milk until creamy. Stir in the flavored tempeh and seasonings. Add the sour cream, then season to taste with salt and additional pepper.

Put the mixture into a baking dish and sprinkle with the pecans and hemp seeds. Bake for 20 minutes. Let cool for a few minutes before eating.

The Plant with a Thousand Faces

Hemp has been cultivated for several millennia, and has literally thousands of uses. Its fibers are strong enough to make durable rope and sailcloth, yet versatile enough to make comfortable clothing. Making paper from hemp rather than timber could save thousands of acres of trees every year. Hemp can be made into biofuel. It can even make plastics as good as those made from petroleum products; *The Hippy Gourmet* uses hemp cases for its DVDs.

Because hemp can be grown fairly easily, and sustainably, it can help save the family farm and the environment at the same time. It could reduce our dependence on petroleum and timber. If hemp were widely grown in the United States, it could benefit industries by providing them with an inexpensively and easily grown commodity. Currently, hemp is grown commercially in dozens of countries, and it could be grown widely in the United States as well. George Washington, the father of our country, grew hemp, and you can't get much more all-American than that!

Hemp products can legally be imported and sold in the United States. Hemp seeds, available in most health food stores, are an excellent source of protein, healthy fats, and iron. Hemp can feed the liberal media—and everyone else who wants healthy, delicious food—for the coming years.

For more information about hemp, check out clips from the upcoming *Hippy Gourmet* documentary about this incredible plant at www.youtube.com/hippygourmet.

Roasted Jalapeño Pepper Salsa

There are millions of salsa recipes out there. We think this one is awesome. If you want to experiment, try different chilies, add a diced cucumber, fresh corn kernels, beans . . . let your mood and your taste buds carry you where they will.

🍄 SERVES 3–6

3 jalapeño peppers
5 roma tomatoes, chopped into small
   pieces
$1/2$ medium red onion, chopped fine
$1/2$ medium white onion, chopped fine
Squeeze of lemon juice
Several sprigs cilantro, chopped
1 teaspoon dried oregano
$1/2$ teaspoon white pepper
1 teaspoon salt
Splash of virgin olive oil

Over an open gas flame, blacken the peppers: Just place them right on top of the flames, turning with tongs when they're blackened—a minute or two per side. If you don't have a gas flame, use a grill or an electric broiler to cook the chilies until their skins are blackened, turning to get all sides; this should take 3 to 4 minutes per side. When the skins are charred, rinse the peppers under cold water. Peel off the skins, cut the peppers in half, remove their inner seeds, and chop. Add them to a bowl along with the tomatoes, onions, lemon juice, cilantro, oregano, and pepper. Mix well. Season to taste with salt, and drizzle olive oil over the salsa.

Jerusalem Artichoke Dip

Most people who watch our show realize that Bruce loves Jerusalem artichokes, tubers that come from a type of large sunflower. The name *Jerusalem* has nothing to do with the Middle Eastern city; it probably comes from *girasole*, the Italian word for "sunflower." It's a wonderful vegetable that grows all over the country, and most people don't even know about it. Try this with a group and help us spread the word about this amazing food.

🍄 MAKES ENOUGH FOR A SMALL GATHERING OF FRIENDS

About 15 Jerusalem artichokes
1 teaspoon plus 2 tablespoons olive oil, divided
Pinch of salt
Freshly ground black pepper to taste
2 shallots, sliced
2 cloves garlic, sliced
Juice of ½ lemon
Hot sauce to taste
1 tablespoon minced chives
Veggie tortilla chips, fresh-cut vegetables such as carrots and peppers, sweet potato chips, or whatever you prefer as a dipper

Rinse the artichokes, and cut off each root at the tip. Cut into about ½-inch slices.

Heat 1 teaspoon of the oil in a pan over a medium-high flame. Add the Jerusalem artichoke slices and a pinch of salt. Cook until the artichokes begin to caramelize slightly, about 5 minutes. Add pepper.

Continue to cook until the artichoke slices are browned, about 5 minutes more. Add the shallots and cook until slightly wilted. Add the garlic and a splash of water. The artichokes should look fully caramelized now, with a nice brown color.

Put the artichoke mixture in a food processor along with the lemon juice and the remaining 2 tablespoons olive oil. Puree. Scrape down the sides of the processor and continue to puree until you reach the consistency you like. Add the hot sauce.

Put the dip into a bowl and let it cool for a few minutes. Garnish with the chives and a slice of lemon before serving with dippers of your choice.

Peanut Dip

ilken tofu makes a good base for creamy soups and sauces, especially this peanut dip. It adds a smooth texture and allows the other flavors to stand out. This dip is good for vegetables, grilled tofu, and grilled shrimp; or you can use it as a sauce with Asian pastas such as lo mein or ramen.

🍄 MAKES ABOUT 1 CUP

$^1/_2$ cup natural peanut butter, chunky
  or smooth
$^1/_2$ cup silken tofu
2 tablespoons lime juice
2 tablespoons tamari or other soy sauce
1 clove garlic, pressed or finely minced
Sprinkling of cayenne pepper, to taste
2 tablespoons brown sugar
1 green onion, chopped fine,
  for garnish

Puree all the ingredients in a blender or food processor until the mixture takes on the consistency of a smooth, thick sauce. Season to taste with pepper and additional tamari, if desired.

If you'll be serving the sauce over hot foods, use right away. If you're using it as a dip, refrigerate for about 30 minutes or until cool. When you're ready to serve, garnish with green onions.

Discovering the World One Plate at a Time

We've been all over the world, by big jet, by biodiesel vegetable oil bus, and on our own feet. The best part of traveling is wandering wherever your heart and feet take you. It's the journey as much as the destination that makes traveling special.

Part of that journey is talking along the way. We've met all sorts of folks and eaten all sorts of food in our travels: noodles from street carts, delicately sauced vegetables off white tablecloths, spicy beans made in a loving grandmother's kitchen. Eating other people's food means tasting the essence of who they believe they are. It's an act that's both intimate and communal. It's a beautiful thing.

We can't pretend we've learned everything about the people we've visited, but we do know that we've shared and learned. The flavors of other people have become a part of our own cooking, our own journey. The flavors we've brought back never really reproduce the food of other cultures. But they can give a hint, a flavor, of that culture—and in this world, every bit of understanding helps.

Bagna Cauda

This traditional Italian dish is communal food at its best—delicious, messy, and fun. It's a simple, salty sauce that highlights beautiful produce straight from the soil. This is the flavor of Italy: joyous, earthy, traditional. Bagna cauda is kept warm over a small flame in the middle of the table, like fondue. You don't need a special pot and candle to serve it, though; your friends will enjoy it out of a nice, thick bowl just as well.

 SERVES 6–8

4 cloves garlic, minced

6 oil-packed anchovies, minced

½ cup extra-virgin olive oil

2 tablespoons butter

Salt and pepper, to taste

Heaping platter of fresh vegetables: endive, celery, peppers, or whatever's fresh

1 loaf crusty bread

Sauté the garlic and anchovies in the olive oil over medium heat until the anchovies melt. Add the butter and let it melt. Add salt (it will take very little, since the anchovies are already salty) and pepper to taste.

Place in a fondue pot or any pot set over a small candle—or simply a hearty, thick bowl. Serve with vegetables and bread, and pass the napkins!

Black Bean Dip

You can make a quick dip out of virtually any kind of bean by pureeing it and some flavorful ingredients in a food processor. If you don't have freshly cooked beans, you can use canned, but be sure to rinse them well first to remove salt and that lingering "canned" taste.

 MAKES 1½ CUPS

2 cups cooked black beans, or 1 can (16 ounces) black beans, rinsed
1 tablespoon fresh lime juice
¼ cup minced fresh cilantro
1 clove garlic, crushed or minced
¼ teaspoon ground cumin
1 small jalapeño, stem and seeds removed
Salt and pepper, to taste

Combine all the ingredients in a food processor and pulse to blend. If necessary, add a couple of teaspoons of water or good olive oil to get the consistency you like. The dip can be chunky or smooth—however you prefer it. Season with salt and pepper. Refrigerate.

Herbed Yogurt Cheese

nce you master the technique of yogurt cheese, try different combinations. Instead of using the herbs in this recipe, for instance, mix with shredded or chopped cucumber and minced garlic for Greek tatziki. Or you can add honey and nuts for a sweet and tart snack, or to a sandwich filling with roasted vegetables.

🍄 MAKES ABOUT 1 CUP

2 cups plain low fat yogurt
$^1/_2$ cup fresh herbs, such as basil, mint, or Italian parsley
Salt and pepper, to taste
1 tablespoon olive oil

Crackers, bread, or fresh vegetables, to dip

Spoon the yogurt into a large colander lined with two layers of cheesecloth. Gather up the edges of the cloth to form a ball, and lift. Twist the edges and fasten with some kitchen twine or a rubber band.

Place the cheesecloth ball back in the colander, setting a bowl underneath to catch the liquid. Let this rest for several hours in the refrigerator.

Unwrap the ball. Mix the yogurt with the herbs, salt, and pepper. Drizzle with the olive oil and serve with your favorite dippers.

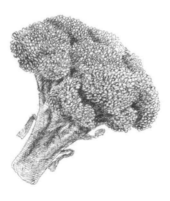

Nuts and Seeds

Is vegetarian food all nuts and berries? Of course not. But since they're so good, why deprive yourself? Set these out for your friends and family to eat whenever the urge strikes.

Pepitas

Many Americans think pumpkin seeds are those nasty, gloopy things they throw away every Halloween. In Mexico, they know better. Available in health food stores, some grocery stores, and Latin markets, pepitas can be eaten on their own or ground up to thicken sauces.

 MAKES 2 CUPS

2 cups green pumpkin seeds (pepitas)
2 teaspoons olive oil
Salt and pepper, to taste

Cook the pepitas in a skillet over medium heat until puffy and a little brown, about 5 minutes. (Keep an eye on them; they'll burn fast.) Remove from the heat. Drizzle with the olive oil while still hot, tossing thoroughly so that the oil is evenly distributed. Sprinkle with salt and pepper. These are great just eaten as is, but you can also try them with a bit of all-natural chili or garlic powder.

Tamari-Roasted Almonds

These are great with cocktails or anytime the munchies hit. Tamari is a dark soy sauce made from soybeans—other kinds may have wheat and other ingredients. Use whatever nuts you like here, though almonds are especially good with the tamari.

🍄 MAKES 1 CUP

1 cup unroasted almonds
1 tablespoon tamari or other soy sauce
Sprinkling of sea salt

Toss the nuts with the tamari in a small bowl. Let them sit for an hour or so.
Preheat the oven to 350 degrees.
Spread the nuts on a baking sheet in a single layer. Save any tamari that has pooled in the bottom of the bowl for rice. Sprinkle a bit of sea salt over the nuts (not too much—the tamari is salty). Bake until the nuts are lightly roasted, 10 to 15 minutes. Watch carefully—nuts burn easily.

Edamame

Here, the chameleon soybean takes another form. Edamame—unprocessed, fresh soybeans, usually served in the pod—are available in health food stores and Asian markets, and these days they're finding their way into conventional supermarkets. Edamame can be a side dish, similar to lima beans, but are often served as a snack. If you can boil water, you can cook edamame.

🍄 MAKES AS MUCH AS YOU LIKE

Edamame, preferably fresh (or frozen
    if that's all that's available)
Salt
Toasted sesame seed oil (optional)

Bring a large pot of water to a boil. Boil the whole edamame pods for about 5 minutes. Drain and sprinkle with salt. Eat by slipping the beans out of the pods, just as you would peas in a pod. If you wish, serve a tiny dish of toasted sesame seed oil on the side. Use it as a dip for the beans.

Bread

Because bread is so delicious on its own, it's easy to make simple yet glorious appetizers with it. Use the very best bread you can make or buy, put a few quality ingredients on it, and you've got a great snack. In fact, a loaf of bread, a few olives, a couple of slices of roasted pepper, and perhaps a little cheese make a meal anyone would love.

Onion Cookies

These should look like small, golden-brown crackers when prepared. Try them with cheese, during cocktail hour, with soups, or as a nice snack. They go perfectly with Jerusalem Artichoke Dip (page 56).

 MAKES ABOUT 4 DOZEN

Neutral oil, such as soy or grapeseed, for greasing baking sheets

2 teaspoons baking powder

1 large white or yellow onion, diced

2 teaspoons raw brown sugar

3/4 cup vegetable oil

1 teaspoon sea salt

3 cups whole wheat flour

1/2 cup orange juice

1 egg (reserve a bit of white in a small bowl)

1 teaspoon sesame seeds

Preheat the oven to 400 degrees. Lightly grease baking sheets.

Blend all the ingredients (except the reserved egg white and sesame seeds) in a bowl until a dough forms. On a lightly floured surface, roll out the dough thinly. Using a small glass or cookie cutter, cut shapes out of the dough.

Mix the reserved egg white with 1 tablespoon water. Using this mixture, "paint" each cookie with a pastry brush. Sprinkle the cookies with the sesame seeds and place them on your prepared baking sheets. Bake for 25 minutes or until golden brown.

Tomato Bruschetta

here must be hundreds of versions of this appetizer across the country, but it's only worth making if you have a really good tomato. This dish shows how lovingly grown ingredients, simply prepared, are far better than the most complicated processed foods.

🍄 MAKES 15–25 BRUSCHETTA, DEPENDING ON LENGTH OF LOAF

1 large loaf high-quality, crusty bread
2 tablespoons extra-virgin olive oil
1 clove garlic, sliced lengthwise in half
2 cups seeded and chopped ripe tomatoes
2 tablespoons minced fresh basil, chives,
    or mint (or a mixture)

1 teaspoon balsamic vinegar
Salt and pepper, to taste

If you'll be using a grill, prepare the coals. If you're using a broiler, preheat it.

Cut the bread into thick slices and either grill it on both sides until it's toasted, or brown it on both sides under the broiler. Either way, it should take just a couple of minutes per side.

Brush olive oil on one side of the toasted bread. Rub with the cut garlic.

Mix the tomatoes, herbs, vinegar, and salt and pepper. Place a heaping dollop on the oiled side of each bread slice. Serve immediately.

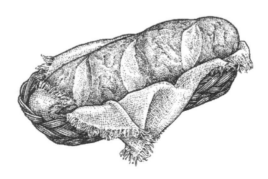

Pear and Gorgonzola Bruschetta

ere's a sweet and salty version of bru-schetta; it's a little yin, a little yang, and all good. Serve this as an appetizer—or when you don't want the evening to end, bring this to the table with a bottle of dessert wine, and you can linger for hours.

MAKES 15–25 BRUSCHETTA, DEPENDING ON LENGTH OF LOAF

1 large loaf high-quality, crusty bread
2 tablespoons extra-virgin olive oil
2 large Anjou pears
4 ounces Gorgonzola cheese, crumbled
Honey, to taste

If you'll be using a grill, prepare the coals. If you're using a broiler, preheat it.

Cut the bread into thick slices and brush both sides of bread with olive oil. Grill it on both sides until it's toasted, or brown it on both sides under the broiler. Either way, it should take just a couple of minutes per side.

Cut the pears into thin slices. Top each slice of toasted bread with pear slices and Gorgonzola. Drizzle honey on the bruschetta slices to taste. Serve as is, or heat the bruschetta under a hot broiler until the honey bubbles and the cheese softens.

Vegan Tortilla Pinwheels

Keep on rolling! These are simple and can be made with almost any filling you like. Substitute tofu cheese spread or cream cheese for the bean dip, and vary the vegetables. If you aren't vegan, try them with cream cheese, lox, and chives.

🍄 MAKES ABOUT 60 PINWHEELS

6 large flour tortillas (any flavor)
1½ cups homemade or store-bought
    hummus (or any vegan bean spread)
1 avocado, peeled and sliced thin
½ cup minced fresh cilantro
4 green onions, chopped fine
2 large carrots, shredded

Cut the edges off the tortillas to form large squares. Spread about ¼ cup of the hummus or bean dip on each tortilla. Don't go quite all the way to the edges. Evenly divide the avocado, cilantro, green onions, and carrots among the tortillas. Roll each one up and slice it crosswise into several pieces. After cutting, each piece should look like a small pinwheel. Lay the pinwheels decoratively on a platter and serve.

Living Simply

Remember when people used to talk about living simply? When life wasn't all about accumulating more than the Joneses? In some countries, people have never forgotten the simple ways of eating. They eat as their ancestors did, and they'll fight any efforts to change. When we visit foreign countries on the show, it often isn't the grand dishes at the hotels that impress. It's the small things, the simple foods that use a few wonderful ingredients.

When we visited Livorno, Italy, on the show, for instance, we ate some amazing Italian snack food at Seghieri Pizza Torta. The dish couldn't be simpler: chickpea flour, olive oil, water, and salt. Yet there's something about the way the ingredients combine over the flames of the pizza oven that makes magic. This is a version that can be made at home, and though it isn't quite the same thing—unless, of course, your home has a pizza oven—it's still a delicious vegan treat.

Chickpea Torta

This dish would be perfect to share with some good Italian wine or your favorite beer. Italian chickpea flour is available at some grocery stores, Italian markets, or over the Internet.

🍄 SERVES 4

²/₃ cup chickpea flour

3 tablespoons extra-virgin olive oil, plus more for oiling pan

About ¾ cup water

1 teaspoon salt

1 teaspoon fresh-ground pepper

Mix the flour, olive oil, water, and salt.

Preheat the oven to 400 degrees. Let the mixture sit while the oven heats. Meanwhile, oil a large pizza pan with a lip, a large oven-proof skillet, or any large round pan with an edge that will allow you to pour the batter in a very thin layer. Preheat the oiled pan in oven for 5 minutes. Pour the batter into the pan and place it in the oven. Be sure that the pan is level.

Bake until the edges begin to darken and torta is golden; begin checking after about 10 minutes. Sprinkle with pepper and serve.

Seafood

Meat-eating guests gobble up seafood on an appetizer buffet before anything else. Clean, wild-caught seafood is a celebration of the ocean and a joy to share with friends.

Seafood Mousse Roll-Up Appetizer

agical, mysterious mousse! This looks complicated and impressive, and it does take some effort, but once you figure out how the process works you'll find it easy to make food that looks like a work of art.

🍄 MAKES ENOUGH FOR A LARGE
GATHERING

½ orange or yellow bell pepper

½ red pepper

A few green onions

½ yellow onion

2 stalks celery

A small amount of butter for greasing

2 pounds raw rock scallops

¼ teaspoon ground nutmeg

Dash white pepper

2 eggs

¼ cup heavy cream, divided

2 pounds raw rock shrimp, cleaned
and de-veined

Cocktail sauce (page 71)
Butterleaf lettuce leaves, for serving

Bring a large pot of water to a boil. Cut the peppers and green onions lengthwise into thin slices. Add them to the water.

Cut the onion and celery into large chunks and add. Let all the vegetables blanch for a couple of minutes, then remove them from the pot with a slotted spoon and pat them dry with a towel.

Spread out aluminum foil in a 9 × 12-inch pan. Place a layer of parchment over the foil, and coat the parchment with a thin layer of butter.

Put the scallops in a food processor. Add the nutmeg, half of the white pepper, and 1 egg. Blend. When the mixture starts to become a paste, add half of the cream. Spread the mousse over the parchment paper, leaving a border of about 1 inch along each edge.

Put the shrimp in a food processor. Add the rest of the pepper and the second egg. Blend. When it starts to become a paste, add the rest of the cream. Spread the shrimp atop the scallops. Swirl the two mousses together a bit for decorative purposes. Lay the blanched peppers and green onion strips in the middle of the mousse.

Pull up both long ends of the parchment paper to form the mousse into a long tube, using the paper to shape it and hold it intact (think of a tamale wrapped in leaves). Wrap the paper in the aluminum foil. Scrunch to remove air bubbles, and twist the ends shut. It should look like a wrapped burrito.

In a poaching pan 3 inches deep, place the mousse in the boiling water in which you cooked the vegetables. Cover the pan and let it cook for 20 minutes.

Remove the mousse to a rack with a pan below to catch any drippings. Poke holes in the wrap to let juices flow out. Chill for 3 to 4 hours.

When you're ready to serve, unwrap the mousse and cut into 1-inch slices, dabbing each with cocktail sauce. Serve on a lettuce leaf.

Cocktail Sauce

This cocktail sauce was created to go with the Seafood Mousse Roll-Up Appetizer, but it's great with most seafood. It has more bite than traditional cocktail sauce because of the addition of wasabi powder. Try it with some steamed shrimp or crab for an impressive appetizer that requires little work.

 MAKES ENOUGH FOR MOUSSE WITH SOME LEFT OVER FOR DIPPING

2 tablespoons wasabi powder
Water
1$\frac{1}{2}$ cups thick tomato catsup
Juice of $\frac{1}{2}$ lemon
1 tablespoon Worcestershire sauce
Salt and pepper, to taste

In a small bowl, mix the wasabi powder and a few drops of water. Keep adding water, a few drops at a time, until it thickens into a nice paste.

In a separate bowl, mix the catsup and lemon juice. Add the Worcestershire sauce, then the wasabi paste, and whisk everything together. Season to taste with salt and pepper.

Fish Dumplings

These little balls of fishy goodness are out of sight. They're fish meatballs, called dumplings because of the way they're cooked in liquid. They're fancy without letting too many tastes interfere with the joy of the fish. These dumplings would also make a good pescatarian main course served with rice and vegetables.

 SERVES 10–12 AS AN APPETIZER, 4–6 AS AN ENTRÉE

2 slices quality white bread, crusts removed

2-pound fillet boneless white fish

2 onions, chopped (about 2 cups)

2½–3½ tablespoons olive oil

2 cloves garlic, chopped

¼ cup finely chopped fresh cilantro

2 large or 3 medium tomatoes, chopped

1 teaspoon garam masala

Soak the bread in water to cover (about 2 cups) for about 10 minutes.

In a food processor, pulse the fish and half the onions. Squeeze the water out of the bread and add it to the fish mixture. Pulse until pureed. Set aside in the refrigerator while you make the sauce.

In a frying pan, heat 2 to 3 tablespoons of the olive oil over a medium-high flame. Add the garlic and the rest of the onion. Cook until softened. Add the cilantro, tomatoes, and garam masala. Cook until the sauce comes together and thickens a bit, about 10 minutes. Add ½ tablespoon olive oil, cover, and reduce the heat to medium low.

Form the fish mixture into balls by the heaping tablespoonful. Add these dumplings into simmering sauce and cover. Cook for about 4 minutes, or until firm.

Gravlax

n Scandinavian languages, *gravlax* means "buried salmon." Historically this dish was, quite literally, cured inside a hole in the ground. These days, our fish doesn't sleep with the fishes; we use a refrigerator instead.

🍄 **Makes a 3-pound fillet, enough for 12–16 people**

2 tablespoons crushed black pepper, divided

2 bunches whole fresh dill, divided

1 cup sea salt, divided

1 cup sugar, divided

3-pound fillet smoked salmon

1 English cucumber, sliced thin

Pinch of table salt

White pepper, to taste

Enough rice vinegar (sweetened) to coat cucumbers

2 tablespoons minced fresh dill

5 tablespoons mayonnaise

½ tablespoon Dijon mustard

1 head butter lettuce

1 loaf Danish pumpernickel bread, sliced half-sandwich size

Enough butter to thinly coat bread

1 grapefruit, divided into segments

1 avocado, peeled and pitted

1 pomegranate

Preparing Salmon:

In a large pan, place half the black pepper, dill, sea salt, and sugar. Place the salmon on top of this mixture, tucking the ingredients under the fish. On top of the salmon, add the rest of the pepper, dill, sea salt, and sugar. Cover with plastic wrap and weigh the salmon down with a heavy skillet or other evenly weighted heavy object. Refrigerate at least overnight and up to 4 days.

Remove the weight and the salmon from the pan. Scrape off any remaining salt, sugar, and dill. Reserve the pan juices. Slice salmon paper-thin at an angle.

Preparing the Platter:

In a bowl, mix the cucumber slices, a pinch of salt, and white pepper to taste. Add enough rice vinegar to coat the cucumber. Add the minced dill and mix.

To make the sauce, in a separate bowl mix the mayonnaise, Dijon, and enough reserved dill juice to make a thin consistency.

Lay large, outside butter lettuce leaves on a serving platter. Butter the pumpernickel bread slices. Lay them over the large leaves, butter-side up. Lay smaller, inside lettuce leaves atop the bread. Arrange the salmon on top of the lettuce. Add the remaining reserved salmon sauce. In the middle of the platter, arrange the marinated cucumbers. Arrange the grapefruit segments, avocado, and pomegranates decoratively over the dish.

To serve, place a fork and spoon on the communal platter, and allow guests to pick out bread, fish, and vegetables in whatever combination they wish.

Fruits and Vegetables

If you want a simple appetizer, go to the farmers' market or your garden, pick a variety of brightly colored vegetables, and arrange them on a platter. With a simple bowl of vinaigrette on the side, you have a thing of beauty to share with your family. Or you can serve a platter of fruit with a dish of yogurt and honey. Nature's bounty doesn't need a great deal of tampering. If you do want something a bit more complicated, though, the following recipes should also impress.

Artichoke Rounds

There's an old story that, during World War II, French women would serve their German "guests" whole, fresh artichokes, then sit back and snicker as they tried to figure out how to eat the crazy thistle. Sounds like a much more civilized form of revenge than carpet bombing.

 SERVES 6–8

Neutral oil, such as soy or grapeseed, to grease pan

1 jar (12 ounces) marinated artichoke hearts

6 green onions, chopped fine

$1/4$ cup chopped parsley

4 eggs, beaten

$1/2$ pound sharp cheddar cheese, grated

6–8 whole wheat crackers, crushed fine

Hot pepper sauce, to taste

Preheat the oven to 325 degrees. Lightly oil an 8 × 8-inch baking pan. Drain the oil from the artichokes, reserving some to cook the onions.

Heat a small skillet over a medium-high flame, add a couple of spoonfuls of the reserved oil, and add the green onions. Cook until they're limp and bright green, about 1 to 2 minutes. Add the parsley and remove the pan from the heat.

In a separate bowl, beat the eggs, adding the remaining ingredients (including the cooked onion) while you do so.

Pour the mixture into the prepared pan and bake for 40 minutes or until set. Use a round metal baking shape to slice out the rounds from the pan while still warm, or cut into small squares. These rounds are best served warm.

Vegan Antipasto Plate

In Italy, antipasto is served as a small bite or two before the meal begins (literally, *antipasto* is "before the meal"). Almost any seasonal vegetable will work in this recipe; if you eat dairy, go ahead and add a couple of slices of good Italian cheese.

 SERVES 4

1 tablespoon chopped Italian (flat-leaf) parsley

1 teaspoon dried oregano

¼ teaspoon sugar

1 tablespoon balsamic vinegar

Salt and pepper, to taste

3 tablespoons extra-virgin olive oil

¾ pound carrots, peeled and sliced into thin matchsticks about 2 inches long

2 cups broccoli florets

2 cups cauliflower florets

1 handful high-quality olives

Whisk together the parsley, oregano, sugar, vinegar, and salt and pepper. Whisk in the oil in a slow stream.

Bring water to a boil in a steamer (using either an electric steamer or a pan with a steamer insert on the stove). Steam the vegetables until just slightly tender, about 5 minutes. In a bowl, toss the vegetables in the vinaigrette. Refrigerate until chilled.

To serve, mound vegetables on a serving platter or individual plates. Sprinkle olives over the vegetables.

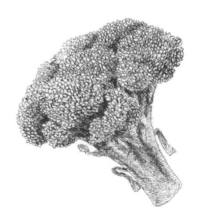

Vegan Sushi

This recipe requires several Japanese ingredients as well as special equipment, but once you master the technique you'll serve this often enough to make the investment worthwhile. We recommend a sushi bin—a small shallow container used to cool and mix sushi rice—made out of cypress, which imparts a delicate flavor to your rice. You will also need a bamboo mat (available at Japanese specialty stores or online) for this recipe.

 MAKES 4 ROLLS

2 cups high-quality sushi rice

2 cups plus 2 tablespoons water

2 tablespoons seasoned rice vinegar, plus extra for coating sushi bin

1 tablespoon neutral oil (such as soy or grapeseed)

2 cloves garlic

1 English cucumber

1 avocado

4 sheets nori (a variety of seaweed)

1 enoki mushroom (omit if unavailable)

1 handful pea shoots

1/2 tablespoon prepared wasabi, plus extra to serve alongside sushi

Sprinkle of hemp seeds

8 strips yama gobo (pickled burdock, a type of root)

Sprinkle of shichimi togarashi (Japanese spice blend) (omit if unavailable)

Sprinkle of ryokua yasai (Japanese vegetable seasoning mix) (omit if unavailable)

Few slices of pickled ginger

Rinse the rice until the water runs clear. Add the rice to a pot along with the water and 2 tablespoons vinegar. Bring to a simmer and cook for 22 minutes, covered. Remove from the heat and let rest for 5 more minutes.

Coat the rice bin in vinegar. Add the cooked rice and stir well to cool to room temperature (it helps if you have an assistant fan the rice for you).

Heat the oil in a small skillet over a medium-high flame. Cook the garlic until golden brown—this will take just a minute or two. Drain the garlic and cool.

Peel and cut the English cucumber and avocado into strips about 1/8 inch thick.

Heat a dry sauté pan over high heat. Toast

the nori in the dry pan for a few seconds on each side.

Lay out a strip of plastic wrap a couple of inches longer than your bamboo mat. Lay the bamboo mat atop the plastic, then place the nori atop the bamboo mat.

Moisten your hands lightly. Place about a quarter of the rice on the nori. Spread to about the thickness of one grain of rice. Leave a small border along the top edge of the nori. In the center of the rice, lay a few strips of enoki and a couple of pea shoots lengthwise. Dab a bit of wasabi in a thin strip down the center. Sprinkle with a bit of garlic and hemp seeds. Lay strips of burdock, avocado, and cucumber down the length of the nori. Sprinkle with the Japanese shichimi togarashi and ryokua yasai.

Slowly roll up the sushi. Since bamboo mats may be hard to roll up neatly on their own, use the plastic wrap to help pull up the mat and get a nice, tight roll. Slice this crosswise down the middle, then cut each half roll at an angle into three pieces. Lay them decoratively on a platter. Serve with a dollop of wasabi, a few slices of pickled ginger, and, if you like, soy sauce.

Vegetable Pot Stickers

When Bruce made this on the show, he served it to his friends as the first course of a vegetarian dinner. It could also be an entrée served alongside a simple vegetable soup. Wonton wrappers are available in the produce section of almost any grocery store.

MAKES 25–30 WONTONS

4 teaspoons neutral oil, such as soy or
    grapeseed, plus additional oil for
    pan-frying if needed
2 cloves garlic, peeled and chopped
$\frac{1}{2}$ cup chopped white onion
1 cup thinly sliced savoy cabbage
1 cup well-chopped mung bean sprouts
4 green onions, chopped small
$\frac{1}{4}$ cup well-chopped sweet red pepper
Salt and pepper, to taste
Enough cornstarch to dust a large tray—
    about 1 tablespoon
25–30 wonton wrappers

Heat 2 teaspoons of the oil in a large skillet over a medium-high flame. Sauté the garlic for about a minute. Add the onion, cabbage, bean sprouts, green onions, and pepper. Cook until lightly browned, about 7 to 8 minutes. Season to taste with salt and pepper.

Bring a large pot of water to a boil.

Dust a large tray, cutting board, or cookie sheet lightly with cornstarch. Place 1 heaping teaspoonful of filling onto the center of each wrapper. Wet the edges a bit, then fold the wrappers in half and pinch the edges to seal. Place the finished wontons on the tray. When all the wontons are done, boil them in the pot for 2 minutes. Drain.

When you're ready to serve, heat the remaining 2 teaspoons of oil in a large skillet over a medium-high flame. Fry the wontons until they're brown on one side, then flip them and brown them on the other. Add extra oil to the pan if needed.

Mushroom Hunting

Mushrooms are amazing organisms. Though we live with them every day, even people who study them still know very little about their mysteries. We do know that what we think of as a "mushroom" is really just the small part the organism uses to reproduce; most of the fungus is a giant network of tiny fibers below ground. One mushroom can occupy acres and live far longer than humans. People think they may have conquered nature, but it's organisms like mushrooms that put us in our place and show us how much we still have to learn.

Wild mushroom hunters really are hunters, and they know every inch of their favorite grounds. When people write about mushroom hunting, they usually focus on the dangers; they rarely mention the excitement of the hunt. It requires a deep knowledge of the land and an intense concentration, almost a meditation. When we went mushroom hunting in California on the show, it was an amazing lesson on the mysteries of wild places.

Some people make a life out of chasing these magical fungi: traveling to where the mushrooms are likely to sprout, supporting themselves through what they can sell. Living off the land without destroying the land is a hippy dream, and mushrooms are a beautiful, delicious hippy food.

Stuffed Mushrooms

*E*ating wild mushrooms you've hunted down in nature can make you feel like a wild and crazy primitive, but even white button mushrooms can be pretty good. These make an out-of-sight vegan appetizer or the beginning of an Italian American spaghetti feast.

 MAKES 20–30

1 red bell pepper

1 green bell pepper

4 cloves garlic

20–30 white button mushrooms

5 tablespoons extra-virgin olive oil, divided

1 red onion

1 yellow onion

1 tablespoon chopped fresh oregano

Enough dried Italian bread crumbs to bind mixture—approximately 1 cup

Salt and pepper, to taste

Remove the caps and seeds from the peppers. Roughly chop them. Mince the garlic. Remove and chop the stems from the mushrooms.

Heat $\frac{1}{4}$ cup of the olive oil over a medium to medium-high flame. Add the garlic, mushroom stems, onions, and peppers. Sauté until soft, about 7 to 8 minutes. Add the oregano and continue sautéing until the mixture is slightly caramelized, about 3 to 4 minutes longer. Place the mixture in a food processor and pulse until finely chopped. Add enough bread crumbs to bind (this will depend upon the moisture of your vegetables); salt and pepper to taste. Continue pulsing until a rough paste forms.

Preheat the oven to 400 degrees. Coat a baking dish with the remaining tablespoon of oil.

Stuff the mushrooms by adding a heaping spoonful of filling to each cap. Mound lightly. Place in a pan and bake until lightly browned, about 15 minutes.

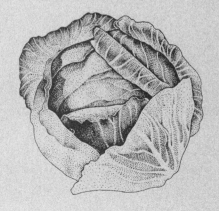

3. Salads and Dressings

What could be simpler or more perfect than vegetables, straight from the garden, untouched by heat? Salads are a celebration of vegetables at their most basic. A salad could be nothing more than a few leaves touched with a splash of lemon juice and a hint of salt. It could be as complicated as a composed salad. Either way, it's a celebration of nature in its purest, most unadorned form. It can be artful without using artifice. This is what comes straight from the earth, people, so love your mother with a salad.

Bruce enjoys wandering through the wild, picking edible plants. It was a skill that came in handy years ago when he was hitchhiking around the country. Harvesting wild edible plants is a way to bring out the hunters-gatherers in our souls. Imagine Bruce wandering through the woods, senses attuned to the smallest differences in green. His eyes focus on a treasure, and he stoops to pick it up. It's the most sustainable form of eating there is: unmolested nature ready to feed us her bounty. All it takes is a gatherer tuned in to her spirit.

Much as we like getting back to nature, it's not really likely that you are going to get most of your produce by gathering in the wild. Still, it's easy to get in touch with the soil. On the show, we're always trying to go out there and get our hands dirty in Mother Nature. Food comes from the earth, in all its crazy, living complexity, not from the produce aisle of the grocery store. Composting, gardening, and foraging are all ways we've gotten down and dirty and felt the life-giving ground. We've seen plants grow from seedlings to the most gorgeous fruits and vegetables that you could imagine. No true hippy gourmet can ever forget that vegetables are living things.

We visited a community garden in San Francisco where people keep alive a bountiful green space in the middle of a metropolis. These great people don't receive city funding, but their loving volunteers keep the garden alive and nourished. Though it's surrounded by buildings and concrete, inside is an oasis of vegetables, fruits, and flowers. These community gardeners know the joy of coaxing life from the earth, and that there's nothing like seeing the perfect product of nature, fresh from the soil, bathed in warm sunlight.

Bruce doesn't simply visit gardens, of course; he has his own. Just outside his dining room, it provides many of the vegetables used on the show. The outdoors and the indoors work together, and in a hippy kitchen neither is really separate.

We've also visited commercial enterprises dedicated to fresh produce, and these professional staffs had the same loving, dedicated spirit as the gardening amateurs. From the organic gardens of the Restaurant De Kas in Amsterdam (a restaurant actually built inside a working greenhouse), to the ridiculously fertile O'o Farms of James McDonald in Maui, Hawaii, we've seen the bountiful harvests of people devoted to making beautiful food by sustainable methods.

Some chefs try to improve upon nature, but one thing that a hippy gourmet knows better than a run-of-the-mill gourmet is that there's nothing you can do to make nature better. Nature will always win over art. One of the most beautiful dishes Bruce made on the show wasn't some complex stew or gooey dessert: It was a simple crudité platter he created for a music festival. Orange, red, yellow, green . . . bright, gorgeous, wild, psychedelic colors for some wild and free music. Bruce arranged them artistically, but it was the vegetables that stole the show.

We've had a lot of salad recipes on the *The Hippy Gourmet*. Some of our favorites, like Bruce's flavorful Caesar Salad, have been featured more than once. We don't know if the Roman emperors enjoyed creations like this, but nobody could eat the combination of anchovies, salty cheese, and, of course, homemade croutons and not feel rich. In this chapter, we've included recipes that are barely garnished and those accompanied by heavy, thick, rich dressings. All are worth tasting and trying.

Many of these recipes are Bruce's specialties, but we also have some of our friends to thank for others. Lara Blank, known for her baked goods from Lara's Delicious here in California, came on the show to make some of the specialties of her native Ukraine. We have her to thank for Salad Olivier, a potato salad with everything but the kitchen sink thrown in, and Beet Salad, which tames the sweetness of the beet with a bit of raw garlic bite, as well as the vegan borscht in our soups and stews chapter.

This chapter includes both side dish and main dish salads. It also features a selection of dressings to gussy up any salad. Dressings are incredibly easy to make, and once you master a couple of basic recipes, you can change them any way you like. You'll never have to buy that overprocessed, overpackaged commercial dressing again. We hope that these salads and dressings help you find joy in nature's bounty.

Salads

From simple side dishes to more complex main courses, here are a variety of vegetable and grain salads to suit any palate.

Mushroom and Artichoke Salad

Go for a wild ride with these 'shrooms. A wild flavor ride, that is. An hour in the refrigerator in a rich, flavorful bath turns ordinary button mushrooms into a rocking salad or side dish.

 SERVES 4–6

10 ounces fresh or frozen artichoke hearts (not marinated)

1 pound (about 5 cups) white button mushrooms

1/2 cup extra-virgin olive oil

2 cloves garlic, crushed

2 tablespoons tarragon vinegar

Touch of lemon juice

1 teaspoon sea salt

1 teaspoon dry mustard

1/2 teaspoon raw sugar

1/4 teaspoon cracked black pepper

1 tablespoon chives or parsley, for garnish

4–6 large butter lettuce leaves

In a steamer or a pan with a steamer insert, bring an inch or two of water to a boil. Add the artichokes, cover, and steam until tender (frozen artichokes need only to thaw and heat up, while fresh artichokes, which must cook, take longer).

In a bowl, combine the artichokes with the remaining ingredients (except the chives or parsley and lettuce).

Marinate the mushrooms and artichokes in the mixture for at least 1 hour in the refrigerator, then toss really well. Season to taste with salt and pepper. Serve family-style on butter lettuce leaves, garnished with herbs, or serve on individual lettuce leaves.

"Aspairgrass" Salad

Asparagus, aspairgrass, asparagross . . . whatever you call it, it's a simple, awesome cold salad. You don't have to wear flowers in your hair, or your food, to be a hippy, but if you choose, they turn a simple green salad into a work of art.

 SERVES 4–6

2 pounds asparagus

1 teaspoon sea salt

1 tablespoon finely chopped fresh gingerroot

$^1/_2$ teaspoon brown sugar

3–4 tablespoons soy sauce

2 tablespoons extra-virgin olive oil

2 tablespoons sesame oil

$^1/_4$ cup fresh nasturtium and calendula flowers, for garnish (optional)

Remove and compost the tough ends of the asparagus. Cut remaining spears diagonally into 2-inch pieces.

Add the sea salt to a large pot of water and bring to a boil over high heat. Drop in the asparagus and blanch for 2 minutes. Remove the spears to a colander and rinse them under cool water to stop the cooking.

Whisk the remaining ingredients (except the flowers) in a glass bowl. Pour this dressing over the asparagus and chill thoroughly. Garnish with flowers, if desired.

Eggplant Salad

This isn't your usual eggplant salad, made with those big, bitter eggplants that look like some kind of giant purple monster's pod. Instead it uses slim, long, graceful Asian eggplants. If your eggplant is shaped like a cucumber, you've found the right vegetable.

 SERVES 4

2 Asian eggplants

2 large tomatoes, sliced as thin as you can

2 tablespoons chopped white onion

6 tablespoons chopped fresh parsley

5 tablespoons olive oil

3 tablespoons vinegar of your choice

Salt and pepper, to taste

Large leaf of romaine or several endive leaves, for serving

Greek olives or sliced radish, for garnish (optional)

Preheat the broiler. Slice the eggplants in half lengthwise and broil until soft, approximately 10 minutes per side. Be sure they're cooked through. Let them cool, then peel off the skin and discard it. Chop the eggplant into bite-size chunks.

Mix the chopped eggplant, tomatoes, onion, parsley, oil, and vinegar. Season to taste with salt and pepper. Serve on either a large romaine lettuce leaf or several endive leaves, garnishing with Greek olives or sliced radishes.

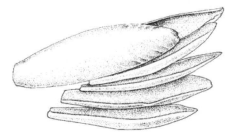

Tabbouleh

This classic Middle Eastern dish is delicious by itself as a main course, but it can also be used to accompany other dishes. Stuff it into a pita or serve with other Middle Eastern favorites. For a less traditional tabbouleh, substitute cooked couscous or millet for the bulgur and skip the soaking step.

 SERVES 6

1 cup bulgur

1¹/₂ cups boiling water

¹/₄ cup olive oil

2 tablespoons freshly squeezed lemon juice

2 tablespoons freshly squeezed lime juice

2 cloves garlic, peeled and chopped fine

1 large tomato or 2 plum tomatoes, chopped

¹/₂ cup chopped flat-leaf parsley

¹/₂ cup chopped mint

2 green onions, chopped

Salt and pepper, to taste

Place the bulgur in a large bowl, pour the boiling water over it, and cover with a kitchen towel. Let this sit for about 15 minutes, or until the water is absorbed and the bulgur is tender.

Fluff the soaked bulgur with a fork to separate the grains. If any water is still standing, cover again and let the mixture sit for an additional 5 minutes.

Stir the remaining ingredients into the grain. Refrigerate to allow the tabbouleh to cool and the flavors to combine, about 30 to 60 minutes. Season to taste with salt and pepper.

Spinach Salad Extraordinaire!

This is a crunchy, dark green sweet-and-sour masterpiece. You'll never want to touch spinach that's been near bacon again. Served with bread or muffins, this could also make a light main course.

SERVES 4–6

1 pound fresh spinach, washed, dried, and torn into bite-size pieces

1/2 pound bean sprouts

2 stalks celery, chopped

1 can (5 ounces) water chestnuts, drained and sliced

1/2 cup raw brown sugar

1/3 cup catsup

1/2 cup extra-virgin olive oil

1/4 cup red wine vinegar

1 teaspoon onion juice

1 teaspoon garlic salt

1 teaspoon paprika

1 teaspoon lemon pepper

Pinch of salt

2 hard-boiled eggs, peeled and sliced thin

Mix the spinach, bean sprouts, celery, and water chestnuts. For a wilted salad, heat a sauté pan over high heat, add the spinach, and stir until just wilted. Remove and mix with the bean sprouts, celery, and water chestnuts.

Mix the brown sugar, catsup, olive oil, vinegar, onion juice, garlic salt, paprika, lemon pepper, and salt in a blender or food processor, or blend by hand with a whisk. Toss the vegetables with the dressing. To serve, top with hard-boiled egg slices.

Gold Rush Salad

 his is a little something for those folks up in the foothills of the Sierras! Real gold is just some cold, hard stuff that's no fun at all on a plate. This is much better: It's gold that you can eat and enjoy with friends.

SERVES 2

1 large orange

1 medium parsnip

1 medium tart apple (such as Granny Smith, Cortland, or Pippin)

2 tablespoons extra-virgin olive oil

1 tablespoon cider or white wine vinegar

1$\frac{1}{2}$ teaspoons raw brown sugar

$\frac{1}{4}$ teaspoon sea salt

$\frac{1}{8}$ teaspoon dry mustard

Dash of cracked pepper

6–8 grated radishes

Peel and remove the white membrane from the orange and cut it into small cubes. Work over a small bowl, reserving any orange juice.

Pare the parsnip and core the apple, then shred them both.

Mix the orange, parsnip, and apple and refrigerate for 30 minutes.

Mix the oil, vinegar, sugar, salt, mustard, pepper, and reserved orange juice together well with a whisk. Toss the dressing with the fruit and vegetables, garnishing with radish shreds.

Beet Salad

This salad has awesome color and lots of flavors jamming together. The garlic bite really plays against the sweet beets and raisins. Make sure to give it plenty of time in the refrigerator for the flavors to mellow.

 SERVES 4–6

½ cup raisins

3 large beets, uncooked

3 cloves garlic, peeled and crushed or
    chopped fine

1 cup chopped walnuts

½ cup mayonnaise (use vegan,
    if you like)

1 tablespoon chopped fresh dill

Salt and pepper, to taste

Soak the raisins, in enough hot water to cover, for about 15 to 30 minutes or until nicely plumped. Drain well.

Peel and grate the beets. You can use your hands and a box grater if you don't mind turning your hands pink. A food processor with a grater attachment will do the same job with a lot less mess and time.

Mix everything together well, then let it sit in the refrigerator preferably at least half an hour. When you're ready to serve, season to taste with salt and pepper.

Asian-Flavored Cabbage Slaw

ou could shred the cabbages with a box grater or food processor rather than cutting them into thin shreds with a knife. The texture will be different, but this slaw will still be delicious. Try serving it with tofu and soba noodles or brown rice.

SERVES 4–6

4 cups thinly shredded napa cabbage
1 cup thinly shredded red cabbage
1 tablespoon coarse kosher or sea salt
2 tablespoons chopped fresh mint
2 tablespoons chopped fresh cilantro
2 tablespoons finely chopped gingerroot
2 tablespoons soy sauce
2 tablespoons rice vinegar

1½ tablespoons neutral oil, such as
    soy or grapeseed
Dash of toasted sesame oil
1 handful chopped peanuts

In a large colander, mix the cabbages and salt. Using your fingers, rub the salt into the cabbage until it has dissolved a bit. Allow the cabbage to sit in the colander over a sink to drain for at least half an hour.

Rinse the cabbage well to remove any remaining salt. A handful at a time, squeeze the shreds dry and place them in a large bowl.

Mix the mint, cilantro, gingerroot, soy sauce, rice vinegar, oil, and sesame oil into the cabbage. Garnish with chopped peanuts and serve.

Caesar Salad

This is the real deal: pungent with raw garlic and anchovies. Add a little more protein, such as cooked fish or tofu, and it's a substantial meal.

 SERVES 4–6

1 egg

Juice of 1 lemon

2 cloves garlic, peeled

1 teaspoon Dijon mustard

Dash of Worcestershire sauce

1 cup Parmesan-Romano cheese blend, grated fine, divided

2 tablespoons balsamic vinegar

Dash of white pepper

1 can (2 ounces) anchovies, packed in oil

1¼–1⅓ cups extra-virgin olive oil

Ends of a loaf of fresh white bread (save the rest for something else)

Pinch of salt

1 head romaine lettuce, chopped into bite-size pieces

Bring 2 inches water to boil over high heat in a small saucepan. Add egg and cook for 1 minute. Drain and rinse under cold running water. In a blender, combine the egg, lemon juice, garlic, Dijon mustard, Worcestershire sauce, ½ cup of the cheese, balsamic vinegar, and white pepper.

In a small bowl, save about a teaspoon of the oil from the anchovies. Add the remaining oil and anchovies to the blender.

Process the dressing ingredients with the blender running; add the olive oil until you reach the desired thickness.

Cut the ends of the white bread into chunks for croutons: Mix the chunks with the reserved anchovy oil, a large pinch of the cheese mixture, and a pinch of salt. Toast the bread on a baking sheet under a broiler or in a dry skillet over high heat on the stove. When the cubes are lightly browned and crispy, remove them from the heat.

In a large bowl, combine the lettuce, remaining cheese, your desired amount of dressing, and croutons. Mix well. Serve the salad with the remaining dressing on the side, or save it up to a couple of days for another salad.

Salad Olivier

Salad Olivier originated in Eastern Europe; it's believed that it was named for a French chef named Olivier. Many fishmongers sell precooked crabs. If you'll be cooking your own, bring a large pot of water to a boil. Plunge the crabs in headfirst. Cover, reduce the heat to medium, and cook for about 15 minutes. When the crabs are done, plunge them into ice water. Crack and remove the meat.

 SERVES 8

4 large russet potatoes, peeled
   and chopped
2 large carrots, peeled and chopped
16 eggs
$^1/_4$ cup table salt
1 cup green peas
Meat from 4 cooked Dungeness crabs
4 dill pickles, chopped
1 cup chopped red bell pepper
1 cup diced cucumber
2 tablespoons chopped fresh dill
2 tablespoons chopped fresh basil
2 tablespoons chopped fresh cilantro
8 green onions, chopped

Bring a large pot of water to a boil over high heat. Add the potatoes and carrots, cover, and reduce the heat to medium low. Cook to your desired tenderness, between 12 and 17 minutes. Drain.

In another pot, bring the eggs, salt, and enough water to cover to a boil over medium-high heat. Cook the eggs for about 5 minutes, then cover the pan, remove from the heat, and let the eggs sit in the hot water for about 10 minutes. Remove the eggs into a bowl of ice water to cool them, then peel and chop.

Bring a pot of water to a boil. Add the peas. Cover, reduce the heat to medium low, and cook until bright green and tender: 1 to 2 minutes for fresh peas, about 5 minutes for peas that are a bit less tender. If you're using frozen peas, follow the package directions. Once they're cooked, drain in a colander under cold water.

Break up the crabmeat and pick through it to make sure there are no shell fragments. In a large bowl, mix the crab with all the ingredients. Season to taste with salt and pepper and serve.

The Magical Soybean

In much of Asia, the soybean provides an almost endless variety of protein and seasonings. It's an excellent source of other nutrients, too, and it's delicious.

Tempeh: Tempeh is made when soybeans are fermented. Sometimes grains such as barley and rice, or flavorings like seaweed, are added. It's chewy and nutty, and Indonesians have eaten it as a staple food for generations. You can coat it with seasonings and bake it for a delicious protein cutlet, add it to stir-fries, put it into soups, or serve it sliced on a sandwich. Grated, you can use it as you would use ground beef in spaghetti sauce, tacos, or even mixed with vegetables as a burrito filling. You can find tempeh in health food stores and some conventional grocery stores. Look for unflavored, seasoned, and even "bacon" varieties.

Tofu: Tofu is made by curdling soy milk. Its texture can range from as soft as custard to almost as firm as fresh mozzarella cheese. Whatever texture you choose, it's milder and softer than tempeh, and so gentle tasting that it complements almost any flavor—without overpowering. Use the very soft varieties as the basis for soups or dips. The firmer varieties can be cut up and added to stir-fries, fried to a crisp, broiled or grilled . . . the possibilities are virtually endless. Tofu is available in most conventional supermarkets and health food stores. Look for unflavored and flavored varieties, and even pungent, cheese-like fermented tofu in some Asian markets.

Miso: Miso is a Japanese condiment made by fermenting soybean paste. It is also made with wheat, barley, or rice. It's highly flavored and salty. In Japan, it is mixed with broth to make a delicious soup. Miso is available in most health food stores and some conventional supermarkets.

Chinese Tofu/Tempeh Salad

With this salad, you can have all the crunch and flavor of a "Chinese" chicken salad, and your bird friends can live to see another day. Because the ingredients can be prepared ahead of time, this is a great dish to make at the last minute for a brunch or lunch with friends. Rice stick noodles are available at Asian markets and many conventional supermarkets.

 SERVES 6–8

2 cups peanut oil

10 ounces dried rice stick noodles

1/4 cup sesame seeds

1 cup roasted peanuts

1/4 cup raw brown sugar

1/4–1/2 cup lemon juice

1/2 teaspoon sea salt

3 tablespoons chopped fresh cilantro

2 tablespoons sesame oil

1 head iceberg lettuce

About 2 pounds savory flavored tempeh
    (any flavor) or BBQ tofu, cut into
    bite-size pieces

1 large red onion, shredded

Heat the peanut oil over a high flame in a wok or large pan. Working carefully, place the rice noodles in the oil in small batches (about a fistful each). In only a few seconds, the noodles will puff and expand. Remove with a slotted spoon and repeat with remaining noodles. Place the finished rice noodles on a platter lined with paper towels for draining. These noodles can be fried days in advance and kept in tight containers.

In a dry skillet over medium-high heat, toast the sesame seeds until fragrant. Remove from the heat. If desired, repeat the toasting procedure with the peanuts.

Combine the brown sugar, lemon juice, salt, cilantro, and sesame oil in a small jar. Shake well. Refrigerate until you're ready to serve.

Tear the lettuce into bite-size pieces.

To serve, mix the tempeh or tofu, lettuce, peanuts, and onion with the dressing. Place on a bed of fried noodles. Garnish with the sesame seeds.

Taco Salad

This is an inexpensive but very filling salad. It's easy to double or triple if you want to serve a large group for a little money. A flour or corn tortilla crisped in a couple of tablespoons of hot oil for a few minutes makes for a crunchy and edible plate to serve the taco salad in; if you try this, omit the corn chips.

 SERVES 6

1 cup kidney beans; or substitute 2 cans
    (16 ounces each) beans, rinsed well,
    and skip the soaking and cooking steps
1 head iceberg lettuce
1/2 cup black olives, pitted and chopped
1 cup shredded sharp cheddar cheese
3 cups corn chips
1/4 cup sour cream
2 tablespoons chopped green chilies (seed
    the chilies for a milder flavor)
2 very ripe avocados, mashed
Chili powder, to taste
Salt and pepper, to taste

If you're using dried beans, soak them overnight in enough water to cover by about 2 inches. In the morning, drain the beans.

In a large pot, cover them with water by about an inch. Bring to a boil over medium-high heat, reduce the heat to medium low, cover, and simmer until tender but not mushy—about 45 minutes. Drain and reserve.

Tear the lettuce into bite-size pieces. In a large salad bowl, layer the lettuce with the cooked beans, olives, cheese, and chips.

In a small bowl, mix the sour cream, chilies, avocado, and chili powder. Season to taste with salt and pepper. Serve with the dressing on the side.

Veggie Cobb

Composed salads—those in which ingredients are carefully arranged rather than tossed together—are often eaten in France, but the Cobb, loaded with just about everything in the kitchen, is all-American. The enjoyment comes from this salad's beauty, so let the artist inside you shine and arrange this composed salad in the way you find most beautiful.

SERVES 4

1½ tablespoons balsamic vinegar

2 teaspoons Dijon mustard

1 tablespoon minced shallot

¼ cup extra-virgin olive oil

Salt and pepper, to taste

4 cups romaine lettuce, torn into bite-size pieces

2 carrots, peeled and shredded

1 beet, peeled and shredded

8 ounces purchased prebaked tofu, any flavor, chopped (or substitute your own homemade baked tofu)

1 avocado, peeled, pit removed, and sliced lengthwise

1 tomato, chopped

2 green onions, chopped

2 hard-boiled eggs, peeled and chopped (omit for a vegan salad)

½ cup crumbled Gorgonzola cheese (omit for a vegan salad)

Whisk together the vinegar, mustard, and shallot. Slowly pour in the olive oil, whisking as you do so. Season to taste with salt and pepper.

Toss about half of the dressing with the romaine lettuce. Place the lettuce on one large platter or on individual plates. Arrange the carrots, beet, tofu, avocado, tomato, green onions, eggs, and cheese around or on top to your liking. Drizzle the remaining dressing on top of the salad and serve.

Quinoa Salad

particularly good on warm days, eaten outside with the sun warming your toes and your heart. If you don't like mangoes or they aren't available, you could substitute 2 medium peaches or nectarines. In smaller portions, it makes a good side dish.

 SERVES 4

1 cup quinoa

$^1/_4$ cup chopped fresh cilantro

1 medium mango, peeled and chopped

$^1/_4$ cup chopped green onions

$^1/_2$ teaspoon lime zest

Juice of 2 limes

3 tablespoons olive oil

Salt and pepper, to taste

Fresh, whole lettuce leaves of your choice

$^1/_4$ cup chopped walnuts

Soak the quinoa for about 10 minutes in enough water to cover it by about 1 inch. Rinse well and drain. If you prefer, rinse the quinoa in several changes of water. This step removes any bitter taste.

Place the quinoa and 2 cups of water in a saucepan. Bring to a boil over high heat. Cover and reduce the heat to medium low. Simmer for about 15 minutes or until the quinoa has absorbed the water and fluffed. Remove from the heat and cool for about 15 minutes.

Mix the cilantro, mango, and green onions into the quinoa. Stir in the zest, lime juice, and olive oil. Season to taste with salt and pepper. Spoon the quinoa onto lettuce leaves to serve sprinkled with walnuts.

Dressings

Many people use nothing more than a squeeze of lemon juice or a dash of vinegar on their salads and with perfect, tender greens, this may be the best approach. We also love a good dressing, though. Use with greens and maybe a vegetable for a side salad. Add fruits, nuts, croutons or toasted bread, and a protein of your choice to make an awesome meal in a bowl.

Vinaigrette

A vinaigrette is basically one part vinegar to three parts oil, plus a bit of salt and some seasonings. Experiment with different vinegars, oils, and seasonings, and use a different ratio of oil to vinegar if you like; don't let yourself get hung up on the rules.

 MAKES ABOUT ¹/₂ CUP

2 tablespoons vinegar (such as balsamic or high-quality wine vinegar)
1 teaspoon Dijon mustard
1 teaspoon minced shallot
6 tablespoons olive oil
Salt and pepper, to taste

Stir together the vinegar, mustard, and shallot in a small bowl with a wire whisk. Slowly add the oil, whisking constantly as you do so. If you think it's a drag to stand there with a whisk, you can instead place all ingredients in a glass jar and shake, shake, shake your groove thang until it's mixed.

To test flavor, dip one of the vegetables you'll be using in the salad into the dressing. Stir in salt and pepper to taste.

Variations:

For an herb vinaigrette, add 1 tablespoon of a single herb or a combination of herbs at the end. Try chives, parsley, basil, tarragon, or whatever grows in your garden.

For a garlic vinaigrette, add 1 clove of minced fresh garlic at the end. Or add a whole clove, peeled and lightly crushed; let it sit in the dressing in the refrigerator for at least half an hour, then remove.

For a cheese vinaigrette, add a handful of blue cheese, feta, or Parmesan at the end.

For a honey mustard vinaigrette, use apple cider vinegar, leave out the shallot, and instead add 2 teaspoonfuls of your favorite honey.

Ginger Vinaigrette

This vinaigrette is perfect for fresh greens with lots of vegetables such as grated or roasted carrots, jicama, beets, or snow peas. It could also be used with pasta, such as soba noodles, or as a marinade for fish or tofu.

 MAKES ABOUT ³/₄ CUP

2 tablespoons roughly chopped gingerroot

¹/₄ cup chopped shallot

1 clove garlic, peeled

¹/₄ cup rice vinegar

1¹/₂ tablespoons soy sauce

¹/₂ teaspoon toasted sesame oil

¹/₂ cup neutral oil, such as soy or
    grapeseed

Salt and pepper, to taste

In a blender or food processor, process the gingerroot, shallot, and garlic until a rough paste forms. Scrape down the sides a couple of times if necessary. Add the rice vinegar, soy sauce, and sesame oil. Process for a few seconds. With the motor running, slowly add the neutral oil. Taste (preferably by dipping one of the vegetables you'll be using in the salad) and, if desired, add black pepper and a bit more soy sauce or salt to taste.

Creamy Herb Dressing

 reamy dressings complement spicy greens, such as arugula, endive, or tender young mustard greens, particularly well. They also are wonderful on garden-fresh tomatoes or slightly spicy radishes. This rich dressing is also great as a dip.

MAKES ABOUT 1¼ CUPS

1 cup buttermilk

2 tablespoons olive oil

1½ tablespoons lemon juice

2 teaspoons Dijon mustard

1 clove garlic, peeled

3 tablespoons chopped chives

2 tablespoons chopped fresh parsley

Process all the ingredients in a food processor or blender. Season to taste with salt and pepper, preferably dipping one of the vegetables you will use in the salad in the dressing to test it.

Variations:

For a blue cheese or feta dressing, omit the parsley and chives, and add ¼ cup crumbled cheese after blending the other ingredients.

For a buttermilk dill dressing, omit the parsley and chives and substitute ¼ cup fresh dill.

Goddess of the Green Dressing

You don't have to hail Caesar all the time; try this twist instead. Offer it on the side, since people prefer to be the master of their own salad dressings when garlic and anchovies are involved. Present it with a beautiful array of organic greens and edible flowers such as stunning purple violets and borage.

 MAKES ABOUT 1¼ CUPS

2–3 spinach leaves, with stems

3 tablespoons finely chopped anchovies

1 bunch green onions, roots removed and roughly chopped

6 mint sprigs

1 roma tomato, stem removed

3 tablespoons chopped chives

1 clove garlic, peeled and minced

1 tablespoon lemon juice

2 tablespoons tarragon vinegar

⅓ cup freshly chopped parsley

1 cup mayonnaise (or substitute 1 egg and 1 cup vegetable oil)

Salt and pepper, to taste

Blend all the ingredients in a blender or a food processor until well combined. If you're omitting the mayonnaise, mix all ingredients except the vegetable oil in a blender or food processor; with the motor running, add the oil in a slow stream.

Season to taste with salt and pepper. Refrigerate for at least an hour. Use within a day or two.

Your Name Here Bottled Salad Dressing

hy would you want a bottled dressing from the store with some other guy's name and picture on it when you could be looking at your own handsome mug? Mix this up, keep it in a bottle in the fridge, and you'll have your very own dressing any time you need it.

MAKES ABOUT 2³/₄ CUPS

¹/₂ cup red wine vinegar

¹/₄ cup brown sugar or honey

1¹/₂ teaspoons sea salt

1 teaspoon onion powder (or granulated onion)

1 teaspoon celery seeds

1 teaspoon paprika

1 teaspoon dried dill weed, or 2 teaspoons fresh

¹/₄ teaspoon fresh-ground pepper

1 cup catsup

1 cup extra-virgin olive oil

2 tablespoons capers

1 tablespoon Worcestershire sauce

2 tablespoons Dijon mustard

2 cloves garlic, peeled

Combine the first eight ingredients in a saucepan and bring to a boil over medium-high heat. Remove from the burner and let cool. Pour into a glass jar and add the remaining ingredients (except the garlic). Shake the jar really well to blend everything together.

Place the garlic cloves on small skewers (large enough so that you can fish them out later without getting your hands too dirty) and place them in the jar. Chill the dressing in the fridge. After approximately 3 hours, open the jar and remove the garlic cloves. Season to taste with salt and pepper.

4. Soups and Stews

When you're cooking for rock stars or television crews, you never know when you're going to be eating or who's going to be at the table. Imagine the craziness of cooking for two teenagers with different schedules . . . then imagine an entire set or concert hall filled with them.

When everything's crazy, soups and stews help you go with the flow. Are four more coming? Soup helps you stretch out the meal. Just throw in a bit of extra stock, break out another loaf of bread, and you're good to go. Are you in the creative groove or is the party too good to break up? Just let it simmer on the burner a little longer, and it's all good. If you make too much, soups and stews are great to share with people in need, and they're always good tomorrow—or better yet as dawn begins to break after an excellent night with friends.

Soups and stews are all about sharing; they're among the foods Bruce found easiest to make for large groups of fellow travelers in the 1960s. The dancing hippies just needed a bowl and a hungry belly, and Bruce always had some food to feed them. Soup is great for gatherings where everyone is part of an extended family. They're also great anytime people need warmth and comfort.

Some people say that too many cooks spoil the pot, but we think all cooking is communal. It's like the old story of stone soup. A traveler comes to a small, quiet town one day. It's the kind of place where people stay indoors and keep to themselves. You don't expect raves or bonfires, or even church picnics; it's so sedate, it's downright boring.

The traveler is carrying nothing but a giant pot and a large stone. He slowly sets the pot in the middle of the town square, then goes about gathering kindling and wood and starts a large fire under the pot. He adds water and the stone. Not much happens in the town, and soon the people start coming from their homes, curiosity a lot stronger than their fear of strangers.

"What are you doing?" the people ask.

"This is a magical stone, and I'm going to make a pot of the most delicious soup in the world . . . stone soup." The people have never heard of stone soup before, so they stay to watch.

The traveler stands quietly for a while and watches the water boil. "Of course," he says after a time, "stone soup is good, but there's nothing as good as stone soup and beans." A woman goes back to her house and fetches a handful of beans. He watches the pot for a while longer.

"And," he says, "nothing beats stone soup with some onions and garlic." A storekeeper goes inside and comes back with a sack of onions and a string of garlic.

"Better yet," the traveler says after watching the pot a little longer, "is stone soup with carrots." And the mayor brings a big bunch of carrots straight from the ground.

For a long time it goes on that way, and pretty soon the stone soup also has cabbage, sweet potatoes, green beans, tomatoes, fresh herbs, and salt. When the traveler judges the soup is done, he tells everyone to get their bowls, and they all marvel at how a simple stone can make such a delicious soup. Everyone smiles and, for once, the townspeople are gathered all in one place, and they couldn't be happier.

All soups and stews are like stone soup in their way—though most don't involve tricking suspicious townspeople into giving you a free meal. We take a little bit from here and a little bit from there, and soon we have a delicious meal for everyone to share.

Don't we take ideas and ingredients from everyone we meet? We learn how to make perfect stock from the French, we learn how to have just the right hand with spices from India, we learn how to make the perfect bowl of beans from Latin Americans. Put it all together, and we have the perfect bowl of soup.

Soups and stews are common to all the cultures that we know. Some are part of the national identity: Mexicans make their menudo, French Canadians make pea soup, the Thais make fragrant broths rich with coconut, and every self-respecting French-woman makes her own stock. They're probably so common because they're so simple. Almost all soups are just a few flavorful ingredients and some liquid simmered together until they become one glorious whole.

On the show, we've cooked soups as different as bean from Brazil, asparagus from France, borscht from the Ukraine, and all-American chili. We love them all. If you're a beginning cook, soup can be your new best friend. It's very forgiving. Too salty? Throw in a couple of potatoes. Too bland? Add a few more flavorful ingredients. Just keep adding and cooking until you've got something you love. Get yourself started with this chapter.

Many of the recipes here are based on beans. Dried beans are almost always superior to canned. They don't have the metallic flavor cans give to beans; worse, canned beans are often cooked to the point of mushiness. Dried beans don't use any excess packaging or additional salt and preservatives. Still, if you're short on time or just prefer not to cook a big pot of beans, substitute one 16-ounce can of beans for each $1/3$ cup of dried beans in the recipe, and skip the steps in which the beans are soaked and cooked.

Come and get it . . . soup's on!

Simple Soups

These soups are easy to make, though none is a meal on its own. This section also contains stock recipes. Stock, the most basic of all soups, is nothing more than flavorful ingredients boiled to extract their essence. It's the basis of countless other dishes, and many simple soups are nothing more than stock and a few added ingredients.

Miso Soup

This simple soup can begin any Japanese meal; it can even be eaten as a warming breakfast. You can change the recipe to your liking by adding mushrooms, tofu, or seaweed. Kombu and bonito flakes are the basis of a broth called dashi, one of the basic ingredients in Japanese cooking.

 SERVES 4

4 1-inch pieces kombu

4 cups water

1 large handful bonito flakes

1 tablespoon miso (any variety)

2 tablespoons minced green onions

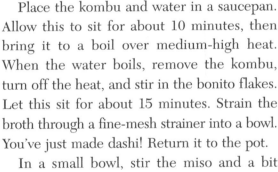

Place the kombu and water in a saucepan. Allow this to sit for about 10 minutes, then bring it to a boil over medium-high heat. When the water boils, remove the kombu, turn off the heat, and stir in the bonito flakes. Let this sit for about 15 minutes. Strain the broth through a fine-mesh strainer into a bowl. You've just made dashi! Return it to the pot.

In a small bowl, stir the miso and a bit (approximately 3 tablespoons) of the cooked broth until it's diluted. Stir the miso mixture into the pot. Heat over a medium-high flame until it's warm, but don't let it boil. Boiling results in a cloudy soup and may destroy healthful enzymes. Add any additional ingredients, such as tofu. Pour into bowls and sprinkle with green onions.

Kom-What?

Many Japanese ingredients seem mysterious to Westerners, but most are barely embellished products of nature. Dashi, the basic stock of Japanese cooking, uses two ingredients that are not well known in the United States.

Kombu: Kombu is a kind of dried seaweed. It comes in large, rectangular dried sheets. You can find it in Asian markets and health food stores. It's rich in nutrients and produces a flavorful broth. To use it, steep it in hot water. Remove and discard the kombu, and use the resulting broth.

Bonito: Bonito is a kind of dried fish, usually found already grated. It's available in Asian markets and many health food stores. Bonito flakes are added to dashi and then strained out. You can discard the bonito flakes or allow them to dry a bit, mix them with some soy sauce, and serve over rice. They're also great straight out of the package over a plate of rice and vegetables.

Vegan Miso Soup

Because dashi contains bonito, made from dried fish, it isn't vegetarian or vegan. This miso soup uses mushrooms instead. They add a meaty quality without using any animal protein.

 SERVES 4

4 1-inch pieces kombu

4 large dried shiitake mushrooms

4 cups water

1 tablespoon miso (any kind)

2 tablespoons minced green onions

Place the kombu, mushrooms, and water in a saucepan. Allow this to sit for about 10 minutes, then place the pan over medium-high heat. When water boils, remove the kombu, turn off the heat, and let the mixture sit for 15 minutes. Remove the mushrooms. Strain the broth through a fine-mesh strainer into a bowl and return it to the pan. Slice the mushrooms and return them to the broth.

Stir together the miso and a bit (approximately 3 tablespoons) of broth in a small bowl until it dissolves. Add this to the broth. If you'll be adding extra ingredients, such as tofu or seaweed, do so now. Heat over a medium-high flame until warm. Do not let it boil. Serve in bowls with green onions sprinkled over.

Cold Cucumber Soup

When it's too hot to move, and too hot to turn on the stove, listen to what your body is telling you. You don't need to make things any hotter. Serve this cool and refreshing soup, and spend the rest of the day skinny-dipping.

 SERVES 4–6

1 quart (4 cups) plain yogurt

2 large cucumbers, washed and ends cut off

¼ teaspoon garlic powder (more if you prefer a zesty garlic flavor); or use 1 clove garlic, peeled and chopped fine

Salt and pepper, to taste

½ cup diced tomato

Sprig of mint

In a blender or food processor, process the yogurt for a few seconds. If you're using full-fat yogurt, be sure that there are no chunks of the fatty layer left. Add the cucumbers and garlic powder. Process until smooth, scraping down the sides if necessary. Season to taste with salt and pepper. Remember that the flavors will get a little more mellow when the dish is chilled. Chill thoroughly, about an hour. Garnish with the tomato and sprig of mint.

What's in Stock

Stocks are about getting to the heart, the very essence, of flavor. We might use meditation or drugs or fasting to reach what's inside ourselves; for food, it just takes some heat and water. Bruce's training is French, and the French know that a good stock can make the difference in a simple recipe. The French wouldn't skimp on an inexpensive stock, and for good reason. Canned and frozen vegetable stocks may be quick and easy, but their quality varies. Most are too salty. All are wasteful.

Most stocks are made by boiling some kind of animal part to pull out the flavor and nutrients, but you don't have to kill anything to get killer flavor. You can make a vegetable stock with whatever vegetables are left over in your vegetable drawer, or even trimmings and ends that you've saved, and it's going to rock the canned stuff. This is true hippy cooking—none of your vegetables has to ever be wasted. Make a lot, and when it's cool, freeze it in zip-top plastic bags in 1-cup portions; you'll always have good stock.

Light stocks are generally better in light-tasting recipes, and dark stocks in heavier recipes. Both are good for replacing water in cooking grains, or as the basis of a simple soup. Just heat up some stock with fresh vegetables and herbs, and perhaps throw in some pasta, beans, or cooked grains, and you have a simple, nourishing meal.

Vegan Vegetable Stock (Light and Dark Versions)

This technique can be used with virtually any vegetables and seasonings. Experiment to find the one that you like best. Mushrooms give a nice, earthy, almost meaty stock; carrots and parsnips a sweet, light one; and leeks and onions make any stock better.

 AMOUNT VARIES

Several of the Following Vegetables:

Onions, unpeeled and roughly chopped
Carrots, roughly chopped
Parsnips, roughly chopped
Leeks, roughly chopped
Tomatoes, roughly chopped
Celery, roughly chopped, including leaves
Mushrooms, roughly chopped
Whole kale leaves
Garlic, unpeeled
Whatever vegetables and trimmings you have (though starchy vegetables such as potatoes will make a thicker stock)

One or More of the Following Seasonings:

Bay leaves
Whole peppercorns
Whole, unchopped herbs, such as parsley sprigs

For Dark Stock Only:

2 tablespoons light olive oil

For Light Stock:

In a large pot, bring the vegetables and seasonings to a boil over high heat with enough water to cover by about an inch. Cover the pot and reduce the heat to medium low. Simmer for 2 to 3 hours. Let the stock cool somewhat, and strain over a bowl. Compost the vegetables and seasonings.

For Dark Stock:

Preheat the oven to 450 degrees.

Toss the large vegetables with the oil. Place in a single layer in one or two roasting pans. Roast until browned, about 40 to 50 minutes. Stir well once or twice during the cooking, and watch carefully to prevent burning.

Add the roasted vegetables, any trimmings, and the seasonings to a large pot. Swirl a bit of water in the roasting pan(s) to get up all the juices and browned bits; add these to the pot, too. Then add enough water to cover the vegetables by about an inch.

Bring to a boil over high heat. Cover and reduce the heat to medium low. Simmer for 2 to 3 hours. Let the stock cool somewhat, and strain it over a large bowl. Compost the vegetables and seasonings.

Bigger Soups and Stews

These soups and stews may be more complex than the basic recipes, but most are super easy. Serve them with a starch such as bread, muffins, crackers, or pita, and most are a full meal on their own. Add a salad and a dessert, and you have a feast.

Brazilian-Style Black Beans

This classic recipe does a tango on your tongue. Black beans are one of the staple foods of the Amazon. Packed with protein and nutrients, they're food to nourish the wild and amazing people who live in or near the rain forest.

 SERVES 6

1½ pounds black beans

2 tablespoons neutral oil, such as soybean

4 large cloves garlic

½ medium onion

1 tablespoon ground cumin

1 teaspoon dried oregano

Salt and pepper, to taste

Soak the beans overnight in enough water to cover by at least 2 inches. Drain.

Coat the bottom of a large pot with the oil. Heat over a medium flame, then add the garlic, onion, cumin, and oregano.

When the onion mixture is tender, add the beans. Cover with just enough hot water to cover the beans by about an inch. Bring to a boil, then cover, reduce the heat, and simmer for about an hour.

When the beans are tender to your liking, spoon about half into another bowl. Mash these, then spoon them back into the pot. Heat until mixture is thickened a bit. Season to taste with salt and pepper.

In the Jungle, the Mighty Jungle

If you can't resist cooking in nature, and break out the grill any chance you can, you've got a little bit of hippy gourmet in you. On the show, we once grilled a vegan feast in the heart of the rain forest, a thousand miles up the Amazon in Brazil.

The cities in Brazil are amazing, but it's the jungle that draws out the *hippy* in *The Hippy Gourmet*. Every inch of the canopy is alive with plants, insects, or animals . . . it's life in all its crazy, untamed profusion. The water running from the distant interior to the Atlantic nourishes just about every form of flora or fauna that you can imagine, and there are still species left for humans to discover. The people are thin and tan and lovely, but it's the rain forest that is the true dark and beautiful jewel of Brazil.

For real Brazilian flavor, serve our Brazilian-Style Black Beans with salsa, yucca, and plantains. Then go out and do what you can to save the rain forest: Donate to conservation groups, recycle and save energy whenever you can, and buy products such as shade-grown coffee that bring money to local people without ruining the Amazon.

Dal

Dal is best served hot over boiled grain (such as brown basmati rice) or alongside Indian bread (like naan) for dipping. With a fruit chutney and a cooling vegetable salad, you have an Indian feast. When cooked, this should look almost like a bright yellow paste, though it tastes a lot better than the stuff we sneaked while the teacher wasn't looking.

 SERVES 4–6

2¹/₂ cups dried yellow split peas

1 small tomato, chopped

1 tablespoon lemon juice

1 tablespoon neutral vegetable oil, such
    as soy or grapeseed

¹/₂ teaspoon ground turmeric

¹/₂ teaspoon ground cumin

Pinch of red pepper flakes

2 cloves garlic, minced

1 teaspoon grated gingerroot

1 small jalapeño pepper, stem removed
    and minced (for a milder dish, remove
    membranes and seeds inside pepper;
    for a hotter dish, use a spicier variety
    of pepper such as habanero)

¹/₄ cup chopped fresh cilantro, for garnish

Salt, to taste

Rinse the split peas, and soak them in 2¹/₂ cups water for 30 minutes. Bring the split peas and water to a boil over medium-high heat. Reduce the heat to medium low, partially cover, and cook for about 20 minutes. Stir occasionally and add water, if necessary, to keep the peas from drying out completely—though the mixture should be thick. When the peas are tender and the mixture is thickened, add the tomato and lemon juice.

Heat the oil over medium-high heat. Add the turmeric, cumin, pepper flakes, garlic, gingerroot, and jalapeño. Heat for 1 to 2 minutes, until fragrant.

Stir the oil and spice mixture into the dal. Taste and add salt if necessary. Garnish with cilantro.

Veggie Chili

Yeehaw, pardner, this is all-American good eating. This makes a whole lot of chili, but it's good the second day. If you don't want just a plain bowl of chili, spoon it over baked potatoes, roasted or baked sweet potatoes, tortilla chips, or corn bread.

 SERVES 8–10

²/₃ cup dried pinto beans
²/₃ cup dried black beans
²/₃ cup dried kidney beans
²/₃ cup dried red beans
1 tablespoon olive oil
1 regular-size onion, chopped, plus
   1 small onion, chopped, divided
1 green bell pepper, chopped, divided
1 red bell pepper, chopped, divided
2 cloves garlic, peeled and chopped,
   divided
3 carrots, cut into chunks
3 stalks celery, chopped (including
   leaves)
2 tablespoons ground cumin
1 tablespoon dried oregano
½ teaspoon black pepper
1 tablespoon paprika
¼ teaspoon cayenne

2 (14½ ounce) cans plum tomatoes
1¼ cups cooked garbanzo beans (chickpeas); you can use canned or some
   left over from another recipe
Salt and pepper, to taste
Cheddar cheese, to taste, grated

Soak the beans (except the garbanzos) overnight or for about 8 hours. The water should cover the beans with about 2 inches of water on top.

Heat the oil in a large pot over a medium flame. Add half the regular-size onion, half the peppers, and half the garlic. Cook until softened.

Add the soaked beans (except the garbanzos), including their soaking liquid. Cook until softened. The cooking time will depend upon the age of your beans; expect an hour or more. Add water if it appears to be running low.

In another pot, mix the rest of the vegetables and the second half of the regular-size onion with the spices. Break up the tomatoes in the can with your hands and add them, along with their juices, to the vegetables. Bring to a boil, then reduce the heat and simmer for about half an hour. Add a bit of water if the mixture dries out.

When both the bean and the vegetable

mixtures are done, take about 4 cups of the bean mixture and pulse in a blender. Put these back into the bean pot and add the vegetable and tomato mixture. Add the garbanzo beans and heat everything together for a few minutes. Season to taste with salt and black pepper. Serve with grated cheese and the rest of the chopped onion.

Mango Bean Soup

This soup sounds a little strange at first, but what good, new idea doesn't? Sometimes the oddest combinations make the most beautiful music if you just let them jam together. Go ahead and try it—open yourself up to something new and wonderful.

 SERVES 6–8

1 pound (about 2 cups) dried navy
    beans
1/2 cup chopped celery
1 cup diced carrots
1 cup canned tomatoes, chopped
1 tablespoon extra-virgin olive oil
1 large white onion, diced
1 pound flavored tempeh,
    cubed
1 teaspoon paprika
2 teaspoons hot prepared mustard
Salt and pepper, to taste
1 mango

1 banana
Juice of 1 lemon

Soak the beans overnight in enough water to cover by 2 inches. Drain.

Combine beans and enough water to cover by about 1 inch in a soup kettle over medium-high heat. Bring to a boil, continue boiling for 20 minutes, then reduce the heat to medium low, cover, and simmer for an hour or so. Add the celery and carrots and continue simmering until the veggies are tender, then add the tomatoes.

Heat the oil in a skillet over a medium-high flame. Brown the onion and tempeh; when the onion is soft, about 10 minutes, add this mixture to the simmering soup. Add the paprika and mustard. Season to taste with salt and pepper.

Dice the mango and banana and mix with the lemon juice. Serve the soup with some diced fruit mixture on top.

Vegetarian North African Stew

From the most ancient part of the world comes rich Old World flavor. This makes a thick, deeply colored eggplant stew surrounded by mixed beans. The spices give it a golden tinge and a delicate, not overpowering spiciness.

 SERVES 10

1 cup dried garbanzo beans

1 cup dried black-eyed peas

1 yellow onion

2 cloves garlic, chopped

1 cup dried lentils

Salt and pepper, to taste

1 red bell pepper, chopped

15–20 baby eggplants, trimmed and chopped

2 cups vegetable stock

1 teaspoon turmeric

1 tablespoon garam masala

1/2 cup raisins

1 teaspoon red pepper flakes

2 tablespoons chopped fresh parsley, for garnish

Soak the garbanzos and black-eyed peas overnight in enough water to cover by about 2 inches.

Peel the onion and mince about 3 tablespoons' worth; slice the rest. Add half the minced onion and about a third of the garlic to each of two saucepans. Add the garbanzos to one pan and lentils and black-eyed peas to the other. Add water to each to cover beans by about 1 inch. Bring both pans to a boil. Cover loosely and reduce the heat to medium low. Cook until tender, skimming any foam if necessary during the cooking. The pan with the lentils and black-eyed peas should be tender first, after about half an hour. The garbanzos should take about an hour. When the beans are done, season with salt and pepper to taste, and set aside.

In a dry skillet, add the remaining garlic, bell pepper, sliced onion, and eggplants. Heat until browned. Add the vegetable stock, turmeric, and garam masala. Stir and cook until the stew starts to thicken a bit. Add the raisins and red pepper flakes. Season to taste with more salt and pepper.

To serve, pour the stew into a bowl, surround it by mounds of cooked beans, and garnish with fresh parsley.

Borscht

There are dozens of versions of borscht across Eastern Europe. This is a gorgeous, warm, vegan version by our friend Lara Blank, of Lara's Delicious. It shows off the awesome, jewel-like beauty of the beet. Served with some thick, dark bread, it's a vegan feast.

 SERVES 10

    4 cups lima beans
    2 large beets, tops sliced off, unpeeled
    3 stalks celery, chopped
    2 Spanish onions, peeled and chopped
    1½ heads green cabbage, cored and
       chopped
    3 sweet peppers (such as red bell
       peppers), seeded and chopped into
       ½-inch pieces
    7 new red potatoes, peeled and cubed
    2 carrots, peeled and cut into ½-inch
       rounds
    ¼ cup grapeseed oil
    2 cups stewed canned tomatoes (choose
       a variety canned with added tomato
       paste)
    4 firm roma tomatoes, cubed
    4 green onions, chopped

    1½ cups finely chopped fresh cilantro
    1 bunch fresh dill, coarsely chopped
    1 tablespoon cayenne pepper
    1 tablespoon paprika
    Dash of sugar
    Salt, to taste

Soak the lima beans for an hour in 1½ gallons (24 cups) water.

In a large pot, boil the beets over medium-high heat in enough water to cover for 30 to 40 minutes, or until tender. Remove the beets, reserving the water.

Place the lima beans, celery, onions, and enough water to cover in a large soup pot. Bring to a boil over high heat. Add the shredded cabbage and stir. Add the beet cooking water, peppers, potatoes, and carrots. Return to a boil, then reduce the heat to medium low and simmer the soup.

Grate the beets. If you do this by hand, you may want to use a kitchen towel or a glove to keep your hands from staining. A food processor will grate the beets quickly without a lot of mess.

In a large skillet, heat the grapeseed oil over high heat. Sauté the beets for about 5 minutes. Add the stewed tomatoes and stir.

Add the chopped tomatoes, green onions, cilantro, dill, cayenne, and paprika. The texture should be thick and slightly watery, like a stew. If mixture seems dry, add a bit of water.

Pour the beet mixture into the lima mixture and stir well. Add the sugar and simmer some more until the soup suits your taste. Add salt and additional sugar to taste.

Ginger Carrot Soup

When you puree simple root vegetables in a soup, something magical happens. Their texture becomes smooth, almost satiny. You could easily make this with a winter squash, such as butternut, as well.

 SERVES 6

2 tablespoons neutral vegetable oil, such as soy or grapeseed

1 yellow onion, peeled and chopped

2 pounds carrots, peeled and roughly chopped (approximately 12–14 carrots)

1 tablespoon grated gingerroot

1 teaspoon garam masala

4 cups vegetable stock or water

1 orange, juiced; or substitute $^1/_3$ cup presqueezed orange juice

Salt and pepper, to taste

Heat the vegetable oil over medium heat. Cook the onion until translucent. Add the carrots and gingerroot. Allow to cook for a few minutes. Add the garam masala. Cook for a minute more. Then add the water or stock, increase the heat to high, bring to a boil, reduce the heat to medium low, and cover. Cook for 10 to 15 minutes, or until the carrots are tender.

Puree the soup in a food processor or blender (it may take a couple of batches); if you have an immersion blender (a stick-like blender that goes directly into liquids), you can use that as well. Be careful, because spattering hot liquids can really hurt.

Return the soup to the pot. Add the orange juice and cook over medium heat until warm. Season to taste with salt and pepper.

Tuscan Bean Soup

When *The Hippy Gourmet TV Show* went to Tuscany, we met people who live surrounded by the living foods they eat every day. The silver-green olive trees that make their gorgeous oils. The grapes warming under the life-giving sun. This soup is simple, but it's alive with the flavors of the land.

 SERVES 8

2 cups dried cannellini beans

2 tablespoons cold-pressed extra-virgin olive oil, preferably Tuscan, plus extra for drizzling

5–6 cloves garlic, peeled but left whole

8–10 leaves fresh sage for soup, plus 8 sage leaves for garnish

$\frac{1}{3}$ cup tomato paste

Salt and pepper, to taste

32 very thin slices high-quality bread

Soak the beans overnight in enough water to cover by about 2 inches. Drain the beans.

Place them in a pot and add water to cover by about 1 inch. Bring to a boil over high heat, cover loosely, and reduce the heat to medium low. Skim any scum, if necessary. Cook the beans for about an hour, or until plump and soft. Remove from the heat.

In a large pan, heat the oil over a medium-high flame. Add the garlic. Tear the sage leaves in two, twisting them slightly to crush them and bring out the natural flavors and oils. Add to the oil. Cook the garlic and sage until the garlic becomes light brown. Remove and discard both the garlic and the sage.

Add the tomato paste to the oil and stir. Add a couple of large ladlefuls of beans and their cooking water to the tomato-oil mixture. Mash.

Drain the remaining beans over a bowl, reserving both the cooking water and the beans; add the beans to the mashed mixture. Stir.

Add enough of the reserved cooking water (or plain water, if you're using canned beans) to the pot to reach the consistency you like. It should be slightly thick but still soupy. Continue cooking until soup is warmed through. Season to taste with salt and pepper.

To serve, lay 2 slices of bread (untoasted) in each individual bowl. Ladle some soup atop, then lay another 2 slices of bread (untoasted) in each bowl. Ladle in the rest of the soup. Drizzle each serving with a bit of olive oil and dress with a sage leave.

Kimchi Soup

Kimchi is made from salted, fermented vegetables, most commonly cabbage. You can find it in Asian groceries and health food stores. In Korea, where every home has kimchi, when it gets a little too strong to serve by itself, it's often made into soup or mixed with rice.

 SERVES 4

5 cups vegetable stock

1/2 tablespoon soy sauce

3/4 cup cabbage kimchi, roughly chopped

1/2 cup chopped green onions, plus extra for garnish

1 teaspoon grated gingerroot

Pepper, to taste

8 ounces firm tofu, cut into small cubes

Place the stock and soy sauce in a large pot. Bring to a boil over medium-high heat. Add the kimchi, green onions, and ginger-root. Cover and reduce the heat to medium low. Cook for about 15 minutes. Season to taste with pepper and additional soy sauce, if desired.

To serve, place tofu cubes in individual serving dishes and spoon hot soup on top. Garnish with green onions.

Mexican Tomato Soup

Fire isn't just for dancing around while your favorite band jams. It transforms ordinary ingredients into something that really shines. Charring the vegetables gives a great depth of flavor to this soup.

 SERVES 4

8 cloves garlic, unpeeled

1 medium red onion, unpeeled and
    cut in half

3 medium tomatoes

½ tablespoon light olive oil

4–5 cups vegetable stock

1 tablespoon lime juice

Salt and pepper, to taste

1 jalapeño pepper, seeded and
    chopped

¼ cup chopped fresh cilantro

1 avocado, peeled and sliced

Preheat the broiler.

Place the garlic, onion, and tomatoes in a single layer on a broiler pan. Sprinkle with oil and toss to coat. Broil, stirring occasionally, until charred—about 10 minutes. Remove the vegetables as they cook. The garlic will be done first, then the onion, then the tomatoes.

When the vegetables are cool enough to handle, peel the garlic cloves and place them in a food processor. Peel and add the onion. Remove the stems from the tomatoes and add. Process until a paste forms. If the mixture is too dry, add a bit of the stock until it begins to move.

Place the blended vegetable mixture in a pot over medium heat. Add the stock and stir. Heat until warm. Stir in the lime juice. Season to taste with salt and pepper.

To serve, garnish with peppers, cilantro, and avocado slices.

Asparagus Soup

 In this soup, nothing goes to waste; recycle, recycle, recycle! The vegetable trimmings go into a stock that concentrates the pure flavor of the vegetables. Although Bruce uses soy milk in this recipe, if you eat dairy, you could substitute heavy cream or milk.

SERVES 4–6

1$\frac{1}{2}$ pounds asparagus

1 large baking potato

1 huge or 2 smaller leeks

2 stalks celery, including leaves

1 tablespoon extra-virgin olive oil

1 clove garlic, peeled and lightly crushed

$\frac{3}{4}$–1 cup soy milk

Salt and pepper, to taste

$\frac{1}{4}$ cup finely sliced green onions, for garnish

1 teaspoon lemon zest, for garnish

Bend each asparagus spear until it snaps. It should naturally break at the point where the woody stem joins the more tender upper part of the asparagus. Put the woody portion of the asparagus in a stockpot. Cut off the top inch or so of the tender portion of the asparagus and reserve. Roughly chop the rest.

Peel the potato and add the skins to the stockpot. Dice the potato.

Carefully wash the leek and cut off the green portion and stem. Roughly chop the green portion. Place both this and the stem in the stockpot. Carefully wash the white portion of the leek under running water to remove any remaining sand. Slice the leek crosswise into thin slices.

Chop the celery stalks; place leaves and tough bases in the stockpot.

Add enough water to the pot to cover the vegetables. Bring to a boil over high heat, then reduce the heat to medium low and simmer while you prepare the rest of the soup.

In a second large pan, heat the olive oil over medium heat. Add the chopped asparagus, celery, and leeks. Stir. After the vegetables have cooked for 2 to 3 minutes, add the garlic. When the veggies are bright green, tender, and beginning to caramelize slightly, add the diced potato. Stir. Place a strainer over the pan and strain in the stock; continue cooking until the vegetables are tender.

In two or three batches, ladle the soup into a blender. Process to the consistency that you like, either completely liquefied or slightly chunky. Pour into a large bowl, and when all the soup is processed, pour it back into the pan. If you have an immersion blender, you can use this directly in the pan.

Bring the soup back to a boil over medium-high heat. While it's heating, bring a small pan of water to boil. Add the asparagus tips. Cook for a couple of minutes, or until bright green. Remove from the heat and drain. Place in ice water to stop their cooking.

Add the soy milk to the soup to taste and heat to thoroughly warm. Season to taste with salt and pepper. To serve, ladle the soup into bowls and garnish with green onions, lemon zest, and asparagus tips.

5. Main Courses— Vegetarian and Vegan

Forget meat and potatoes. There are many wonderful, colorful, and flavorful foods to be eaten and enjoyed that don't involve animal protein.

A lot of chefs create fabulous, well-thought-out menus filled with a variety of colors, tastes, and textures . . . then they get to the vegetarian selection and throw in a vegetable pasta or portobello mushroom burger. Hey, there's nothing wrong with pasta and portobello mushrooms—try Bruce's Mushroom Stroganoff on top of pasta for a delicious taste of both—but the dishes in this chapter show that vegetarian and vegan food can be a whole lot more.

Even chefs who specialize in meat are

putting vegetarian-friendly main courses on their menus. Here in California, we have Millennium Restaurant in San Francisco, one of the best restaurants in the country to be both gourmet and hippy at the same time. On the show, we've visited Ravens Restaurant (part of the Stanford Inn in Mendocino) and seen the chef prepare a dish of Roasted Corn Sopes with Tomatillo Salsa that would make any portobello burger blush with shame. Chef Glenn Chu of Indigo Restaurant in Honolulu prepared savory, rich tofu for us when we traveled to Hawaii. The menu in his restaurant includes plenty of meat, but he doesn't limit himself to animals; he cooks delicious vegetarian food as well. In Tuscany, Italy, we dined at Osteria del Contadino. Though meat and pasta are local specialties—and they brought some out for the nonvegetarians on the *Hippy Gourmet* team—the talented chefs produced some of the most delicious pasta imaginable, such as a ravioli with four cheeses that made our mouths sing . . . with not a speck of bland pasta primavera in sight. All these chefs cook excellent food, vegetarian or not. Bruce even showed the great chefs of Italy how to prepare his famous Vegan Ratatouille, lighting up the Tuscan night sky while cooking outdoors on an open flame at the Miramare, a beachside resort near Livorno.

Bruce doesn't need meat to create feasts fit for any palate. His dishes may not satisfy someone who consumes only meat and martinis—but then does anything satisfy someone who consumes only meat and martinis? He creates food that satisfies the body and soul of anyone open to eating delicious food.

All the dishes in this section have a story behind them. Bruce cooked the warmly spicy, rich Vegan Veggie Thai Curry for the Performing Animals Welfare Society (PAWS) animal sanctuary. PAWS provides refuge for performing animals that have been abused or abandoned, including several Asian elephants.

Maybe the elephants got a little whiff of the jungles of Asia and thought of home. In any case, we can be sure that they didn't smell any of their animal cousins getting cooked.

Bruce cooked his Mushroom Stroganoff for Jihyun Kim and Thu Tam, the lovely ladies who changed Bruce's look to help him transition from cable access to PBS several years ago. They trimmed his beard, darkened his hair, and changed his loose hippy shirt for a just-so-slightly younger model. He may have been a bit doubtful about changing his looks—he believes in the natural way after all, not a lot of vanity and false appearances—but he came away looking ten years younger thanks to their talents. Using *his* talents to cook Mushroom Stroganoff for them was the least that he could do.

For the annual Bay to Breakers race, Bruce went outdoors to prepare Veggie Fried Rice over an open fire. Living the hippy way, Bruce loves to get outdoors to do his cooking. Nothing adds flavor to food the way that smoke, and an appetite from moving your body in nature, does. The show's fans even got into the act to help with the rice, and of course to help eat it.

Bruce got back to his roots when he made Grilled Tofu. On the show, he and his friends traveled in a '64 VW bus, then built a campfire down by the river and lived the old-fashioned hippy way. If you think that grilled chicken or burgers are great, try tofu. You can make it while camping—hippy buses optional—or on your own back porch. Not only is it delicious, but no animals were harmed in the making of this dish!

Whether you know the stories behind them or not, these dishes can get you started on a vegetarian cuisine that's no stranger to gourmet. It isn't hard to be creative when you have all the colors of the rainbow at your disposal. Use the recipes as a starting point, and you'll soon be making vegetarian dishes more creative than those on the menu of most American restaurants. Perfect the portobello mushroom burger if you'd like, but don't limit yourself. Expand your horizons, man, and your taste buds.

Even if you are a carnivore, when there are so many amazing foods out there, why limit yourself to steak, chicken breasts, and fish fillets? Think instead of a balance of colors, textures, and temperatures that please body and soul. And since many of these foods cost only pennies, you can afford to feast your friends even if you aren't a big shot. This chapter offers vegan and vegetarian options that you can build a meal around—or serve as meals all on their own.

Tofu Dishes

Tofu is magical. It's a shimmering, versatile, nourishing food, and it all comes from a little bean.

"Wild" Rice and Steamed Veggies

This recipe gets a bit wild with the addition of an entire head of garlic. Ginger juice brings up the heat and the flavor. You can buy ginger juice in health food or some high-end cooking stores.

 SERVES 4

2 cups short-grain brown rice

4 cups water

1 teaspoon salt

2 tablespoons sesame oil

1 head garlic, peeled and sliced

2 cups broccoli, including tops and
   peeled stems

1 medium zucchini, sliced

1 medium yellow crookneck squash, sliced

3 medium carrots, peeled and chopped

1 package (8 ounces) seasoned tofu (any
   flavor); or marinate your own in your
   favorite recipe

1 teaspoon ginger juice

Place the rice in a dry pan over medium-high heat to toast. Mix constantly until you hear a slight crackling sound, about 2 to 3 minutes. Add the water and salt. Stir. Bring to a boil, boil for 1 minute, then reduce the heat to low and cover. Let this simmer for 45 minutes.

Heat the sesame oil in a small pan over a medium flame. Add the garlic and stir until golden brown. Remove from the heat, and strain the garlic. Reserve the oil.

Add enough water to the bottom of a pot with a steamer insert to cover by about 1 inch. Bring to a boil, and put the vegetables in the steamer. Cover and cook for about 7 minutes, or until vegetables are steamed to your liking.

Add half of the reserved sesame oil to a small pan, then add the tofu. Cook until just heated—2 to 3 minutes—flipping once. Slice the tofu into thin pieces after it is cooked.

In a serving dish, layer the rice, vegetables, tofu, and garlic. Sprinkle with ginger juice.

Grilled Tofu

Let the fire do its magic. You can use any marinade you like for grilled tofu. If you don't want to make your own, a bit of commercial or homemade barbecue sauce or leftover vinaigrette salad dressing will work as well. Serve with rice or noodles, or use in place of meat as a sandwich filling.

 SERVES 3–4

1 package (14–16 ounces) firm tofu

3 tablespoons tamari or other soy sauce

1 teaspoon toasted sesame oil

2 cloves garlic, minced

1 teaspoon finely minced gingerroot

1/2 teaspoon red pepper flakes

1 teaspoon dark brown sugar

Oil to brush grill or grill pan

Cut the tofu lengthwise into three or four large rectangles. Lay the chunks on a clean kitchen towel on top of a cutting board. Top with a second towel. Weight the tofu with another heavy cutting board or a heavy skillet. Tilt the bottom cutting board a bit toward a sink to allow draining. Let the tofu sit for an hour or two. Changing the towels once during the draining process will give you a firmer tofu, but it isn't necessary. When it's drained, place the tofu in a shallow pan.

Mix all the remaining ingredients (except the oil for the grill) in a small bowl, then pour the mixture over the tofu. Lift the tofu a bit to make sure that marinade gets all over it. Let it marinate, refrigerated, for 30 to 60 minutes.

While the tofu marinates, prepare a grill or grill pan (a heavy pan that allows you to "grill" food indoors) over medium heat. Lightly oil the grill or grill pan.

Cook the tofu for about 3 minutes on each side, turning once. Avoid turning more than once to keep the tofu from breaking up.

Variation: Oven-Baked Tofu

Follow the recipe for Grilled Tofu, but when you get to the step of heating the grill, preheat the oven to 350 degrees instead. Lightly oil a baking sheet and top with the tofu. Bake for 10 to 15 minutes or until thoroughly heated and dry.

Vegan Veggie Thai Curry

We recommend the Chao Thai brand of powdered coconut milk, available in Asian markets and over the Internet. To prepare, mix one of the 2-ounce packets with 1 cup water. Thai green curry pastes vary tremendously in their strength; taste a bit to see if the amounts recommended in the recipe will work for you.

 SERVES 4–6

1 package (14–16 ounces) firm tofu

3½ tablespoons neutral vegetable oil, such as soy or grapeseed, divided

2 tablespoons minced garlic, divided

1 tablespoon chunky peanut butter

1 tablespoon Thai green curry paste, divided

1 cup coconut milk (homemade, prepared from a powder, or canned), divided

2 cups white jasmine rice

1 medium eggplant, cubed

2 carrots, sliced

2 cups trimmed and chopped string beans

1 red bell pepper, sliced

1 green bell pepper, sliced

1 medium yellow onion, cut into large chunks

1 medium zucchini, cubed

1 tablespoon honey

1 shot dry sherry (optional)

1 cup chopped fresh cilantro

1 cup chopped basil (the Thai variety is preferable, but use whatever is fresh and available)

Mango and papaya slices, for garnish

Cut the tofu into 1-inch cubes.

In a small frying pan, heat 1 tablespoon of the oil over a medium-high flame. Add the tofu along with ½ tablespoon of the garlic, and sauté until lightly browned. Remove the tofu cubes from the oil and set aside.

Heat another small pan over a medium-high flame. Add 1 tablespoon of the oil, ½ tablespoon of the garlic, and the peanut butter. Mix well. Add about ½ tablespoon of the Thai green curry and enough coconut milk (about ¼ cup) to make a thick sauce. Mix well. When it's heated, pour it over the tofu.

Add the rice and 3 cups of water to a pot. Bring to a boil over medium-high heat, then cover and reduce the heat to medium low.

Cook for about 15 minutes, or until all the water is absorbed.

Heat a sauté pan over a medium-high flame and add 1 tablespoon of the oil. Add the eggplant and stir continuously to sauté. Dribble the remaining ½ tablespoon oil over the eggplant while you sauté.

Add the carrots and string beans. Cook for a couple of minutes. Add the remaining garlic, along with the peppers and onion. Cook for another couple of minutes. Add the zucchini. Cook for a couple of minutes. Add the remaining curry paste and coconut milk. Mix well and let everything simmer for a few minutes, until all the vegetables are done to your liking. Add the honey and sherry, combining well.

To serve, heap the rice on a platter. Cover with the vegetables. Top with the herbs, mango, and papaya. Serve the tofu and sauce on the side.

Cuisine Without Heat

Many people today are interested in an idea called raw food. They believe that cooking destroys many of the beneficial enzymes in food. Whatever the truth to that claim—and we've said before that *The Hippy Gourmet* isn't qualified to dispense nutritional advice—cooking will remain part of our repertoire. Gathering around the fire is a magical, primitive rite that's part of the wonder of being human. Bruce loves nurturing his inner caveman by cooking in front of a raging fire.

Nevertheless, using less fuel is always a good idea for the environment. Eating a mixture of raw and cooked foods also helps your body get all of the nutrients it needs. One way to cook without fire is the solar oven, which uses reflectors to concentrate the power of the sun so that you can cook without any other source of energy. Another is to enjoy foods both hot and cold.

Japanese-Style Tofu

This incredibly simple tofu recipe is great when the weather is hot. It wouldn't qualify as raw food, but it does show how you can be a gourmet cook without ever turning on the oven. Serve it with rice and a simple vegetable for an easy meal. Vegans can leave out the bonito flakes, and it will still be delicious.

 SERVES 4

1 block (14–16 ounces) silken tofu
1 teaspoon grated fresh gingerroot
1 medium green onion, minced
2 tablespoons dried bonito flakes
2 tablespoons shoyu or other soy sauce

Place the tofu on a serving platter. Garnish with the gingerroot, green onion, and bonito flakes. Sprinkle with soy sauce.

Vegetables

Forget brussels sprouts boiled until they're gray, or dingy iceberg lettuce drenched in gooey dressing. Think rich Mushroom Stroganoff, elegant Beet Tarts, or sweet and satisfying Baked Stuffed Acorn Squashes instead. The vegetables in this section are substantial enough to eat as a meal on their own, with a grain or bread on the side.

Mushroom Stroganoff

On the show, Bruce cooked this dish outdoors over a roaring open fire. You can't beat cooking in nature, but you could also make this on a stove indoors. Use a big pan or wok over high heat. For a vegan version, just leave out the sour cream.

 SERVES 8

1 tablespoon extra-virgin olive oil

1 yellow onion, sliced thin

4 large portobello mushrooms, cut into chunks

5 cups shiitake mushrooms, cut into chunks

5 cups white button mushrooms, cut into chunks

1 teaspoon paprika (preferably high-quality Hungarian)

1 cup vegetable stock

1 cup sour cream

Salt and pepper, to taste

Heat a pan over a fire or over a high flame until it's hot. Add the oil. Add the onion and stir for 1 to 2 minutes. Add the mushrooms. Stir for 1 or 2 minutes. Sprinkle the mushrooms with the paprika and stir. Add the vegetable stock. Continue to cook until the mushrooms are tender and a nice gravy has formed.

In a small separate bowl, stir some of the mushroom mixture into the sour cream to raise its temperature. Once the sour cream and mushrooms are well combined, stir them into the hot stroganoff. This process is called tempering, and it keeps the sour cream from curdling in the finished dish. Allow the dish to warm a bit and season to taste with salt and pepper.

Baked Stuffed Acorn Squashes

corn squashes are as American as apple pie. They are so named because their shape resembles acorns, but you won't be fighting any squirrels for these big boys. You can use any or all of the fillings in this recipe—just adjust your quantities.

🌶 **SERVES 8 AS A SIDE DISH, 4 AS A MAIN COURSE**

4 acorn squashes

2 teaspoons neutral oil, such as soy or grapeseed

$\frac{1}{2}$ cup chopped dried plums

$\frac{1}{4}$ cup chopped pecans

$\frac{1}{4}$ cup chopped sweetened dried cranberries

$\frac{1}{4}$ cup pine nuts

$\frac{1}{2}$ cup chopped dried apricots

$\frac{1}{4}$ cup brown sugar

Preheat the oven to 375 degrees.

Cut each acorn squash in half lengthwise and scoop out its seeds and strings. Oil two baking sheets and spread some of the oil on the cut side of the squashes. Place the squashes, cut-side down, on the baking sheets, and bake for 30 minutes. Remove the squashes and turn them cut-side up.

Mix the plums, pecans, cranberries, pine nuts, and apricots, and stuff this mixture into the cavity of each squash half. Sprinkle brown sugar on top. Bake for another 30 minutes, or until the squashes are tender and the filling is bubbling hot.

Fine Dining, Hippy-Style

Hippy? Formal dining? Those two things usually belong together like *compassionate* and *conservative*. All those starchy white tablecloths and starched shirts make nature-loving free spirits just a little uncomfortable. But any hippy could comfortably eat in the Restaurant De Kas in Amsterdam. It's a dream come true for a hippy and for a chef.

Part of the restaurant is a greenhouse, and when Martijn Kajuiter, head chef, made his Beet Tarts on our show, he harvested the beets himself moments before beginning preparation. Between April and December, the restaurant, together with a few local farmers, grows all its own produce. The food is truly local, and it celebrates the beauty of seasonal produce. The chefs aren't at the end of some industrial food chain; they need only walk out their door to see what foods they'll cook that day.

If you have the opportunity, visit this extraordinary place. You'll have to make a reservation and plan ahead—a drag, we know—but it's worth it.

Beet Tarts with Herb Salad

Simple, slightly sweet, and completely delicious, this tart—from Restaurant De Kas's chef Martijn Kajuiter—could be either a main course (served with a simple but substantial bean soup) or an appetizer. Beets look like dirty, boring roots when you dig them from the ground, but they turn bright, jewel-like, and gorgeous when you cook them.

Chef Martijn includes several edible flowers in the herb salad as well. If you have access to organically grown edible flowers, use them, but do not substitute commercially raised flowers, which are loaded with pesticides. If you omit the flowers, the recipe will still be delicious.

The dish also includes a white horseradish cream sauce and a red beet reduction. The sauces are quite beautiful, but if you're making this as a simple meal, feel free to omit one or both. Without the sauces, this is a simple but gorgeous meal. With them, it's gourmet vegetarian dining at its best.

 SERVES 2 AS A MAIN COURSE,
4 AS AN APPETIZER

4 squares puff pastry (frozen or homemade) large enough to cover beet halves
2 large red beets

1 cup freshly squeezed beet juice, homemade from a juicer or purchased from a juice bar (optional)
1 tablespoon extra-virgin olive oil, plus ½ tablespoon if making beet reduction, divided
2 teaspoons fresh lemon thyme, roughly chopped (or substitute your favorite herb)
1½ cups mixed fresh herbs (and edible flowers, if using)
Salt, to taste
¼ cup heavy cream (optional)
1 tablespoon freshly grated horseradish or prepared horseradish (optional)
1 tablespoon freshly squeezed lemon juice (optional)
Pepper, to taste

Preheat the oven to 400 degrees. If you're using frozen pastry, remove it from the freezer and let it thaw for at least half an hour.

Cut the leaves off the beet roots, leaving a couple of inches of stem intact. Cutting too close to the root will cause the beets to bleed as they cook. Wash the beets well, removing the dirt.

Over a high flame, heat a pot of water to a boil. Add the beets. Reduce the heat to medium low and simmer the beets for about 30 minutes, or until a knife slips into them easily.

If you're making beet juice sauce, place the beet juice in a pan over medium-high heat and cook until it's reduced to the consistency of a thick syrup, about 15 to 20 minutes. Remove it from the heat and let it cool.

Rub the skin off the beets. If some skin sticks, cut it off with a knife. Slice the beets in half lengthwise.

Spread about ½ tablespoon of the olive oil on a baking pan. Sprinkle with the lemon thyme. Place the beets, cut-side down, on top. Cut the puff pastry into squares large enough to fit over the rounded sides of the beets, and place atop. Bake for about 20 minutes, or until the pastry is crisp.

Toss together the fresh herbs (and edible flowers, if desired), about ½ tablespoon of the olive oil, and salt.

If you're making horseradish cream sauce, whisk together the cream, horseradish, and lemon juice, seasoning to taste with salt and pepper. If you're making beet reduction, whisk together the reduced beet juice with ½ tablespoon olive oil, seasoning to taste with salt and pepper. Drizzle either sauce (or both) decoratively on serving plates. Place the tarts, beet-side up, on the plates, then add herb salad, either alongside or on top of the tarts. Serve hot.

Veggie Fried Rice

Who says vegetarian barbecues have to be nothing but tofu dogs and soy burgers? Bring that wok outside for an international-style cookout! We suggest preparing this over an outdoor charcoal grill, but you could also use the highest setting on your stove.

 SERVES 8

¼ cup soybean oil, divided (half for
   cooking vegetables, half for caramelized
   sugar sauce)
1 yellow onion, peeled and chopped
6 cloves garlic, peeled and chopped
2 red bell peppers, seeded and chopped
½ of 1 finely chopped hot pepper, such as
   jalapeño, Thai, or habanero—different
   colors if available
4 cups mushrooms (any variety), cleaned
   with brush and chopped
1 bunch asparagus, tough ends removed
   and remainder chopped
2 tablespoons white sugar
8 cups cooked long-grain white rice
Soy sauce, to taste
1 cup chopped green onions,
   for garnish

Coat two large frying pans with 1 tablespoon each of the soybean oil. Heat to high over an outdoor charcoal grill or the highest setting of your indoor stove.

Add the vegetables in the order listed, half in each pan, sautéing for a minute or so after each addition. Continue to cook until the veggies are tender, then push them out toward the sides of the pans, making a space in the center. Pour in the remaining oil. Add the sugar to the oil.

When the sugar starts to caramelize—about 3 to 4 seconds—add the cooked rice. Mix thoroughly and keep cooking until the rice is warmed through. Stir in soy sauce to taste. Garnish with green onions.

Buckminster Fuller

How do we survive on this planet? Not by going through the same routines and slogging along in the same grind. It takes people who are willing to look at things in new ways, to have a vision and carry it through. Buckminster Fuller was one of those people. He was always trying to make a little more with a little less. In an era of gas guzzlers, he designed a car that was the most fuel-efficient of its time. Invented in 1933, the three-wheeled car got thirty miles to the gallon. Fuller also designed a flat map of the world with far less distortion than most. He looked around and saw, in a world of poverty and war, hope for the future. He devoted his life to making "spaceship earth," as he called it, a place that would be livable for many generations.

Most people have heard of him because of his invention of the geodesic dome. This amazing structure makes the most of very little. The dome is nature's perfect shape, allowing the most interior space with the fewest building materials. Easy to build— simply a matter of putting up and covering a simple frame—these domes are made by interlocking shapes, often triangles, and can be constructed out of virtually any material. Bruce built them on the grounds of his high school in California, and on a plot of land in Nova Scotia, Canada. He and his friends did it so quickly, even Bucky himself was impressed. The temperature outside might have been twenty degrees, but inside, with a minimum of heating, it was seventy.

Buckminster Fuller is a spirit that we all could follow. That's why we paid tribute to him on the show. Bruce cooked spaghetti squash in his honor and served it in its own shell, a perfect dome. If we just pay attention, nature shows us the way to follow.

Spaghetti Squash Marinara

This vegetable looks a bit like a yellow watermelon. The flesh of this member of the pumpkin family separates into pasta-like strands. Cleaned and dried, the shell makes a dome-like bowl. When you cook this, think of Bucky.

 SERVES 6

1 large spaghetti squash

15 roma tomatoes

$^1/_3$–$^1/_2$ cup extra-virgin olive oil (reserve 1 tablespoon)

6 cloves garlic, peeled and chopped

1 large white onion, peeled and chopped

1 large green bell pepper, peeled and chopped

3 cups white button mushrooms, quartered

1 tablespoon fresh or 1 teaspoon dried marjoram

1 tablespoon fresh or 1 teaspoon dried basil

1 tablespoon fresh or 1 teaspoon dried oregano

Salt and pepper, to taste

2 medium carrots, sliced into large strands

1 medium zucchini, sliced into large strands

Freshly grated cheese of your choice, if desired

In a pot large enough to fit the squash, bring about 2 inches of water to a boil. Cut the spaghetti squash in half and remove its seeds and strings. Add the squash to the pot. Cover and reduce the heat to medium low. Cook until the squash is tender, then remove it and let it get cool enough to handle.

Bring another large pot of water to a boil. Remove the stem ends from the tomatoes and cut a small X in the other end. Boil the tomatoes for 1 to 2 minutes, then remove them from the water. Peel off the skins, squeeze out and discard the seeds, and roughly chop.

Heat the oil in a pot over a medium-high flame. Add the garlic and cook for a minute or so. Add the onion and green pepper. Cook for a couple of minutes. Add the mushrooms, marjoram, basil, and oregano. Cook until the mushrooms release their liquid and reduce a little. Add the tomatoes. Cook until the sauce has thickened a bit. Season to taste with salt and pepper.

With a fork, pull apart the spaghetti squash. It should form spaghetti-like strands. If you'll be serving it in the shell, wipe the shell's exterior clean with a damp towel.

Heat the reserved tablespoon of olive oil in a large skillet over medium-high heat. Add the carrots and zucchini. Cook until they soften a bit, about 4 or 5 minutes. Add the spaghetti squash and stir. Add most of the tomato sauce, reserving a bit to spoon on top of the finished dish. Stir the mixture until it's warmed through. Season to taste with salt and pepper.

If desired, spoon the squash mixture into the shell and spoon on the reserved sauce. If you prefer, you may simply serve it in a bowl. Sprinkle with cheese, if you like.

Chard Spheres

 ippies like slow and gentle people and slow and gentle cooking. This dish is worth breaking out the steamer and waiting for. Serve it over pasta or on its own for a warm and satisfying main dish.

SERVES 8

1 cup short-grain brown rice

2 cups water

1 white onion, minced

1 clove garlic, peeled and minced

10 sprigs parsley, minced

$\frac{1}{2}$ teaspoon Worcestershire sauce

1 egg

$\frac{1}{2}$ teaspoon dried rosemary

$\frac{1}{2}$ teaspoon dried oregano

Salt and pepper, to taste

8–10 large chard leaves, washed,
    stems intact

In a dry pan over high heat, toast the rice until it's fragrant and light brown. Add the water, bring to a boil, reduce the heat to medium low, cover, and simmer for about 45 minutes. Set aside.

In a bowl, mix all the ingredients, including the cooked rice, except the chard. Season with salt and pepper.

In a steamer or a pan with a steamer insert, bring a couple of inches of water to a boil over medium heat.

Place a nice heaping spoonful of the rice mixture at the end of each chard leaf. Roll and wrap the leaf around the mixture, and place in the steamer on a rack with the seam side down. Once all the chard leaves are rolled, steam for about 20 minutes or so. Remove the steamer from the heat and let it sit until the chard is slightly cooled—5 to 10 minutes.

Serve the Chard Spheres on a plate like dumplings, or add a side of hot pasta and red sauce.

Amaranth and Jambalaya

n the show, we prepared this over an outdoor grill. You could do the same thing and have your friends over for an outdoor bayou feast. If you'd rather stay inside, you could cook this on a stove as well. Either way, let the good times roll.

SERVES 4

1 cup whole-grain amaranth

1½ teaspoons sea salt, divided (or to taste)

3 cups water

1 yellow bell pepper, seeded and cut into chunks

1 red bell pepper, seeded and cut into chunks

1 green bell pepper, seeded and cut into chunks

2 medium yellow squashes, cut in half lengthwise and then cut into chunks

5 stalks celery, including leaves, cut at an angle into medium chunks

1 large yellow onion, peeled and diced large

5–6 cloves garlic, peeled and chopped

1 large can (32 ounces) tomatoes, broken up into bite-size pieces

5 green onions, for garnish

2 tablespoons virgin olive oil

½ teaspoon red pepper flakes

½ teaspoon dried marjoram

½ teaspoon dried thyme

¼ teaspoon white pepper

Prepare a hot fire on an outdoor grill. In a saucepan, add the amaranth, 1 teaspoon of the sea salt, and the water. Mix well and place on the flames or the stovetop, over high heat. Bring to a ripping boil, cover, and simmer for 25 minutes. If on the stove, bring to a boil over high heat, cover, reduce the heat to medium low, and simmer for 25 minutes.

Place all the vegetables (except the tomatoes and green onions) in a bowl. Drain the tomatoes and place them in a second bowl.

Cut off the tips of the green onions. Make a couple of long, lengthwise slices—being careful not to cut the green onions apart—through the green part, until the greens splay apart. Place on ice until ready to use.

Preheat a skillet over the fire and pour in the oil. If you're using the stove, preheat it over a high flame and add the oil. Sauté the vegetables until they're tender, then add the tomatoes and spices. Mix well and simmer. Season to taste with salt and pepper. Serve the veggies over the amaranth, garnishing with the green onions.

Succotash

There are hundreds of versions of succotash, but all contain corn and beans, staples of the Native peoples in the Americas. Serve with whipped squash and corn bread for a celebration of native American foods.

 SERVES 4

1 tablespoon light olive oil

Kernels cut from 4 ears corn (or substitute 1½ cups frozen, defrosted corn)

4 green onions, chopped

2 cups fresh or frozen baby lima beans

2 tablespoons chopped fresh sage

Salt and pepper, to taste

Heat the oil in a skillet over a medium-high flame. Add the corn, cooking until it's lightly browned, about 5 to 7 minutes. Add the green onions and cook for a minute or so more. Remove from the heat.

Bring 6 to 8 cups of water to a boil in a large saucepan. Add the lima beans and cook until tender, about 10 minutes. Drain.

Add the lima beans and sage to the corn mixture. Heat all the ingredients well over a medium-high flame. Season to taste with salt and pepper, and serve.

Casseroles

A casserole doesn't have to be your aunt Ethel's mystery-meat and canned-soup surprise. Originally, the term *casserole* referred to the large, deep ceramic pans most casseroles are made in, but now it also refers to the food itself. A casserole is simply a mixture of ingredients cooked by moist, slow heat. A casserole can be a rich and warming lasagna, a cheese-laden gratin, or a deeply satisfying grain dish. A hippy cook knows that when you take natural ingredients and let them mellow together in a casserole pan until they're one delicious whole, a casserole can be a beautiful thing.

Millet Casserole

Be free and make this your own thing; you just need to adjust the amount of water and cooking time in the second step if you use a different grain. Try these variations: barley with grated butternut squash and carrots, brown rice with a mixture of hot peppers and bell peppers, or quinoa with a mixture of lima beans and corn.

 SERVES 4

1 cup millet

3 cups water

2 tablespoons olive oil, plus extra for oiling pan

1 yellow onion, peeled and chopped

4 cloves garlic, peeled and chopped

1 red bell pepper, peeled and chopped

2 cups chopped mushrooms of your choice

2 cups chopped zucchini

2 cups chopped tomatoes

1/2 cup grated Parmesan cheese, divided (half for casserole, half for topping)

2 eggs

1/2 cup chopped flat-leaf parsley

2 tablespoons chopped fresh basil or
  2 teaspoons dried basil (or other
  herb of your choice)
Salt and pepper, to taste

Preheat the oven to 350 degrees.

In a saucepan, combine the millet and water. Bring to a boil over high heat. Cover and reduce heat to medium low. Cook for 20 to 30 minutes, or until the millet absorbs the water and softens.

Heat the olive oil in a large skillet over a medium-high flame. Add the onions and cook until they're translucent. Add the garlic and pepper. Cook for another couple of minutes. Then add the mushrooms and zucchini, and cook until all the vegetables are softened. Remove the veggies from the heat.

Oil a 9 × 9-inch casserole with a bit of olive oil.

Mix together the millet, cooked vegetables, tomatoes, half the Parmesan, eggs, parsley, and basil. Season with salt and pepper.

Spoon the mixture into the prepared casserole. Bake for about 20 minutes. Top with the remaining cheese, then bake about 10 minutes more, or until the casserole is warm and cheese is melted.

Green Chile and Rice Casserole

Even hippies can't live on plain brown rice and tamari every day; healthy, earth-friendly diets need indulgences, too. When you feel that you need something creamy, cheesy, and decadent, turn to this vegetarian main dish.

SERVES 4–6

1 cup short-grain brown rice

2 cups water

3 medium zucchinis, sliced thinly

Oil to grease 3-quart casserole

7$\frac{1}{2}$ ounces canned whole green chilies, drained and chopped

12 ounces (3 cups) grated Monterey Jack cheese, divided

1 large tomato, sliced thin

2 cups sour cream

1 teaspoon dried oregano

1 teaspoon garlic salt

$\frac{1}{4}$ cup chopped green pepper

$\frac{1}{4}$ cup chopped green onions

2 tablespoons chopped fresh parsley, for garnish

In a dry pot over high heat, toast the rice for a couple of minutes until it's fragrant and slightly browned. Add the water and bring it to a boil. Cover, reduce the heat to medium low, and simmer the rice for 45 minutes.

Preheat the oven to 350 degrees.

In a separate pan, cook the zucchinis in a little bit of salted water (about 1 cup) over medium-high heat until they're tender but still crisp. Drain and set aside.

Place the rice in a 3-quart oiled casserole (approximately 12 inches in diameter for a circular casserole, or 13 × 9 inches if it's rectangular). Cover with the chopped chilies. Sprinkle half the cheese over the chilies and arrange the zucchini slices over the cheese. Add the tomato slices. Combine the sour cream with the remaining ingredients (except the parsley) and spread evenly over the tomato layer. Scatter the remaining cheese all over.

Bake for 40 to 50 minutes, or until heated through. Sprinkle the parsley on top as a garnish at the end.

Baked Beans

ippies know that everything tastes better baked. This is an awesome main course served with squash and brussels sprouts on a cold day; or you can make smaller portions for a side dish. Add vegan "hot dogs" during the last 15 minutes of cooking and you have beanie weenies.

Serves 3–4

1/2 tablespoon extra-virgin olive oil

1 small white onion, chopped

1 clove garlic, minced

1 teaspoon grated gingerroot

1 can (8 ounces) tomato paste

1 tablespoon dark brown sugar

1 tablespoon molasses

1/2 teaspoon dry mustard

1 bay leaf

1/2 tablespoon cider vinegar

2 cups cooked small white beans, such as cannellini, navy, or great northern

Preheat the oven to 300 degrees.

Heat the oil in a small skillet over a medium-high flame. Add the onion and cook until soft and very light brown. Add the garlic and gingerroot and cook for about 1 minute more, then remove the pan from the heat.

In a small baking dish, combine the onion mixture with the remaining ingredients. Bake, uncovered, for 2 to 3 hours. Check occasionally, and if the mixture is drying out, add a bit of water.

Mushroom Lasagna

This is a thin, simple lasagna with a few flavors that blend together into one glorious whole. Use any kind of mushroom that you like. A blend of wild mushrooms would create an intense, earthy mushroom lasagna, but plain button mushrooms will create a deeply flavored dish as well.

 SERVES 8

1 cup (about an ounce) dried porcini mushrooms

2 tablespoons extra-virgin olive oil, plus extra for oiling pan and drizzling on top

1 large yellow onion, peeled and chopped fine

2 cloves garlic, peeled and chopped

5 cups chopped mushrooms (plain button or mixed)

¼ cup chopped fresh flat-leaf parsley

½ tablespoon finely chopped fresh rosemary

1 cup dry white wine

1 can (28 ounces) Italian plum tomatoes

Salt and pepper, to taste

12 lasagna noodles

1½ cups grated Fontina cheese

1½ cups grated Parmesan cheese

In a small bowl, pour about 1½ cups boiling water over the porcini mushrooms. Let this sit for about 30 minutes, or until the porcinis are softened, then remove them from the water and chop. Reserve the soaking water.

Heat the oil over a medium-high flame in a large skillet. Add the onion and cook until lightly browned, about 7 to 8 minutes. Add the garlic. Cook for another minute or so. Add the fresh mushrooms and cook until they're lightly browned, about 5 minutes more. Add the reserved porcinis, the parsley, and the rosemary. Cook for about 1 minute more.

Add the wine. Cook until most of the wine has cooked off and the mixture is just a little moist. Add the reserved porcini water—but be careful not to include any dirt that has settled at the bottom of the bowl. Cook until mostly dry.

Drain most of the water from the tomatoes. Crush them lightly with your hands—nature's perfect tool! Add the tomatoes to the sauce and cook until it's nice and thick. Season to taste with salt and pepper.

While the sauce is cooking, cook the pasta according to package directions. Preheat the oven to 350 degrees.

When the pasta and sauce are both ready, lightly oil a casserole dish large enough to fit the lasagna noodles, about 9 × 13 inches. Add a couple of spoonfuls of sauce to the bottom of the pan and spread it around. Mix the cheeses together.

Lay 3 noodles over the sauce. Spread about a quarter of the remaining sauce atop the noodles, then sprinkle lightly with cheese. Repeat until all of the noodles and sauce are used up. Sprinkle remaining cheese on top. Cover with foil or a lid and bake for about half an hour. Uncover and bake for about 15 minutes more. Let the lasagna sit for about 10 minutes before eating.

Navy Bean Gratin

This dish is soft and crunchy at the same time, rich and yet simple. Perfect for those days that are cold, dreary, and foggy, it'll leave you feeling warm all over. Because of the hominess of this dish, it's an inexpensive way to make your friends feel pampered.

 4–6 HEALTHY PORTIONS

2 cups navy beans (or substitute other white bean of your choice)

3 tablespoons olive oil, divided

1 large white onion, chopped

2 large carrots, peeled and chopped small

4 cloves garlic, chopped

1 tablespoon fresh or 1 teaspoon dried thyme

Salt and pepper, to taste

$^3/_4$ cup dry bread crumbs

$^3/_4$ cup grated Parmesan cheese

Soak the beans overnight in enough water to cover by about 2 inches. Drain.

Bring the beans and enough water to cover by about 1 inch to a boil in a large pot over high heat. When the beans boil, reduce the heat to medium low and cover loosely. Skim if necessary. Cook for about an hour, or until the beans are tender. Remove from the heat and drain, reserving about $^3/_4$ cup of the cooking water.

Preheat the oven to 350 degrees.

Heat 1 tablespoon of the oil in a skillet over a medium-high flame. Cook the onion until light gold. Add the carrots and cook a few minutes longer, or until the carrots are lightly softened. Add the garlic. Cook another minute. Remove the vegetables from the heat and stir in the thyme.

Mix the cooked vegetables, beans, and reserved cooking water in a baking dish. An 11 × 7-inch pan should hold the beans well, but use a larger or smaller pan if that's all you have. Season to taste with salt and pepper.

In a separate bowl, mix together the bread crumbs, cheese, and remaining 2 tablespoons of olive oil. Season with a bit of pepper (the cheese should provide plenty of salt). Sprinkle this topping over the beans. Bake for 20 to 30 minutes, or until the filling is piping hot and the topping is golden and crispy. If the topping is starting to get a bit too brown, cover it with foil to finish baking.

Breads and Pastas

Many nutritionists hate sandwiches and pasta, and it's often true that they can be nothing more than a big heaping helping of refined starch topped by saturated fat. Yet meals based on bread and pasta are staples worldwide: Pasta begins every large meal in Italy, tiny stalls sell falafel in handmade flat bread in the Middle East, roti come wrapped around spicy, savory fillings in India, street vendors in Thailand sell fresh, spicy noodles, and American mothers feed their children macaroni and cheese. These foods are simple, they please almost everyone, and, made with all-natural ingredients, they can be nourishing and healthy. The dishes in this chapter, unlike most American sandwiches and pastas, begin with a whole-grain base and use unprocessed, healthy toppings. All are an easy way to make a vegan or vegetarian main dish that everyone will like.

Taking It Easy

The Stanford Inn in Mendocino, California, is a peaceful and inviting inn on the coast. Its owners, the Stanfords, sought to create an inn based upon an easier, gentler way of living on the land. The inn's warm, natural interiors are echoed in the gorgeous organic gardens that surround it. You won't find any pesticides here, but you will find a variety of wild and tame animals. Everything is recycled, including organic waste. The Stanfords seek to give a natural, authentic experience to all their guests. People and their animals are both welcomed equally in this relaxing retreat.

Ravens, its restaurant, shows how eating sustainably doesn't mean giving up pleasure. Its food leaves guests happy, satisfied, and energized. Chef de cuisine Gunnar Thompson was kind enough to prepare the following beautiful and satisfying recipe for our viewers.

Roasted Corn Sopes with Tomatillo Salsa

When prepared, sopes should look like small, thick, cornmeal-colored patties a little smaller than the palm of your hand. They are made from masa, the main ingredient in tortillas. Served with bright green salsa and brownish red beans, this dish has all the colors of the earth.

 SERVES 6–8

1½ cups pinto beans

1 cup fresh corn kernels

1 tablespoon plus 1 teaspoon olive oil, divided

¼ cup sliced green onions

2½ cups corn masa (available in most grocery stores or in Latino markets)

2½ teaspoons salt, divided

3 tablespoons or more vegetable oil

1 jalapeño pepper, seeded and ribbed

2 cloves garlic, peeled

1 pound fresh, whole tomatillos, papery outer skin removed

4 sprigs cilantro

2 tablespoons lime juice

Edible flowers, for garnish (optional)

Soak the beans overnight in enough water to cover by about 2 inches. Drain.

Put the beans in a pot and add water to cover by about 1 inch. Bring to a boil over medium-high heat. Cover loosely and reduce the heat to medium low. Skim any foam if necessary. Cook the beans for about an hour and a half, or until tender. Drain, season to taste with salt and pepper, and set aside.

In a skillet, sauté the corn kernels in 1 teaspoon of the olive oil over medium-high heat until they're a little browned, about 5 minutes. Mix the kernels with the green onions, masa, remaining tablespoon of olive oil, and 1½ teaspoons of the salt. Add enough warm water to make the mixture come together into a ball. Form the dough into small cakes.

Heat the vegetable oil over a medium-high flame. Cook the sopes until they're golden on both sides, turning once—about 5 minutes per side.

Add the pepper, garlic, tomatillos, cilantro, lime juice, and remaining teaspoon of salt to the bowl of a food processor. Process until the salsa is the consistency that you like.

To serve, place sopes on a serving plate along with the pinto beans and salsa. If you like, garnish with edible flowers.

Solar Living

The time has come for us to power our cars, homes, and factories with sustainable alternative energy. The Institute for Solar Living in Mendocino, California, shows how using the sun to power our homes is not only possible, but can be practical and comfortable as well. These folks had a dream of turning a wasteland into something beautiful, and they did so at the Solar Living Center, a place built so that visitors could see the practicality of solar living in action. It's also the home of Real Goods, a company that sells solar panels. More than two hundred thousand people a year visit to see how solar power can be used in their own homes and buildings. The building is designed to receive maximum solar light and heating during the winter, while creative overhangs and hemp screens keep out excess energy in the summer. Grape arbors and an evaporative drip system provide additional cooling so that air-conditioning isn't required, even in summers that can reach a hundred degrees. The walls were built of rice straw bales, a material that would otherwise go to waste. The building is surrounded by gardens full of organically grown plants.

When architects focus on making buildings fit with their environment, whether they're in Phoenix, Arizona, or Greenwich, Connecticut, they can drastically reduce energy consumption. Not to mention that their buildings will be beautiful for generations and will leave a small footprint on the land.

We visited the solar institute on the show because if we're going to survive on this planet, we've got to walk the walk of sustainable living. To show that you can actually use the knowledge that they teach, Bruce cooked with no power other than the light shining down from the sun.

You can make your own solar oven fairly easily from kits available on the Web, and several manufacturers sell ready-made ovens at outdoor stores or over the Internet. When we cooked on the show, we used an oven from the Solar Oven Society, a wonderful organization that uses 100 percent recycled materials in building their ovens. They donate tens of thousands of these ovens to needy villages in the developing world. By using the sun rather than wood to purify water and heat food, solar ovens help prevent deforestation. The best part is how simple it all is: The ovens use reflectors to concentrate the power of the sun and allow the temperature to rise to 325 degrees inside a small, black box with a glass lid.

Solar Pizza

We love solar ovens on *The Hippy Gourmet TV Show*. Because they're really nothing more than boxes with reflectors, they're highly portable, and we see it as our mission to leave them behind for the local people when we visit developing countries. On a rainy day, you could make this pizza in a conventional oven.

 MAKES 2 PIZZAS

1 tablespoon active dry yeast

³/₄ cup lukewarm water

2 cups unbleached white flour

1 teaspoon sea salt

1 tablespoon olive oil, plus a bit for oiling bowl and pans

Cornmeal to dust pans

1¹/₂ cups pizza sauce, homemade (just simmer a 16-ounce can of crushed tomatoes with a bit of garlic, salt, and pepper until slightly thickened) or store-bought

¹/₂ cup grated medium-sharp cheddar cheese

¹/₂ cup grated Swiss cheese

¹/₂ cup grated mozzarella cheese (or more, for extra-cheesy)

1 medium yellow squash, sliced thin

1 medium zucchini, sliced thin
$^1/_4$ cup grated Parmesan or Asiago
    cheese
$^1/_4$ cup grated Romano cheese
Pinch of dried oregano

Mix the yeast, lukewarm water, and a dash of the flour in a bowl. Stir to dissolve, and let sit for about 5 minutes.

Mix the flour and salt in a large mixing bowl. Make a small dent in the middle and add the olive oil. Mix. Add the water-yeast mixture. Mix with a wooden spoon until it forms an elastic ball. Fold the dough a few times until it starts to become stretchy and develops a nice consistency. Add a little olive oil (about $^1/_2$ teaspoon) to the bowl, and turn the dough to oil it lightly. Cover with a kitchen towel and let it rise for about an hour in a warm spot.

Halve the dough. Work with one half at a time, keeping the other half covered until you're ready to use it. Form the dough into a circle by gently pulling it outward with your hands, pressing down the center if necessary, to the thickness that you like—about $^1/_8$ to $^1/_4$ inch.

Preheat the oven to 400 degrees.

Place the crust on a pan that has been prepared by lightly oiling and dusting with cornmeal. Spread half the pizza sauce evenly atop. Add a quarter of the cheddar, Swiss, and mozzarella. Add half the yellow squash and zucchini, then another quarter of the cheddar, Swiss, and mozzarella. Sprinkle with half the Parmesan and half the Romano. Sprinkle with oregano.

Place the pizza in the oven and bake until the cheeses melt and the crust is golden, about 25 to 30 minutes.

Repeat with the second pizza.

Gourmet Pesto Pizza

New Yawkas like plain old red sauce on their pies, but out here in California we're a little more free and easy. We go with what's good for us, and that means pesto on our pizza. These awesome pies are topped with homemade pesto for deep herb flavor and green color.

 MAKES 2 PIZZAS

2 cups stone-ground unbleached flour

1 tablespoon wheat germ

$1/2$ teaspoon salt

1 tablespoon brown sugar

1 tablespoon olive oil, plus extra for bowl and pans

$3/4$ cup warm water, divided

1 tablespoon active dry yeast

2 cloves garlic, peeled

2 ounces pine nuts

1 large bunch basil

1 cup grated Parmesan-Romano blend cheese

$1/4$ –$1/2$ cup olive oil

1 teaspoon white pepper

1 tablespoon cornmeal

2 cups grated cheddar cheese

2 cups grated Swiss cheese

In a large bowl, mix the flour, wheat germ, salt, brown sugar, 1 tablespoon of the olive oil, and $1/2$ cup of the warm water.

In a separate small bowl, dissolve the yeast in the remaining $1/4$ cup of warm water. Stir the yeast mixture into the flour. Mix by hand until the dough pulls clean from the bowl. If you're using a mixer with a dough hook attachment, mix on low until it pulls clean from the bowl. Knead the dough until it's smooth and elastic.

Place a splash of olive oil in a clean bowl and add the dough, turning to coat it with oil. Cover with a clean cloth and let rise in a warm spot for an hour.

In a blender, pulse to chop the garlic, pine nuts, basil, and Parmesan-Romano blend. While pulsing, slowly add $1/4$ to $1/2$ cup olive oil until it reaches a consistency that you like. Add the white pepper and pulse. If desired, add salt to taste (the cheese will make the mixture salty).

Preheat the oven to 400 degrees. On two pizza pans or large baking sheets, smear a bit of olive oil. Dust the pans with the cornmeal.

Cut the dough into two pieces. Working with one half at a time, stretch and shape the dough to get approximately the shape that you like, then use a rolling pin to roll to your desired thickness (about $1/8$ to $1/4$ inch).

Place the crust on the baking sheets. Add three large spoonfuls of pesto (or more, if you like) to each pizza. Coat the crusts to $1/4$ inch from the edge. Sprinkle with the cheddar and Swiss. Bake for 25 minutes or until the crust is golden. You may want to rotate the pans during baking to ensure that they cook evenly.

Gourmet Vegetable Pizza

Pizza can be whatever you want it to be. It's like a blank canvas, and you're the artist who can make your spirit shine through your creation. Don't let the recipe limit you; make these with whatever vegetables in your garden look best.

  MAKES 2 PIZZAS

2 cups stone-ground unbleached flour

1 tablespoon wheat germ

$1/2$ teaspoon salt

1 tablespoon brown sugar

2 tablespoons olive oil, plus extra for bowl and pans, divided

$3/4$ cup warm water, divided

1 tablespoon active dry yeast

4 cloves garlic, diced small

1 white onion, chopped small

2 small red bell peppers, seeded and chopped small

2 small green bell peppers, seeded and chopped small

2 portobello mushrooms, sliced large

1 tablespoon cornmeal

1 cup store-bought marinara sauce

2 cups grated cheddar cheese

2 cups grated Swiss cheese

Sprinkle of dried oregano

In a large bowl, mix the flour, wheat germ, salt, brown sugar, 1 tablespoon of the olive oil, and $1/2$ cup of the warm water.

In a separate small bowl, dissolve the yeast

in the remaining $1/4$ cup of warm water. Stir the yeast mixture into the flour. Mix by hand until the dough pulls clean from the bowl. If you're using a mixer with a dough hook attachment, mix on low until it pulls clean from the bowl. Knead the dough until it's smooth and elastic.

Place a splash of olive oil in a clean bowl and add the dough, turning to coat it with oil. Cover with a clean cloth and let rise in a warm spot for an hour.

In a large skillet, heat 1 tablespoon of the olive oil over a medium-high flame. Add the garlic, onion, peppers, and mushrooms to the pan. Cook, stirring occasionally, until caramelized, about 10 minutes.

Preheat the oven to 400 degrees. On two pizza pans or large baking sheets, smear a bit of olive oil. Dust the pans with the cornmeal.

Cut the dough into two pieces. Working with one half at a time, stretch and shape the dough to get approximately the shape that you like, then use a rolling pin to roll to your desired thickness (about $1/8$ to $1/4$ inch).

Place the crusts on the baking sheets. Spread marinara sauce up to $1/4$ inch from the edge of the pizza. Spread the cooked vegetables over the sauce. Sprinkle with the cheddar and Swiss cheeses, then the dried oregano. Bake for 25 minutes or until the crust is golden. You may want to rotate the pans during baking to ensure that they cook evenly.

Kasha Varnishkes

This is Eastern European peasant food. It's a good introduction to buckwheat, a grain many Americans are unfamiliar with. Buckwheat groats are kernels of buckwheat, a grain common in Eastern Europe, and kasha is buckwheat groats that have been toasted. You can find kasha in health food stores, some supermarkets, and Eastern European specialty stores. The completed dish should look like bow-tie pasta coated with rich brown grains.

 SERVES 4

1 cup kasha

1 egg (vegans can substitute the equivalent egg replacement)

1½ tablespoons light olive oil

½ cup chopped yellow onion

½ cup chopped red bell pepper

2 cups vegetable stock or water

1 cup bow-tie pasta

Salt and pepper, to taste

¼ cup minced fresh Italian parsley

In a small bowl, mix together the kasha and egg or egg replacement.

Heat the oil in a skillet over a medium-high flame. Add the onion and pepper and cook until tender and starting to brown.

Bring a large pot of water to a boil for cooking the pasta.

When the onion mixture is ready, remove it to a bowl. In the same skillet, cook the kasha and egg for 2 to 3 minutes, or until dry.

Add the vegetable stock or water and reserved onion mixture to the kasha. Bring to a boil. Cover and simmer until the kasha is tender, about 15 minutes.

Cook the pasta according to package directions. Drain.

Toss together the hot pasta and kasha. Season to taste with salt and pepper. Sprinkle with parsley.

Veggie Knish

Fugetaboutit! This whole-grain version of the classic New York street food is stuffed with garden-fresh leeks and potatoes. It should look like a thick, slightly flattened disk of pastry when done.

SERVES 8

2 cups whole wheat pasta flour
Pinch of salt
1 cup Spectrum Spread (a solid, nonhydrogenated butter substitute made from canola oil)
1 cup ice water
2 medium potatoes, peeled and diced
1 tablespoon extra-virgin olive oil, plus extra to grease the baking sheet
2 leeks (white part only), cleaned well and sliced on the diagonal
1 clove garlic, chopped
Salt and pepper, to taste
1 block (14–16 ounces) tofu, cut into squares
Juice of 1 lemon
Small amount of soy milk (about ¼–⅓ cup)

In a large bowl, mix the flour and salt together. Cut in the Spectrum Spread with a pastry cutter or two knives. Slowly mix in the ice water. Roll into a smooth ball and cut into eight slices (as you would cut a pie). Place the slices on a plate, cover with plastic wrap, and refrigerate while you make the filling.

Bring a large pot of water several inches deep to a boil. Place a steamer rack in the pot, add the potatoes, and steam for about 15 minutes or until soft in the center.

Heat the olive oil over a medium flame in a medium skillet. Sauté the leeks and garlic until just tender, about 3 to 4 minutes. Season with salt and pepper, and add to the boiled potatoes. Add the tofu and lemon juice. Mash everything together, adding just enough soy milk to give everything an even consistency. Season with salt and pepper to taste.

Preheat the oven to 425 degrees.

Lightly grease the baking sheet. Leaving the dough in the plastic wrap, flatten each piece into a fairly thin round with a rolling pin. Unfold the plastic wrap and fill the center of the dough with a scoop of filling. Fold the right and left sides over the filling, then fold up the bottom and top. Pinch to seal. Place on the prepared baking sheet and bake until golden brown with slight cracks on surface.

"Meat" Balls and Pasta

Mama mia! They'll never miss the meat with these rich and cheesy rice and almond balls. These look like traditional meatballs, but they'll make everyone happy, including the cows.

 SERVES 8

2 cups short-grain brown rice

4 cups water

2 eggs

$^1/_2$ cup 2 percent milk

1 tablespoon mustard seeds

1 clove garlic, peeled and chopped

$^1/_2$ teaspoon sea salt

$^1/_2$ teaspoon ground black pepper

$^1/_2$ cup ground almonds

4 ounces (about 1 cup) grated Parmesan cheese

2 pounds (about 1 large can) whole peeled tomatoes, drained and slightly crushed with your hands

16 ounces canned tomato sauce

2 small yellow onions, peeled and sliced thin

1 pound spaghetti or linguine, prepared according to package directions

Preheat the oven to 350 degrees.

In a dry pan over high heat, toast the rice for a couple of minutes, until it's fragrant and slightly browned. Add the water and bring to a boil. Cover, reduce the heat to medium low, and simmer the rice for 45 minutes.

In a large bowl, mix the cooked rice, eggs, milk, mustard seeds, garlic, salt, and pepper. Add the ground almonds and grated cheese. Mix well. Roll the mixture into balls the size of a large walnut. Place the balls in a casserole dish.

Combine the tomatoes, tomato sauce, and onions, and pour over the balls. Cover and bake for 1 hour.

Prepare the pasta according to package directions. Drain. Season to taste with salt and pepper. Serve the balls and sauce over the pasta.

Pasta with Vegan Butternut Squash Sauce

Pureed butternut squash gives a creamy consistency to dishes without using any dairy. This dish is both sweet and savory. If you're not vegan, the earthy saltiness of a bit of cheese, such as a few Parmesan shavings or some crumbled Gorgonzola, complements this dish well.

 SERVES 4

1 medium butternut squash

½ pound whole wheat spaghetti (or other long, thin pasta of your choice)

2 tablespoons extra-virgin olive oil, plus extra for oiling pan

3 cloves garlic, peeled and chopped

Several fresh sage leaves, chopped

1 teaspoon red pepper flakes

Salt and pepper, to taste

Water or vegetable stock, as needed

¼ cup chopped hazelnuts

Preheat the oven to 375 degrees.

Cut the squash in half and scoop out its seeds and strings. Lightly coat a baking sheet with oil, rubbing some on the cut sides of the squash. Place the squash cut-side down on the sheet. Bake the squash until it's tender and the cut side is browned, usually between 45 minutes and an hour.

While the squash is cooling a bit, bring enough water to a boil to cook the pasta according to package directions.

Heat the olive oil in a small skillet over a medium-high flame. Cook the garlic for a minute or so, until it's very lightly browned.

Scoop out the flesh of the squash into the bowl of a food processor or, if you prefer an immersion blender, into a bowl. Add the garlic, sage, and pepper flakes. Puree. Use water or stock to adjust consistency. Season to taste with salt and pepper.

Cook the pasta.

While it boils, cook the hazelnuts in a dry pan over medium-high heat until fragrant.

Drain the pasta and toss it with the squash mixture. To serve, sprinkle with hazelnuts.

Vegan Vegetable Sandwich

This recipe showcases fresh grated vegetables tossed in a simple vinaigrette. Substitute any shredded vegetables that you like—say, raw beets—add slices of tofu or soy-based meat substitutes, or add some mashed beans to personalize this sandwich.

 SERVES 4

8 slices whole-grain bread

2 teaspoons balsamic vinegar

1 teaspoon Dijon mustard

2 tablespoons extra-virgin olive oil

Salt and pepper, to taste

2 carrots, peeled and grated

4-inch slice daikon radish, peeled and grated

1 cup fresh spinach or arugula

1 avocado, peeled and sliced

Toast the bread.

While it's toasting, whisk together the vinegar and mustard in a large bowl. Slowly whisk in the olive oil. Season to taste with salt and pepper.

Toss the carrots, daikon, and spinach with the dressing.

To assemble, divide the avocado slices among 4 slices of bread. Top with the vegetable mixture. If any dressing remains in the bottom of the bowl, drizzle it over the vegetables. Top with the remaining bread.

Our Favorite Fava Bean Sandwich

nce you make the fava bean spread, this sandwich is an initiation to jam any way that you want. For large groups, set out the spread, the bread, and a whole heap of toppings. Let everyone go wherever their inspirations, and their stomachs, carry them.

 MAKES ABOUT 4 CUPS

20 ounces (about 3$\frac{1}{2}$ cups) dried fava beans

$\frac{1}{4}$ cup tahini (sesame butter)

1 tablespoon extra-virgin olive oil

1 tablespoon lemon juice

1 teaspoon garlic powder

$\frac{1}{4}$ cup (or less) water

Salt and pepper, to taste

Fresh whole wheat multigrain bread, sliced

Sliced tomato, lettuce, pickle wedges, radish slices, arugula, alfalfa sprouts, and/or avocado slices to garnish (optional)

Soak the beans overnight in enough water to cover by about 2 inches. Drain.

Put the beans in a large pot and add water to cover by about an inch. Bring to a boil over high heat, then cover, reduce the heat to medium low, and simmer until tender, about 45 minutes to an hour. Drain and let cool.

Blend the beans, tahini, olive oil, lemon juice, and garlic powder in a food processor or blender until creamy smooth. Add water, if necessary, to reach the consistency you like. Season to taste with salt and pepper. Spread each slice of bread with a generous portion of the fava bean mixture, garnishing with any or all of the optional toppings.

Bean Burgers

These are best cooked on a stovetop rather than a grill to prevent them from falling apart. Use any kind of beans and flavorings that you like. Try white beans with mint, oregano, and lemon zest (leaving out the cilantro, jalapeño, and dried spices); black beans with orange zest and garlic (again omitting the cilantro, jalapeño, and dried spices); or chickpeas with curry powder, shredded sweet potato, and ginger (leaving out the dried spices).

 SERVES 4

½ cup dry bread crumbs

2 green onions, chopped

¼ cup chopped fresh cilantro

1 jalapeño pepper, seeded and chopped

½ teaspoon ground cumin

¼ teaspoon ground coriander

About 1 teaspoon salt

2 cups cooked pinto beans

1 large egg

1 tablespoon extra-virgin olive oil

4 whole wheat hamburger buns

4 romaine lettuce leaves

1 avocado, peeled and sliced

Hot pepper sauce, to taste

Mix together the bread crumbs, green onions, cilantro, pepper, cumin, coriander, and salt. Add the pinto beans and mash the mixture together. Leave some lumps for texture. Add the egg and mix well. Form the mixture into four patties and refrigerate for about 15 minutes.

Heat the oil in a large skillet over a medium-high flame. Cook the patties, turning once, until they're browned on both sides and heated through. Serve on buns with lettuce, avocado, and hot sauce to taste.

Veggie Potpies

et your chickens run free and try vegan potpies instead. These pies take a little effort, but they're warm, comforting, and worth every minute of your time. You will need six ramekins (7–8 ounces each) or other small dishes of about the same size to make these pies. Maggi is a vegetable protein sauce similar to soy sauce; if you can't find it, use your favorite soy sauce instead.

 SERVES 6

1/2 cup (8 ounces) shortening
1 cup whole wheat flour
1 1/2 cups all-purpose flour
1 teaspoon salt
25–30 baby onions
2 turnips
2 carrots
1/4 red bell pepper
1 parsnip
2 large heads broccoli
10 dark mushrooms, such as cremini
2 tablespoons light olive oil
6–8 cloves garlic, peeled and sliced
2 baking potatoes, peeled and roughly
     chopped into cubes

1 cube vegetable bouillon dissolved in
     1 cup water
1 tablespoon chopped fresh thyme
2 tablespoons chopped fresh flat-leaf
     parsley
Salt and pepper, to taste
Dash of Maggi (or substitute soy sauce)
1 tablespoon flour or arrowroot mixed
     with 2 tablespoons water
1 cup fresh peas
Enough extra-virgin olive oil to brush
     top of each pie

In a large mixing bowl, combine the shortening, flours, and salt with a pastry cutter or two knives. Starting with a cup of ice water, mix water in a little at a time until the dough starts to come together. You will not use all of the water. Wrap the dough in plastic wrap and refrigerate as you prepare the vegetables.

Bring a large pot of water to a boil. Blanch the onions in boiling water for about 2 minutes. Pour the onions into a strainer, then put them in a bowl of cool water to cool. Snip off the root ends of the onions and squeeze each until the center pops out of its outer layer.

Peel the skin off one turnip. Leave the

other unpeeled. Roughly chop both turnips. Peel the carrots and roughly chop. Slice the pepper. Peel the parsnip and cut off the stem end; quarter. Peel the woody stalk ends of the broccoli and thinly chop the stems. Cut the top into florets. Prepare the mushrooms by chopping the larger ones into six pieces and the smaller ones into four.

Heat the oil in a heavy skillet over a medium-high flame. Sauté the garlic for a minute or so.

Add the vegetables in the following order, stirring after each addition: onions, turnips, carrots, red pepper, parsnip, broccoli, and mushrooms. Cover with a lid and cook until the vegetables are slightly tender and the colors have changed a bit, about 8 to 10 minutes. The onions should be slightly blackened. Add the potato cubes to the center of the pot along with a third of the vegetable bouillon. Cook until tender, about 10 minutes. Add the thyme and parsley. Season with salt and pepper.

Add another third of the stock. With a potato masher, crush the potatoes (it's fine if

you mash a few of the other vegetables, too) and add the rest of the stock. Add a splash of Maggi and mix well. Continue to cook the vegetables until tender, about 5 minutes more. Add the flour or arrowroot mixture. Mix well.

Unwrap the chilled dough on a lightly floured board. Roll to $1/4$-inch thickness. Using a small bowl (slightly larger than the top of your ramekins) as a template, cut the dough into six circles.

Pour the vegetables into the ramekins. Add the peas to the top for color.

Preheat the oven to 350 degrees.

Gently moisten the bottom of each dough circle with water to help it adhere to the top of the ramekin. Cover each ramekin with dough and pinch the edges down lightly over the rim. Prick each with a fork for ventilation. Using a pastry brush, moisten the dough on top of each ramekin with a bit of water. Bake for 25 to 30 minutes. After removing the pies from the oven, baste the top of each with a bit of olive oil to add a nice sheen.

6. Main Courses–Pescatarian

Being a hippy is about always exploring and stretching your horizons. It's about being open and ready for adventures. Eating like a hippy means never letting yourself fall into a rut but instead letting the tastes of the world flow through your cooking and your soul.

Variety and exploration are among the reasons we love sustainably caught fish. When we travel, one of the best parts is tasting varieties of seafood we've never seen before. We've tried salt-crusted orata, triglie, cuttlefish, and many others that you'd find in few American kitchens. It's a big, crazy world out there in the oceans and rivers, and the creatures we harvest from it come in all shapes, colors, and sizes. From giant crea-

tures that look like aliens to succulent little morsels, there's something for everyone.

And just like being a hippy gourmet means tasting new things, it means cooking new things. Some people are scared of cooking fish. If you're one of those, just relax and try something new. The worst thing that could happen is that your fish is a little dry. The best that could happen is that you make the tastiest meal your friends and family have ever eaten. You might just discover that you love cooking fish, then you have many roads to wander, my friend.

When you buy fish, tread with care. With current levels of overfishing, fish cannot reproduce fast enough to sustain their populations; sadly, there are several species we could lose entirely within a generation. That means gone forever with a few passes of a net.

We don't blame the poor fishermen who are just trying to earn a living. They feel that they have to use the new technologies just to support themselves, and they're probably right. Greater harvests mean lower prices for fishermen, who then need bigger and bigger harvests just to keep their incomes stable. But by using our power at the checkout counter, we can make planet-friendly seafood choices that will encourage the fishing industry and world governments to act in a way that is ecologically and financially viable for all concerned.

Not all factory-farmed fish are bad, but it's important to buy only those that are raised sustainably. There are plenty of seafood farms around the world that care very much about their local environments, as well as making sure that their seafood is hormone- and antibiotic-free. We see a great opportunity for fisheries in developing countries to do the right thing—and again, your purchasing power makes all the difference in the world.

Like everything else in this world, it's good to diversify your diet, which includes varying the kinds of seafood you cook and eat and how many times a week you have it.

Because many of the larger fish species contain mercury and other toxins, it's wise for people who are sensitive to them, such as small children, to be extra careful about the fish they consume.

But, hey, we don't want to bum you out. For all the negatives, fish is still one of the healthiest, most delicious sources of protein, and the Hippy Gourmet is going to continue cooking it. Just as we take care to buy organic produce, though, we also take care to buy sustainably caught and produced fish. A lot of delicious choices still exist, more than we can eat in a lifetime. In fact, expanding our horizons may be good for the oceans. It's when we limit ourselves to one fish—such as cod or Chilean sea bass—that we threaten the whole species. There's a wild profusion of seafood out there, and we should enjoy nature in all its abundant diversity. Check out the Monterey Bay Aquarium's Seafood Watch Program (www.mbayaq.org/cr/seafoodwatch.asp) to make sure you're buying seafood caught in a sustainable way.

We've had a lot of good times with fish on the show. Hippy cooking isn't just about taking care of the footprints we're making; it's about having a good time, too. On one episode, Bruce used the entire fish, head and all, to make a Mediterranean Whole Baked Fish that made us want to run in the surf with joy. Ya, mon, he felt the island rhythms and the island heat when he made Jerk Fish. Then he came down a few notches and explored the Zen of cooking homemade Shrimp Ravioli. He even took the batteries out of the smoke detector to make Blackened Shrimp and Salmon!

Enjoying fish is about just that . . . enjoying it. Have fun, relax, and savor the journey. Included are a handful of recipes to get you started. A few introduce ways of cooking that you can use on almost any fish. If a particular variety is a stranger to you, it's almost never a bad idea to broil, grill, or pan-sear it simply, and top with just a bit of sea salt or lemon. Eat it unembellished to see what its true taste is. If you like the fish, then you can get fancy next time. Have fun and start fishing.

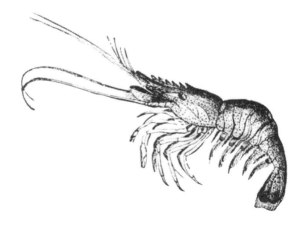

Herb-Steamed Halibut

Steaming fish on a bed of herbs or flavorful ingredients, such as ginger or green onions, adds deep flavor without adding any fat. This dish works with most kinds of fish and virtually any herb you choose.

 SERVES 4

1 bunch fresh dill
1 bunch fresh flat-leaf parsley
4 halibut fillets, 6–8 ounces each
Drizzle of olive oil (optional)
Salt and pepper, to taste
1 lemon, cut into wedges

Bring a couple of inches of water to a boil in a pan large enough to hold your steamer of choice.

Chop about 1 tablespoon dill and 1 tablespoon parsley and reserve. Leave the rest of the herbs whole.

Lay half of the whole dill and the parsley atop the steamer. Lay the fish on top of the herbs, then top the fish with the remaining whole herbs. Place the steamer on top of the boiling water and cover the pan. Cook for about 7 minutes, then carefully lift the lid (steam will burn you more easily than just about anything in the kitchen) and check the fish. When it's done, it'll be firm to the touch and should have just lost its translucency. Don't cook longer or the fish will dry out. Remember that fish will continue to cook a bit as you carry it to the table.

Take the fish from the steamer and discard the whole herbs. Drizzle the fish fillets with a bit of olive oil, if desired, sprinkle with salt and pepper to taste, and sprinkle with the reserved herbs. Serve with lemon wedges.

Count Bouilla-baisse!

Here's a classic French dish made hippy-style. It's fun to serve it in hollowed-out bread "bowls," but serving this in a plain old bowl will taste just as good. Large prawns are often factory-farmed, so if they aren't available from a sustainable source in your area, substitute an equal amount of another shellfish.

 SERVES 8

2 pounds white fish

$\frac{1}{2}$ cup crab

$\frac{1}{2}$ pound shrimp

$\frac{1}{2}$ pound prawns

$\frac{1}{2}$ pound scallops

$\frac{1}{2}$ cup coconut oil (or substitute peanut oil)

1 clove garlic, peeled and slightly crushed with the side of a knife

1 cup canned, stewed tomatoes

1 cup chopped white or yellow onions

$\frac{3}{4}$ cup chopped celery

$\frac{1}{2}$ cup chopped fresh parsley

$\frac{1}{2}$ bay leaf

$\frac{1}{8}$ teaspoon thyme

$\frac{1}{4}$ teaspoon saffron

$\frac{1}{4}$ teaspoon paprika

1 can (8 ounces) tomato paste

$\frac{1}{2}$ cup white wine (preferably Sauternes)

Sea salt, to taste (about $\frac{1}{2}$ teaspoon)

8 miniature or 1 full-size loaf sourdough bread (optional)

Scale and de-bone all the fish and shellfish (if you don't know how, request that the fishmonger do this for you when you're buying it).

Heat the oil over a medium-high flame in a deep saucepan. Place the garlic in the oil until golden brown (1 to 2 minutes), then remove and discard the clove. Stir in the tomatoes, onions, celery, parsley, bay leaf, thyme, saffron, paprika, and tomato paste. Cook for 10 to 12 minutes, stirring occasionally.

Layer the fish and shellfish—thicker pieces on the bottom—in the tomato base. Pour the wine atop, then sprinkle on a little sea salt to taste, but do not stir.

Bring all the ingredients to a very slow boil, reduce the heat to medium, cover, and cook for 20 minutes. Do not stir.

If you're using bread "bowls," cut off the tops of the mini loaves and scoop out the soft inner bread, saving this for another use; serve the stew in the crust. Otherwise, spoon into bowls and serve with bread at the table.

Crabby Cioppino

One of our Mediterranean-style favorites—with a twist, of course. Cioppino was probably created in San Francisco by Italian immigrants. Peeling the shellfish after it's simmered in a dark tomato base is just part of the fun; hippies know getting your hands dirty is one of life's great joys! This is delicious served with a hearty, dark whole-grain bread rubbed with some raw garlic.

  SERVES 4

¹/₂ cup olive oil
1 white onion, chopped fine
2 cloves garlic, peeled and chopped fine
¹/₂ cup chopped fresh parsley
2 cans (28 ounces each) whole tomatoes,
    drained and crushed
1 whole clove
1 cup dry red wine

Salt and pepper, to taste
1–3 cooked crabs
¹/₂ pound prawns
1 pound clams

In a large pan, heat the oil over a medium-high flame and add the onion, garlic, and parsley. Cook for about 10 minutes, or until the onion is light brown.

Add the tomatoes, clove, wine, and salt and pepper to taste. Bring to a boil, then reduce the heat to medium low and simmer, covered, for 30 minutes. Stir to prevent browning.

Rinse the crabs, prawns, and clams, and scrub the clams with a stiff brush if they have any visible dirt.

Increase the heat to medium high. Add the crab, prawns, and clams to the pan. When the mixture reaches a boil, cover, reduce the heat to medium low, and cook for about 20 minutes.

Clams and Mussels with Wine and Herb Broth

Native Americans loved clams and mussels so much that they left piles of shells several feet high near the best beds, many still visible today in places such as the Florida Keys. We think they're pretty good, too. Use whatever varieties of bivalves are freshest and most readily available in your part of the country.

 SERVES 4

2 dozen clams

2 dozen mussels

1 tablespoon extra-virgin olive oil

$^1/_4$ cup finely chopped shallots

2 cloves garlic, peeled and chopped

1 bay leaf

$^1/_4$ cup chopped fresh flat-leaf parsley

1 cup dry white wine

Salt and pepper, to taste

Sourdough or crusty bread

Rinse both the clams and the mussels under running water. They may require a stiff brush to remove excess dirt on the shells. Discard any that have an open shell that will not close. If the mussels have "beards"—a clump of fibers sticking out from the shells—pull these off.

In a large pot, heat the olive oil over a medium-high flame. Add the shallots and garlic and cook until softened, about 4 to 5 minutes. Add the bay leaf, parsley, and wine. Bring to a boil. Add the clams and cover. Let steam for about 5 minutes. Add the mussels and cover again. Allow to steam for about 5 minutes more.

When both the mussels and the clams have opened, remove them from the pot with a spoon. Discard any that have not opened. Season the cooking liquid with a bit of salt and pepper and serve alongside the seafood. Sourdough or crusty bread is a must to soak up the broth!

Asian Shrimp

The corn syrup in this recipe helps high-light the natural sweetness in shrimp. Corn syrup—and any other product made with corn—is one ingredient you should definitely buy in an organic version. Many of the "regular" corn products sold in the United States are bioengineered; if you don't want Frankenfood, go organic.

 SERVES 3–4

1/4 cup dark corn syrup

1/4 cup water

2 tablespoons soy sauce

2 tablespoons sherry

1 tablespoon cornstarch

1 clove garlic, minced

1/4 teaspoon ground dried ginger

1 pound medium shrimp

2 tablespoons corn oil

1 tomato, cut into wedges

1/2 cup red and/or green peppers, seeded and cut into chunks

In a bowl, combine the corn syrup, water, soy sauce, sherry, cornstarch, garlic, and ginger.

If desired, peel and de-vein the shrimp. Peeled shrimp will be less messy to eat. Unpeeled shrimp will be more flavorful, and, as every toddler knows, being messy is half the fun.

Heat the corn oil in a skillet over a medium-high flame until it shimmers. Add the shrimp and cook, stirring occasionally, for 3 to 4 minutes. Add the sauce and the remaining ingredients and bring to a boil. Cook for 1 or 2 minutes, stirring gently. Serve with brown or wild rice, or a combination.

Spinach and Mushroom Sole

This is one classic rolled fish recipe that totally rocks! It's great for your body, and once you taste it you'll see that it's also great for your "sole."

 SERVES 2–4

1 bunch spinach, thoroughly washed

1 tablespoon olive oil (or butter)

2 green onions, chopped

8–10 mushrooms of your choice, chopped

Pepper and sea salt, to taste

1 pound fresh sole fillets

$\frac{1}{2}$ lemon

1 jar (25–28 ounces) pasta sauce
 of your choice

Preheat the oven to 350 degrees.

Heat a large, dry pan over a medium-high flame. No oil is necessary since the water on the spinach leaves will prevent sticking. Cook the spinach until completely wilted, about 2 minutes, then set aside to cool. Drain the spinach well and chop. If you want to make sure it's totally dry, press it in a clean kitchen towel.

Heat the olive oil over a medium-high flame. Sauté the onions and mushrooms together. When the onions are soft and lightly brown, add the spinach. Cook for 1 to 2 minutes. Season with a bit of pepper and sea salt.

In a casserole dish, lay out the slices of sole, squeezing a little lemon juice over the tops of the fillets. Spoon a nice mound of spinach on each fillet, then roll it up around the spinach, leaving the end under the bottom of the roll-up. Pour tomato sauce on top of each fillet. Sprinkle with a bit more sea salt and pepper. Bake for 25 to 35 minutes, or until fillets feel slightly firm to the touch.

Monterey Bay and Legal, Safe, Sustainable (and Good) Fishing

Some people refuse to eat fish for environmental reasons, some are frightened by the high mercury content or pesticide residues in some species, and some refuse to eat other living creatures. We respect those reasons, but we also love fish. Those of us who do eat it can minimize our impact on the planet by avoiding those fish, such as farm-raised salmon, that have the most negative impact on the environment.

One of the many reasons that *The Hippy Gourmet* supports the Monterey Bay Aquarium, and has featured it on the show, is because it's more than just an aquarium. As you can see from the way the interior and exterior of the aquarium flow into each other, these folks don't believe that an aquarium's role is limited to its walls. They're dedicated to preserving healthy oceans.

One way they help is to publish easy guides for consumers who want to eat environmentally friendly fish. For a complete list of sustainable choices in your area, check one of the aquarium's guides. They're available online (www.mbayaq.org/cr/seafood watch.asp) or through the mail. Here are some planet-friendly choices that you can make: wild-caught salmon, farm-raised catfish, Pacific halibut, Dungeness crab, farm-raised tilapia, and farm-raised mussels or clams. Some choices to avoid: Chilean sea bass, red snapper, imported shrimp, Atlantic cod, and grouper.

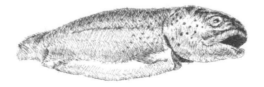

Grilled Salmon

Meyer lemons are rounder and sweeter than regular lemons. If they are unavailable, substitute regular lemons; the recipe will be just a bit more acidic. On the show, we served this dish with mixed stir-fried vegetables cooked in olive oil and sweet white rice.

 SERVES 6–8

2-inch chunk raw gingerroot

6 cloves of garlic

1 cup soy sauce

Splash of light olive oil

Juice of 1 Meyer lemon

Juice of 1 lime

1½ pounds salmon cut into large fillets about 1 inch thick, skin removed

Remove the peel and hard knobs of the gingerroot with a paring knife. Blend the garlic, soy sauce, and gingerroot in a blender for 1 minute. Add a splash of oil. Blend. Add lemon and lime juice, blending again.

Put the salmon fillets in a bowl. Add the marinade and let them sit for about half an hour (but no longer, or the acidic juices will cook the fish).

While the salmon is marinating, heat a grill to medium to high. Wipe a bit of marinade on the grill with a paper towel to flavor its surface.

Remove the fish from the marinade and place on the grill. Cover and cook for 5 minutes. Using tongs and a spatula, and being careful not to tear the fish, flip the fillets. Continue grilling until done, about 7 to 8 minutes. The fish should be firm to the touch and have just turned opaque.

Mediterranean Baked Whole Fish

Just imagine that glorious Mediterranean sun on your skin as you cook this. This recipe works with any whole fish that you prefer: a small salmon, arctic char, or even a freshwater fish such as large-mouth bass. If your fish are quite small—anticipate about a pound of whole fish per person—you may want to bake more than one.

    EACH HALF POUND OF FISH
SERVES 1

1 whole fish, cleaned and scaled,
   but not de-boned
Salt, to taste
3 tablespoons lemon juice
2–3 tablespoons extra-virgin olive oil
2 green peppers, seeded and sliced thinly
1 yellow onion, peeled and chopped
4 cloves garlic, peeled and chopped
2 tablespoons ground turmeric
1 teaspoon ground cumin
1 red chile pepper, seeded and sliced
1 green chile pepper, seeded and sliced
2 cups crushed tomatoes

¼ cup pine nuts
2 green onions, cut however you prefer,
   for garnish

Preheat the oven to 350 degrees.

Place the fish in a baking pan. With a knife, poke a few small holes in it. Sprinkle with salt and pour lemon juice on top. Set aside.

Heat the oil in a frying pan over a medium-high flame. Add the green peppers, onion, and garlic. Cook for a minute or so. Add the turmeric and cumin. Mix well. Add the chilies and tomatoes. Cook for about 5 minutes, or until the mixture is reduced somewhat.

On a baking sheet in the preheated oven or in a dry skillet on the stove over high heat, toast the pine nuts until fragrant and remove from the heat (they will continue to darken somewhat in the pan). Reserve 2 teaspoons.

Remove the fish from the baking pan. Put the pine nuts in the pan, then top with the fish. Place the cooked vegetable-spice mixture atop. Bake for 30 to 40 minutes.

Serve the fish on a platter garnished with the reserved pine nuts and green onions.

Dominica

Located in the Thousand Islands of the West Indies, Dominica is almost 98 percent undeveloped. A hippy paradise! Visitors to the untouched coastline can see miles of crystal blue and turquoise waters surrounding the mountainous island. Only the occasional Native fishing family interrupts the pristine beauty. Inland, a rain forest canopy reveals an abundance of tropical fruits, nuts, and vegetables ready for the picking. The sound of rushing water in the distance draws you closer to Twin Falls, which rain sweet, fresh water into the Emerald Pool below.

Like many former colonies, Dominica has had its growing pains, but it's still beautiful and largely untouched. With so much abundance, Dominican farmers don't use fences on their diverse plantations. They invite anyone to come and take what they need. The people of Dominica glow with health; they get all they require from the sea and land around them.

Jerk Fish

Spicy, casual, and oh so good . . . just like the amazing people we met in the islands. This fish celebrates Dominica. On the show, we served it with coconut rice, Mango Papaya Chutney (page 252), and sautéed vegetables.

 SERVES 6–8

2 tablespoons ground allspice

2 teaspoons ground black pepper

1 teaspoon ground cinnamon

¼ teaspoon ground nutmeg

1 teaspoon dried thyme

2 teaspoons salt

5 tablespoons neutral oil, such as soy or grapeseed

¼ cup red wine vinegar

2 finely diced Scotch bonnet peppers (habaneros) (use 1 for medium hot)

10 diced green onions

3 pounds fish of your choice, skin removed, cut into bite-size pieces

Blend all of the ingredients except the fish in a food processor or blender.

In a large bowl, mix the fish and the spice blend. Toss the fish with your hands to coat. Let it sit for at least 1 hour and up to 3 or 4. Beware! If your hands are in the marinade, don't touch your eyes or any other sensitive part of your body . . . ouch! Wash carefully.

Heat the grill to medium or high. On a charcoal grill, wait until the coals are coated in white and very hot. Rub a bit of oil on the grill with a paper towel. Be careful not to drip on the coals, which will cause flare-ups that could burn you.

Place the fish on the grill. If you like, you can thread the fish onto metal skewers or wooden skewers that have been soaked in water for easier handling. Grill for about 8 minutes on the first side. Flip the pieces and grill for another 3 or 4 minutes on the second.

Variation:

If you wish to cook the fish on a stovetop, you can, though it won't have all the authentic jerk flavor. Heat a pan over a medium-high flame, add a tablespoon of neutral oil, such as soy or grapeseed, and cook the fish for about 3 to 4 minutes on each side, or until it's cooked through.

Blackened Shrimp and Salmon

Blacken it with Louisiana flavor, baby, and you'll be rocking Bourbon Street–style. On the show, we served this with buttered noodles and steamed yellow squashes and zucchinis. The plain noodles and vegetables are a good balance with the hot, spicy seafood.

 SERVES 4–6

1 tablespoon salt

1 tablespoon dried thyme

1 tablespoon paprika

1 tablespoon dried oregano

1 tablespoon garlic powder

1 tablespoon ground black pepper

1 tablespoon ground white pepper

1 tablespoon cayenne pepper

1 pound tiger shrimp, peeled and de-veined

1 tablespoon butter, melted

1 pound salmon fillets, skin removed, cut into large pieces

$1/2$ lemon

Mix the salt with all the spices on a large piece of brown paper, such as a flattened grocery bag. If you lived through the 1960s, you may have done something similar on an album cover. If not, take our word for it: This is the way to do it. Bend the paper and use it to pour the spice mixture into a bowl.

Heat a frying pan over a high flame.

Split each shrimp by making a cut through the head end to about halfway down the body. Dredge the shrimp in the melted butter, then into the spice mixture.

Add the shrimp to the very hot pan. Cook the shrimp for about 2 minutes, or until dark brown, turning once, then remove them from the pan.

Use vent fan on high and be aware smoke detectors may go off.

Dredge the salmon in the melted butter, then into the spice mixture.

Add the salmon to the hot pan along with remaining butter. Sear until dark brown, about 2 to 3 minutes, then flip and sear the second side for another 2 to 3 minutes until dark brown. Squeeze a bit of fresh lemon over the seafood and serve.

Orange Trout and Prickly Pear Cactus

The cactus might prickle at your touch, but it hides a succulent interior. Cactus leaves, or nopalitos, are available at Latino markets and in some grocery stores. They have a slightly tart taste that matches well with seafood and citrus. On the show, we served this with potatoes and sautéed mushrooms and spinach.

 SERVES 4

4 prickly pear cactus leaves

2 tablespoons butter, divided

4 whole trout (about 1 pound each), cleaned, boned, and scaled, with head and tail removed (if you don't know how, have the fishmonger do this when you buy the fish)

$1/2$ cup all-purpose flour

1 teaspoon salt

$1/2$ teaspoon ground black pepper

Juice of $1/4$ large orange

1 tablespoon chopped fresh flat-leaf parsley

Wearing gloves, snip the spines, if any, off the cactus leaves, and cut off the bases. Using a vegetable peeler, scrape the leaves around the edges and nubs. Cut into small strips across the grain, then cut the small strips in half.

Heat half the butter in a small pan over a medium-high flame and sauté the cactus until just tender, about 4 to 5 minutes. Season to taste with salt and pepper.

Wash the trout thoroughly. Place the flour, salt, and pepper in a paper bag. Add the fish and shake.

Heat the remaining butter in a skillet over a medium-high flame. Remove the fish from the bag, shaking off any excess flour. Starting with the flesh side down, cook the trout until brown on both sides, turning once, about 7 to 10 minutes total. Sprinkle with the orange juice and chopped parsley. Serve with the cactus.

Seviche and Salsa

This dish combines the flavors of Peru and Japan—two cultures that know the beauty of raw or barely cooked fish. In this dish, the fresh fish is "cooked" in a combination of citrus juices. Use only the highest-quality, never-frozen fish that is available to you.

 SERVES 4–6

2 pounds fresh lean fish, such as halibut, Pacific line-caught cod, or pollack

Juice of 6 lemons

Juice of 6 limes

4 tomatoes, seeded and chopped

1 medium red onion, peeled and chopped

1 bunch cilantro, chopped fine

1–2 cloves garlic, peeled and crushed

2 tablespoons sesame seeds

4 packages ramen noodles, flavor of your choice (preferably a high-quality Japanese brand)

2 tablespoons bonito flakes

2 tablespoons tamari or other soy sauce

Chop the fish into small pieces (two to three pieces per bite). Combine the fish and lemon and lime juices in a large nonreactive bowl. Make sure that all the fish is submerged. Cover and marinate in the refrigerator for at least 1 and up to 12 hours.

In another bowl, combine the tomatoes, onion, cilantro, and garlic. Mix well.

In a small, dry skillet over high heat, toast the sesame seeds. When they become fragrant, in approximately 1 or 2 minutes, remove them from the heat and let them cool. Grind the seeds in a small, clean coffee grinder or blender to form a powder.

In a large pot, boil 5 cups water. Add the noodles and their seasoning packets. Boil for 5 minutes, or until tender.

To serve, spoon the salsa into bowls. Top with ground sesame seeds. Add the seviche and its juice. Add the noodles and their juice. Top with a pinch of bonito flakes, and sprinkle with tamari.

Fish Chowder

This dish uses the fish itself, as well as the trimmings from the vegetables, to form its own stock, so be sure not to throw anything out when you prepare your vegetables. This simple fish chowder doesn't have the gummy saltiness of its canned counterparts. Leftovers will keep for only a day or two, so make this when you're expecting a crowd.

 SERVES 10–12

¹/₄ pound (1 stick) butter

¹/₂ cup all-purpose flour

5 stalks celery, including leaves, diced large

1 teaspoon whole black peppercorns

1 bay leaf

6 medium russet potatoes, peeled and diced in large chunks

2 white onions, peeled and diced large

2 carrots, peeled and diced large

4–5 pounds white fish fillets, such as halibut, Pacific line-caught cod, or pollack

1 tablespoon salt

1 tablespoon light olive oil

6 cloves garlic, peeled and chopped fine

¹/₂ teaspoon crushed black pepper

1 teaspoon dried savory

1 teaspoon dried tarragon

1 can (12 ounces) evaporated milk

In a saucepan over medium heat, melt the butter. Whisk in the flour and continue to cook until the mixture lightly foams. Remove from the heat.

Place 2 quarts (8 cups) water in a large stockpot. Add 1 stalk of the celery along with the whole peppercorns, bay leaf, and trimmings from the celery, potatoes, onions, and carrots. Bring to a boil. Add the fish fillets and bring back to a boil for 2 minutes. Remove from the heat. Strain the stock into a large bowl, pouring the liquid back into the pan. Lay the fish out to cool a bit and discard the remaining solids.

Over medium-high heat, bring the liquid to a simmer. Add the potatoes and salt. Add the butter-flour mixture (called a roux) to the liquid and stir until it's mixed in well. When the mixture reaches a boil, reduce the heat to medium-low, cover, and simmer until the potatoes are soft and the stock is slightly thickened.

While the potatoes cook, remove any remaining bones from the fish fillets. Chop them into large pieces.

In a separate pot, heat the oil over a medium-high flame. Add the garlic and onions. Let this cook for 3 to 5 minutes. Add the carrots and remaining 4 stalks of celery, and the crushed pepper, savory, and tarragon. Cook until the onions are translucent, about 3 to 5 minutes more. When they're cooked, add the vegetable mixture to the stock. Add the fish and stir well, then add the evaporated milk. Heat through. Taste, adjust the salt and pepper, and serve.

Shrimp Ravioli in Saffron Cream Sauce

When you want to relax by losing yourself in the calm Zen of cooking, this is the thing to make. Ravioli requires a lot of time and attention, and it's well worth it. You'll need to break out the pasta maker for this dish; if you don't have one, you can roll the dough by hand. It goes well with a side of fresh asparagus.

  SERVES 10

1¼ pounds shrimp, peeled (reserve
   the shells)
2 stalks celery, chopped
1 pinch tarragon
2 pinches saffron, divided
2 pinches grated lemon peel, divided
1 thin slice lemon
3 cups unbleached white flour

4 large egg whites
1 tablespoon extra-virgin olive oil
   (optional)
1 teaspoon powdered celery seeds
1 large pinch white pepper
1 tablespoon butter
6 shallots, peeled and chopped
½ cup cream
Salt and pepper, to taste
1 bunch parsley, leaves only,
   chopped

Bring 4 to 6 cups water to a boil in a large pot over high heat. Reduce the heat to medium, and add the shrimp shells, celery, and pinch of tarragon. Simmer for 10 minutes. Add 1 pinch saffron, 1 pinch grated lemon, and the lemon slice. Simmer for 10 minutes more. Pour the liquid through a strainer and set aside. Discard the solids.

On a clean surface or in a bowl, make a pile of the flour. Dip a large cup in the middle to make a well. Add the egg whites and the olive oil (if desired) to the well. With a spatula, begin to fold in the flour, beginning along the top outside perimeter. Once the flour and egg are incorporated, knead until you have a firm dough.

Cut the dough into four sections and run each section through a pasta machine. Begin on the largest setting, and keep running through on successively smaller settings. Before the final setting, let the dough sit, covered by a kitchen towel, in a large bowl or on the counter.

While the dough relaxes, add half the shrimp, along with the celery seeds and white pepper, to a blender. Pulse.

Run the dough through the thinnest setting. Lay out half the dough for the bottoms of the ravioli, and reserve the remaining dough for the top. Lay small dabs of shrimp puree on the dough, leaving about an inch on all sides. On top of each dap of paste, place 1 whole shrimp. With a pastry brush, brush a small amount of water on the exposed pasta. Lay the top pieces of pasta on the bottoms. Press down around all sides of the filling. Using a pasta cutter or serrated edge cutter, cut out raviolis.

Bring a large pot of water to a boil. Adding a small amount of oil to the water will help prevent sticking. Add the ravioli. Cook for about 10 minutes, or until the pasta is tender. Drain and place on a platter.

While the water is boiling and the ravioli is cooking, melt the butter in a skillet over low heat. Add the shallots and any shrimp left over from the ravioli. Let this cook until the shallots are soft and the shrimp are pink, about 3 to 5 minutes. Add the saved liquid from the shrimp shells along with the cream. Keep simmering until reduced, about 5 to 10 minutes. Just before taking the pan off the heat, add the remaining saffron and lemon peel. Season to taste with salt and pepper. Serve the sauce over the drained pasta. Sprinkle with parsley.

Quiche Me, Seafood-Style!

Do real men eat quiche? There's no doubt when you taste this dish. This is a healthy brunch dish to impress the ladies, the men, or just yourself. Serve it with fresh fruit or a small salad on the side.

 SERVES 3–4

$^2/_3$ cup short-grain brown rice

$1^1/_3$ cups water

$^1/_4$ cup ($^1/_2$ stick) butter, melted, plus
    1 teaspoon unmelted

$^1/_2$ cup grated Swiss or cheddar cheese
    (or a blend of the two)

$^1/_2$ pound crabmeat, lobster meat, or
    peeled shrimp

$^1/_2$ cup 2 percent milk

3 eggs

1 teaspoon chopped chives

$^1/_4$ teaspoon sea salt

$^1/_8$ teaspoon white pepper

In a dry pot over high heat, toast the rice until it's fragrant and lightly browned. Add the water, bring to a boil, reduce the heat to medium low, cover, and simmer for 45 minutes.

Preheat the oven to 375 degrees.

Combine the rice with the melted butter and press into a shallow baking pan (about 10 × 10 inches). The rice should cover the bottom and come up about $^1/_2$ inch on the sides. Spread the cheese over the rice.

In a skillet, heat the teaspoon of butter over a medium-high flame. Add the seafood and cook for just a minute or two.

In a separate saucepan, heat the milk until it just begins to steam. Remove from the heat and let it cool slightly.

Whisk together the eggs, chives, milk, and salt and pepper to taste.

Spread the cooked seafood over the rice-cheese layer at the bottom of the pan and pour the custard ingredients over the top, making sure to cover it all up. Bake for 35 to 40 minutes, or until the top is golden brown.

Lavash Sandwiches

Lavash is a form of bread that comes in very large, thin sheets that look something like an overgrown tortilla. It's available in many health food stores, some conventional groceries, and Middle Eastern bakeries; if you can't find it, you could substitute large tortillas. When rolled and cut into slices, it makes a beautiful presentation.

 SERVES 2–4

1 red bell pepper
1 yellow bell pepper
1 piece whole-grain lavash
1 pat butter, melted
2 cups spinach leaves
1 can water-packed tuna, drained
2 avocados, peeled and sliced thin
   lengthwise
1 cup grated cheddar cheese
Salt and pepper, to taste

Preheat the oven to 350 degrees.

Bring a pot of water to a boil over high heat. Add both peppers and cook for about a minute to blanch. Drain, seed, and chop into slices.

Lay a piece of lavash on a large cooking sheet. Brush with the melted butter. Spread the spinach on the lavash, followed by the tuna, avocado, peppers, cheese, and salt and pepper to taste.

Place in the oven for about 2 minutes, or until the cheese melts and the spinach wilts a bit. Remove from the oven. Slide the lavash onto a sheet of foil about the size of the pan. Roll the bread lengthwise, then wrap it in foil and twist the ends shut. It should look like a giant burrito. Let it rest at room temperature for about 10 minutes, then remove the foil and cut the roll into $1\frac{1}{2}$-inch slices.

Smoked Salmon Crepes

This is a simple, elegant dish that you can serve as a first course or, alongside some steamed vegetables or a salad, as a main dish. Crème fraîche is a French delicacy found in gourmet stores and some supermarkets. You could use sour cream or make your own by adding 1 tablespoon of sour cream to 1 cup of scalded milk and allowing the mixture to sit out unrefrigerated overnight.

 SERVES 6–8

½ pound smoked salmon
1 recipe buckwheat crepes
   (see page 33)
1 tablespoon butter, melted
1 cup crème fraîche
¼ cup finely chopped chives

Preheat the broiler.

Divide the salmon among the crepes. Fold over the left and right sides of the crepes, then the top and bottom, to form rectangular packages. Place the crepes, folded-side down, in a baking pan. Brush the tops with melted butter and broil until light brown, just a couple of minutes.

Mix the crème fraîche and chives. To serve, place a dollop of the crème fraîche mixture over each crepe.

7. Bean and Grain Side Dishes

Beans, beans, the magical fruit . . . that's no joke. Beans and grains together make the perfect food, and as Bruce points out, "Beans helped fuel the hippie movement!" You can get all of the protein necessary for health from beans, plus lots of nutrients, fiber, and good taste. The impact on the environment you make by eating these vegan protein sources pales in comparison with what animal protein does to the planet. Beans and grain are inexpensive enough to feed you, not the food industry's bank account. And in their dried form, they'll keep indefinitely. That's food that really grooves. Beans and grain are such an easy solution to the problem of finding healthy, environmentally friendly food that they really do seem almost magical.

Nutritionists used to think that you had to eat "complementary proteins" together. That is, you had to figure out which legumes, grains, and nuts, eaten together, would provide all the amino acids that your body needs. Planning a meal required a big stack of reference books, graphs to monitor your protein intake, and a full-time book-keeper complete with calculator and eye-shades to keep everything straight.

Thankfully, they now say that as long as you are eating a balance of proteins through-out the day, you'll get all that your body needs. Bruce didn't become a hippy so that his life would be governed by even more rules than before. It's all about freedom, and if we want to eat our black beans without a side of brown rice, we're going to walk on the wild side and do that.

In this chapter, we'll try to get beyond the idea of beans as a mere side dish and think of them as a main event. A simple bean dish and a simple grain dish together from this chapter add up to one main course. Even if the only cooking you've done before now is microwaving burritos, this chapter will show you how to cook any kind of bean and grain.

Basic Bean and Grain Cooking

Cooking beans and grains is not difficult. If you don't know the amount of water or cooking times, check your bulk bins; many tell you how to cook what you're buying. Keep in mind that the cooking times are approximate. Natural foods are always a little different, like anything in nature, so don't expect 100 percent conformity. Most of all, have fun experimenting. Gather the family around the table for your new creations; even if they don't like 'em, you can all have fun learning.

Beans are incredibly easy to make. Served with a starch—rice, tortillas, quinoa,

or whatever you like—and a vegetable, they make an easy, satisfying meal. For vegetarians and semi-vegetarians, and anyone else who likes good food, they're a delicious source of inexpensive protein. The technique is simple: Soak, boil, season, and eat. Some varieties take a little less or more time to cook; for any variety you haven't cooked before, cook as directed, then start checking for doneness at about an hour. Once your beans are cooked, they can be eaten as is or used as a basis for soups and stews, casseroles, dips and purees, or any dish calling for canned beans (a typical 16-ounce can of beans equals about $1\frac{1}{2}$ to $1\frac{3}{4}$ cups of freshly cooked beans).

You can substitute canned beans in most recipes calling for dried, but we don't recommend doing so unless you're really pressed for time. To save time, you can always cook up one large pot of beans and use them in a variety of ways during the week. Canned beans do not have the same flavor and texture as dried beans, and they are far more wasteful. With canned beans, you do not control the quality of the cooking or the ingredients that go into the product. If you do substitute canned beans, be sure to rinse them well to remove excess salt as well as the canned taste.

Most grains are incredibly easy to cook. Most of the time, you boil them. You can't go wrong using grains as a background for a highly flavored sauce or stew. Think of them as a very tasty blank canvas to which you add your colors—the vegetables, fruits, and proteins. If you've never experienced a grain before, boil up a batch, taste a bit plain or with just a little salt, and decide what'll taste good on top of it.

Many people find grains a bit more intimidating than beans. No matter how exotic a bean might be, it's still usually a simple matter to figure out how to use it. Grains, on the other hand, look like a bit more of a mystery. Don't be afraid to ask questions at your natural food market or grocery store, and don't worry if you don't like your first batch; you can always try again with a new grain tomorrow.

A Guide to Grains

Here's a quick guide to grains, common and less common, to get you started.

Amaranth: This grain was widely used by the Aztecs. It's slightly nutty, a little bit sticky, and mild. It can be combined with honey, fruit, and nuts for a hot breakfast cereal.

Barley: Originally from the Middle East, barley can thrive all over the world. It can be eaten by itself, or you can throw a handful into a simmering stew as a thickener. Hulled barley (barley with the outer husk removed) will take a little more time to cook; pearled barley (barley with both the outer hull and the bran removed), a little less.

Brown Rice: Brown rice is white rice without all the bran processed off. It can be substituted for white rice, though you'll have to cook it a bit longer. Different varieties of brown rice will have different cooking times, so watch your pot carefully. Also look for black and red rice; they're delicious, with a deep, nutty flavor.

Buckwheat: Buckwheat has a strong flavor, so it goes well with strong-tasting foods. Roasted, hulled buckwheat is called kasha, and it's a favorite in Eastern European cooking.

Couscous: Couscous is actually a pasta, usually made from semolina flour. It's available in whole-grain varieties. Traditionally, it's slowly steamed in a special pot, but most of the couscous available in the United States has been precooked and dried, and it cooks very quickly.

Millet: Though a lot of Americans think of millet as that round stuff you find in bird-seed, it's a very important grain in much of the world, especially Africa and parts of Asia. It's nutritious, it's delicious, and it can be used for everything from a hot breakfast cereal to a substitute for rice.

Quinoa: Quinoa is an excellent source of multiple amino acids. The Incas, who didn't eat much animal protein, virtually lived off this stuff. It can contain a bitter coating that must be thoroughly removed before eating, though this has already been removed in most of the quinoa sold in the United States. It's light, delicious, and nutritious; for many vegan cooks, it's a favorite.

Wheat: Cracked wheat is whole wheat berries that have been coarsely broken. Bulgur is very similar, but it has been cooked and dried. Bulgur takes a bit less time to cook than cracked wheat, and it's the grain that you'll most commonly see in tabbouleh.

Once you master your simple bean and grain recipes, experiment by trying them together. Beans and grains love to groove in concert; their tastes are almost always in harmony. And if the combinations you like aren't the classic ones, go ahead and eat them anyway. Who says you can't have Japanese edamame sprinkled on your Latin American quinoa? Go with what works for you. It's magical. It's musical. It's all good.

The Basic Recipes
These recipes are all you need to get started.

A Very Simple Big Pot of Beans

This simple recipe can be used with most beans: navy, white, black, pinto, kidney . . . the list goes on. One cup of dried beans yields about 2 to 3 cups of cooked, but you may get more or less depending upon the variety you're cooking.

 MAKES 3–4 SERVINGS

1 cup dried beans
Water

Wash the beans. Discard any small stones or dirt. Place the beans in a bowl with enough water to cover them by about 2 inches.

Let the beans soak for about 8 hours or overnight. You can do this on the counter if your kitchen is cool, or use the refrigerator. If you need to cook the beans the same day, you can bring the beans, plus enough water to cover by about 2 inches, to a boil over high heat in a covered pan; when they reach a boil, take them off the heat. Then let them sit for a couple of hours, and proceed with this recipe.

Drain and rinse the beans in a colander.

Place them in a pot and cover with water by about an inch. Bring to a boil over high heat. Reduce the heat to medium low and partially cover the pot—use the lid, but put it on loosely so that steam can escape. Let the beans cook at a gentle simmer for between 45 minutes and 2 hours. After 45 minutes, begin to taste them. Most beans will take 1 to 1½ hours. See the table that follows for approximate cooking times for some common bean varieties. When they reach the softness you like, take them off the heat.

Beans have a tendency to boil over. To avoid a mess, stir occasionally, and be sure to leave them partially, not fully, covered.

Beans may form a layer of scum while they're cooking. It isn't harmful, but if it bothers you, skim it off with a spoon and throw it out.

Acids, such as tomatoes and citrus, will keep the beans from softening, and salt may cause them to toughen. If you want your beans to absorb maximum flavor, cook the seasonings with them for a few minutes after the beans are done.

Approximate Cooking Times for Common Beans

Bean	Cooking Time	Yield (per 1 cup dried)
Adzuki	45 minutes	3 cups
Black	1¼ hours	2¼ cups
Black-eyed peas	1 hour	2 cups
Cannellini (small white)	50 minutes	2½ cups
Chickpeas (garbanzos)	2 hours	2 cups
Fava beans	1 hour	2 cups
Great northern	1½ hours	3 cups
Kidney beans	1 hour	2¼ cups
Lentils (brown)	45 minutes	2¼ cups
Lima beans	1 hour	2½ cups
Navy beans	1 hour	3 cups
Pinto beans	1½ hours	3 cups
Soybeans	3 hours	3 cups
Split peas	45 minutes	2 cups

A Simple Pot of Grain

his recipe is applicable to most, but not all grains. Bulgur wheat, for example, is cooked by pouring hot water over the wheat and allowing it to sit until it swells and softens. See the table that follows for the appropriate cooking times and amounts of liquid.

SERVES 4

1 cup grain of your choice
Water

Bring the grain and water a to boil over medium-high heat. Cover the pan and reduce the heat to medium low. Don't close the lid too tightly—grains have a tendency to boil over. Try to leave the lid slightly askew. If the liquid does boil over, remove the lid for a moment, stir, and then continue to cook. Cook until the liquid is absorbed and the grain is tender.

Cooking Methods for Common Grains

Grain (1 cup)	Amount of Liquid	Cooking Time	Yield
Amaranth	3 cups	15–20 minutes	$2^2/_3$ cups
Barley, hulled	4 cups	$1^3/_4$–2 hours	$2^1/_2$ cups
Barley, pearl	3 cups	45–60 minutes	3 cups
Brown, red, or black rice	2 cups	45–50 minutes	$2^1/_2$ cups
Buckwheat groats	2 cups	15 minutes	3 cups
Millet	3 cups	20–30 minutes	3 cups
Oats, rolled	2 cups	5 minutes	2 cups
Oats, steel-cut	$3^1/_2$ cups	20–30 minutes	2 cups
Quinoa	2 cups	15–20 minutes	2 cups
Wheat, bulgur	$1^1/_2$ cups	15 minutes (pour boiling water over and steep)	3 cups

Flavoring That Big Pot of Beans

The following are very simple recipes showing how you can turn a simple pot of beans into a side dish or meal. Use them as a way to get started, then go ahead and use your imagination. Vegans may leave the cheese out of any recipes that call for it or substitute a soy cheese equivalent; the dish will still have plenty of flavor.

Mexican-Style Beans

 Que bueno! If you like it spicy, add more hot pepper, or try a spicier pepper such as a habanero—now, that's spicy, baby. With plain boiled grain or tortillas and a small salad, this makes a generous meal.

 SERVES 3–4

2 cups cooked black, pinto, or kidney beans

2 tablespoons minced fresh cilantro

1 generous squeeze lime or other citrus juice

1 clove garlic, minced or pressed in garlic press

1 hot pepper, minced

$^1/_2$ cup fresh or frozen corn

Salt and pepper, to taste

$^1/_2$ avocado, chopped

Toss together all the ingredients except the avocado. Season to taste with salt and pepper. If you like, you can heat the ingredients together; this dish may also be served at room temperature. Garnish with the avocado.

Greek-Style Beans

Oompah! To serve as a sandwich, stuff this mixture into whole-grain pitas and garnish with lettuce, tomato, and/or sprouts. To serve as a salad, spoon the mix over salad greens and top with a couple of kalamata olives.

 SERVES 3–4

  2 cups cooked garbanzo, lima, or fava beans

  2 tablespoons minced fresh mint

  2 tablespoons minced fresh parsley

  1 tablespoon extra-virgin olive oil

  1 clove garlic, minced or pressed in garlic press

  Generous squeeze of fresh lemon juice

  1 small tomato, chopped

  Salt and pepper, to taste

  A generous sprinkling of feta cheese

If you'll be serving the beans at room temperature, toss together all the ingredients except the feta cheese. Season with salt and pepper to taste. Garnish with the cheese.

If you'll be serving this hot, heat the oil over a medium-high flame. Cook the garlic for 1–2 minutes, or until it just begins to brown. Add all the remaining ingredients except the cheese and heat until warm. Season to taste with salt and pepper, then garnish with the cheese.

Taking It Slow

Why take the time to cook your own beans when they're available in a can in any grocery store? Or better yet, already spread on a burrito for you? Because eating isn't just about getting nourishment; it's about pleasure. The slow-food movement is about taking time to eat, dining with loved ones rather than wolfing down food on the run. It's about making foods by hand at home or buying from small producers, about enjoying local and unique flavors, not eating the same mass-produced, preseasoned beans, whether you're in Arizona or Maine. It's about buying foods that have traveled the shortest distance possible to your table, and that have made the least impact on the earth. It's about seeing yourself not as an anonymous consumer but as an active participant in the process of making, preparing, and most of all enjoying your food.

The slow-food movement has spread across Europe, but its birthplace is Italy. The movement began in the 1980s because of concern that industrialization was standardizing taste and eliminating many worthy, unique dishes. The movement has paid off by helping to save many incredible local foods. One of the reasons we've visited Italy so many times on the show is that it's the home of the slow-food movement, and of so many artisinally produced products.

People take the time to make the cheese or olive oil or pasta made by their great-grandparents, and the wonderful thing is that it will be just a little bit different from the one made just over the hill. When we visit Italy, we see the fruits of the slow-food movement, and it energizes us to do our part in the United States.

In this country, the slow-food movement is spreading; there are already thousands of members. Check out the Slow Food USA Web site at www.slowfoodusa.org, or contact a local chapter. Or just make a few tiny changes in your own life: Get to know your producers by visiting a farmers' market or joining a CSA, set aside an evening to cook for your family and friends rather than just eating on the run, and, when you're shopping, seek out locally made products rather than something shipped across the continent or the world. Enjoy yourself, eat well, and take it slow and easy.

Coconut Beans

This is reminiscent of an East African dish made with pigeon peas. Pigeon peas aren't common in the United States, but this recipe is good made with any bean that you have available. It's excellent served with millet.

 SERVES 3–4

½ tablespoon neutral oil, such as soy
    or grapeseed
1 small white onion, minced
2 cloves garlic, minced
1 small hot pepper, minced
1 teaspoon ground turmeric
2 cups cooked chickpeas, pigeon peas,
    or black-eyed peas
1 cup prepared coconut milk (homemade,
    mixed from powdered coconut milk,
    or from a can)
1 small tomato, chopped
Salt and pepper, to taste

Heat the oil over a medium flame. Add the onion and cook until it's softened and light brown. Add the garlic and hot pepper and continue to cook until the pepper is softened. Add the turmeric and cook for about 1 minute more. Add the cooked beans, coconut milk, and tomato. With a spoon, mash some of the beans against the side of the pot. Continue cooking until the mixture is warm and somewhat thickened. Season to taste with salt and pepper.

Southern-Style Beans

This dish has soul, brother. Southern or soul food has a reputation for being unhealthy, but it doesn't need to be. Its basic elements—beans, cornmeal, and greens—are sustaining, healthy vegan foods.

 SERVES 3–4

1 tablespoon neutral oil, such as soy
   or grapeseed
1 cup chopped yellow or white onions
2 cups cooked black-eyed peas or field
   peas
4 ounces smoked tofu (optional)
Salt and pepper, to taste
Pepper vinegar to taste (optional)
Chopped raw onion to taste (optional)
Sweet relish to taste (optional)
Hot sauce to taste (optional)

In a pot, heat the oil over a medium-high flame. Add the onions and cook until tender and slightly browned. Add the beans and heat. If desired, dice the smoked tofu and add it to the mixture. Cook for 2 to 3 minutes, or until thoroughly heated. Season with salt and pepper. Serve with one or more of the garnishes, if you like.

Japanese-Style Beans

This is comfort food from the other side of the planet. Serve with plain rice or another favorite grain. With sautéed vegetables garnished with a bit of tamari, you have a complete meal.

 SERVES 3–4

2 teaspoons sesame seeds
2 cups cooked adzuki beans or black
   soybeans
1 tablespoon tamari or other soy sauce
1 teaspoon rice vinegar
Salt and pepper, to taste
$1/4$ cup minced green onions
$1/2$ cup chopped cucumber

In a dry pan over medium-high heat, cook the sesame seeds until fragrant. Remove from the heat and reserve. Heat the beans over a medium-high flame. Add the tamari and rice vinegar. Season to taste with salt and pepper (remember that tamari is salty). Garnish with the green onions, toasted sesame seeds, and cucumber.

Simple Grain Recipes

A simple, ungarnished grain does well with virtually any vegetable or bean stew, but seasoned, it makes a delicious dish all on its own.

Coconut Grain

Go coconuts for grains. Rich, soothing coconut milk is sweet and refreshing. This is especially good served with curries or other spicy foods; in Dominica, we ate a similar dish with Jerk Fish, and that's spicy, mon.

 SERVES 4

Water

1 cup coconut milk

1 cup grain

$\frac{1}{2}$ teaspoon grated lime zest

Salt and pepper, to taste

Add enough water to the coconut milk to equal amount of liquid necessary to cook grain. For example, 1 cup brown rice requires about 2 cups water, so add 1 cup to the coconut milk.

Heat the water, coconut milk, and grain in a saucepan over a medium-high flame. When the mixture reaches a boil, cover and reduce the heat to low. Cook until tender. Fluff the grain, stir in the lime zest, and season with salt and pepper.

Herbed Grain

What hippy doesn't like herbs? This dish is good when you're serving it with a simple, lightly flavored dish of beans or vegetables . . . and it's wonderful with a platter of boiled corn, bean salad, and sliced tomatoes at the height of summer.

 SERVES 4

1–2 teaspoons light olive oil
1 clove garlic, peeled and chopped
2 cups cooked grain
½ cup minced fresh herbs, such as basil, marjoram, sage, parsley, mint, or tarragon
Salt and pepper, to taste
Optional: 1 teaspoon flavorful oil, such as extra-virgin olive oil or avocado oil

In a skillet over medium-high heat, add the oil and garlic. Cook until tender, just a minute or two. Add the garlic to the cooked grain, mix in the herbs, and season with salt and pepper. If you wish, drizzle a bit of flavorful oil on top.

Rice Pilaf

This is far better than any packaged product that claims to be from San Francisco. The technique of toasting grains in a hot pan with a little oil before adding the liquid transforms them into a much more complex dish with only a bit of added work; try it with other boiled grains.

 SERVES 4

1 tablespoon extra-virgin olive oil
¾ cup long-grain white rice
¼ cup small pieces of broken vermicelli pasta
1 clove garlic, minced
2 cups water
2 teaspoons fresh herbs of your choice (try oregano or sage)
Salt and pepper, to taste

Heat the oil in a pan over a medium-high flame. Add the rice and pasta, stirring constantly. Cook until both are slightly browned. Add the garlic and cook for a minute longer. Add the water and bring to a boil. Cover and reduce the heat to medium low. Cook for 15 minutes or until the water is absorbed and the rice is tender. Stir in fresh herbs and salt and pepper to taste.

Barley Risotto

Traditionally, risotto is made with arborio rice, but you can use any grain that's relatively high in gluten. When slowly cooked with liquid and stirred often, these grains will become creamy. Try this technique with steel-cut oats, bulgur wheat, and, of course, arborio rice.

 SERVES 4

¼ cup dried mushrooms, such as porcini, shiitake, or mixed

1 cup hot water

2 tablespoons extra-virgin olive oil

1 small white onion, minced

2 cups fresh mushrooms of your choice, cleaned and chopped

½ tablespoon finely minced fresh rosemary

2 cloves garlic, minced

1 cup pearl barley

½ cup dry white wine

2–3 cups water

Salt and pepper, to taste

½ cup freshly grated Parmesan cheese

Combine the dried mushrooms and hot water. Set aside to soak.

Heat the olive oil over a medium-high flame. Add the onion and cook until slightly softened. Add the fresh mushrooms and cook until they start to brown. Add the rosemary and garlic. Cook for about 1 minute more.

Drain the dried mushrooms, reserving the liquid. Add the dried mushrooms to the pan, then the barley, stirring to coat. Add the wine. Stirring, cook until the liquid has boiled away, about 5 minutes.

Add the mushroom liquid. Again, cook until the liquid has boiled away, stirring constantly, about 5 minutes. Add water, ½ cup at a time, until the barley is tender. This should take 2 to 3 more cups and about 30 to 40 minutes. Stir often as the barley cooks. Season to taste with salt and pepper. Serve with grated cheese.

Orange-Spiced Whole Wheat Couscous

 t's a pasta, it's a grain . . . who cares, it's good. This simple couscous recipe would be great with a spicy vegetable stew with chickpeas. Many people believe that whole wheat couscous tastes almost identical to the refined variety.

SERVES 4

3/4 cup fresh orange juice

1/4 teaspoon ground cinnamon

1/4 teaspoon ground cumin

Dash of red pepper flakes

1/4 teaspoon ground coriander

2 tablespoons raisins

3/4 cup water

1 cup whole wheat couscous

Salt and pepper, to taste

Combine the orange juice, cinnamon, cumin, red pepper flakes, coriander, raisins, and water in a saucepan. Cook over high heat until the mixture boils. Stir in the couscous, cover, and remove from the heat. Let sit for about 5 minutes, or until the liquid is absorbed and the couscous is puffed and tender. Fluff with a fork and season to taste with salt and black pepper.

Fruity Bulgur Pilaf

How sweet it is. This dish is especially good on cool fall and winter evenings. Serve it with mixed roasted vegetables such as winter squashes, potatoes, sweet potatoes, turnips, and rutabagas.

 SERVES 4

1 tablespoon light olive oil

$\frac{1}{2}$ cup chopped yellow onion

1 cup bulgur

$2\frac{1}{2}$ cups water

1 teaspoon orange zest

2 tablespoons raisins

2 tablespoons dried cranberries

$\frac{1}{4}$ cup pecans or other nut of your choice

Salt and pepper, to taste

1 tablespoon minced fresh Italian
   parsley

Heat the oil in a pan over a medium-high flame. Cook the onion until soft but not brown, 3 to 4 minutes. Stir in the bulgur and cook for about 1 minute more.

Stir in the water, orange zest, raisins, and cranberries. Bring to a boil. Cover and reduce the heat to medium low. Cook, covered, until the liquid is absorbed, about 10 minutes.

Meanwhile, heat a dry saucepan and add the pecans. Cook until fragrant, watching carefully—nuts tend to burn.

Season the pilaf to taste with salt and pepper. Sprinkle with the parsley and nuts.

Herbed Quinoa

 uinoa is that brand-new grain that's been around for thousands of years. On the show, we served this dish with Mushroom Stroganoff (page 137) made over the fire, but it would be great with any rich vegetable stew.

SERVES 8

2 cups quinoa

1 red bell pepper, seeded and chopped fine

1 green bell pepper, seeded and chopped fine

1 yellow bell pepper, seeded and chopped fine

$^1/_4$ cup minced fresh mint

$^1/_4$ cup minced fresh cilantro

$^1/_4$ cup minced fresh parsley

$^1/_2$ cup minced green onions

Salt and pepper, to taste

Soak the quinoa in enough water by a couple of inches for about 10 minutes. Swirl it around a bit to make sure that it's well rinsed, then drain.

Add the quinoa and 4 fresh cups of water to a pan over high heat. Bring to a boil, cover, and reduce the heat to low. Cook for about 15 minutes or until all the water is absorbed.

Toss the quinoa with the peppers, herbs, and green onions. Season to taste with salt and pepper.

8. Vegetable Side Dishes and Condiments

We love the big, whirling, swirling cosmos, but you've got to be mindful of the little things to really get into the magic of the world. Look closely at a Romanesco broccoli and get lost in its fractal forms. Talk to the people working their land and jamming to their music. Sit quietly in a field and feel the wind blowing your hair against your face and listen to the insects humming by your ear. And when you cook, pay attention to the small dishes, and realize that it's the details that make something truly special.

Just because vegetable side dishes aren't the main event, people think that they don't deserve special attention. But side dishes can give as much pleasure as the main event—or more. Think about the typical Thanksgiving dinner. Is it the turkey everyone loves, or the sweet potato casserole, mashed potatoes, dressing, green beans, and cranberry sauce? This year, let that bird go free, and focus on the foods that people really love.

Vegetables are gorgeous and come in infinite varieties. There's no reason for them to ever be repetitive or bland. Plain steamed broccoli or carrots are delicious, especially fresh from the ground in season, but though they can be sweet as candy, they're boring night after night. One of the reasons children might claim to hate vegetables is that they see their parents push them aside on their plates, and they learn about what adults really believe is delicious and fun to eat. Though it might come in handy when you're homebound during a blizzard, a package of frozen lima beans isn't going to tempt anyone.

Some of the most interesting recipes that we've made on the show are the everyday side dishes. Ratatouille—*rat-ta-touille*, as Bruce likes to say—isn't some dance step you'd see on Broadway. It's a slow-cooked medley of beautiful summer vegetables at their peak. The Yucca and Plantains we made in the Amazon aren't even recognizable to most Americans; one looks like a mysterious tuber, the other like a crazy, overgrown banana. And then there are those sweet-and-sour chutneys; they make the plainest dish of rice and beans into something out of sight.

It's a big, beautiful world out there, full of every shape, size, and texture you could want. Explore a little. Try that strange, funky root you've wondered about. Find out if that stuff that looks like overgrown celery can rock your world. Experiment with the heirloom tomatoes that are as far from the red, round things in the supermarket as a fresh raspberry is from raspberry chewing gum. Chances are, whatever you choose won't bite, and if it does, hey, that's another experience. Part of the hippy mind-set is being open to whatever comes your way, opening your eyes, and letting loose.

Even if you do want to make one of your well-known standbys—and most vegetables have enough going on that you can enjoy them again and again—give it a new treatment. Break out the soy sauce, garlic, and ginger, and don't be shy with the flavors that you love. Most vegetables love to get wild and funky, and they're just waiting for a cook's loving hand to really shine.

People in other parts of the world know that when flavorings are done right, they enhance food rather than cover it up. Sure, you can never improve upon nature, but you can dance with it. When people think of French food, they think of sauces, but saying that the French pour cream and butter over everything is unfair. They love food too much to smother it. A sauce doesn't have to be heavy to be good; what it does need to do is add a concentrated bit of flavor to food and to heighten, not drown, what is being seasoned.

If you learn a couple of basic sauces—and we're talking about not cream sauces but good, honest flavors such as citrus, yogurt, and herbs—then you can make even the quickest, simplest meal a thing of beauty that you want to share with your friends and family.

On *The Hippy Gourmet*, we love condiments. Not catsup and chili sauce, of course—though those have their place, too—but the deeply colored flavors that you can get only in your own kitchen. In Dominica, we were digging mango and loving papaya, and Bruce married the two in a wild and swirling blender ceremony. The outrageously red and orange combination tasted tangy and delicious on its own, but it tamed the fire of even the spiciest dishes. Back home in the Haight, he made a Spinach Chutney so good, and with such a gorgeous bright green color, that you'd be happy to eat it by itself as a side dish. We share these recipes with you in this chapter because, like vegetables, they are culinary stars that too often get ignored.

Some of these dishes are vegetable sides. Some are warm and comforting starchy vegetables. Some are sauces for tingling that tired tongue a little. Some defy classification. Serve them alongside a simple grain or legume, and you have a meal fit for a king or, even better, the people you love.

Vegetables

The easiest ways to cook vegetables are steaming or a simple sauté or stir-fry. Neither method has to be plain or boring. A well-done sauté or stir-fry is a celebration of nature's beauty: crisp-tender, slightly caramelized, and retaining all the flavor of the earth. Simple steamed vegetables make a delicious meal when you add seasonings such as soy sauce, a bit of grated gingerroot, and toasted sesame oil.

Stir-Frying and Sautéing

Stir-frying and sautéing are techniques in which food is cooked rapidly over high heat. Both require that the food be moved continuously about in a very hot pan. The difference? Stir-fried foods are stirred. Sautéed foods are tossed about. Stir-frying is a bit neater when you're just starting out in the kitchen, but sautéing, once mastered, makes you look much more suave. Would those fancy French chefs look quite so debonair if they used spatulas rather than expertly flipping their food with a flick of the wrist? Imagine your date melting as you show your expert technique, and you just might be cooking the French way.

For both techniques, try to cut your vegetables in approximately the same size. It's no good to taste one big chunk of hard sweet potato in one bite, a piece of mushy one in another. Use a bit of oil, and, if the vegetables threaten to burn, add a small amount of liquid. Neither technique requires any special equipment. As long as your pan is large enough to accommodate all your vegetables, it will serve for either stir-frying or sautéing. Add vegetables in order of their cooking time: Long-cooking vegetables, such as onions and root vegetables, go first; faster-cooking vegetables like broccoli and cabbage are next; the quick cookers, such as spinach and peas, go last.

Veggie Stir-Fry

Stir things up! Zucchinis have a lot of water, so this recipe calls for covering the pan and allowing things to steam a bit. You could use the technique with other vegetables that contain a lot of water, such as mushrooms or leafy greens. Once the vegetables cook in their own juices, uncover the pan and let everything brown.

 SERVES 4–6

¹/₂ cup light olive oil

¹/₃ cup chopped garlic

4 Chinese eggplants, sliced lengthwise and cut into chunks

3 heads bok choy, quartered and cut into large chunks

2 zucchinis, sliced lengthwise and cut into chunks

1 yellow bell pepper, seeded and sliced

1 red bell pepper, seeded and sliced

Soy sauce, or salt and pepper, to taste (optional)

Heat a wok or other large pan over an outdoor grill or indoor stove with a high flame. Add the oil and heat until very hot. Add the garlic and stir until it sizzles. This will take only a couple of seconds—let the garlic just kiss that heat. Add the eggplant chunks and stir. When the eggplant begins to soften, add the bok choy, zucchinis, and peppers. Stir-fry for a couple of minutes, then cover the pan and let the veggies steam for about 2 minutes. Remove the cover and keep stirring until tender.

Season to taste with soy sauce or salt and pepper.

Sautéed Leafy Greens

This is a great way to get a little bit more of that sweet, sweet green. Use any or all of the greens called for here, and adjust the quantities and cooking times accordingly. Collards take the longest, then chard; spinach barely needs to be touched by heat.

 SERVES 4–6

1 large bunch collards

1 large bunch Swiss chard

1 large bunch spinach

2 tablespoons extra-virgin olive oil

Dash of red pepper flakes

4 cloves garlic, peeled and chopped

2 tablespoons water

Optional ingredients: ¼ cup raisins soaked in enough hot water to cover for about 20 minutes, 2 tablespoons toasted pine nuts, ½ cup cooked chickpeas

Salt and pepper, to taste

Wash the collards, chard, and spinach well, making sure to remove all grit. Remove the stems from each of the greens and roughly chop.

Heat the oil in a large pan over a medium-high flame. Add the pepper flakes and garlic and cook until the garlic sizzles, about 30 seconds. Add collards and water, and stir for a couple of minutes. Cover and steam for 5 minutes. Add the chard and stir well for a minute or two, then cover again and steam for 2 minutes. Add the spinach, cover, and steam for about a minute.

Uncover the pan and stir the greens together well. If you're using any of the optional ingredients, stir them in and heat. Season to taste with salt and pepper.

Stir-Fried Snow Peas with Sesame Seeds

uts and seeds aren't just for the squirrels. Stir-frying with seeds or nuts adds a different element of crunch to your dishes as well as healthful fats and proteins. You could substitute or add tender asparagus, sugar snap peas, or thin green beans as well.

 SERVES 4

3 cups snow peas

1 tablespoon neutral oil, such as soy or grapeseed

1 teaspoon minced gingerroot

2 cloves garlic, peeled and minced

1 tablespoon sesame seeds

$^1/_2$ tablespoon soy sauce

Salt and pepper, to taste

$^1/_2$ teaspoon toasted sesame oil

Trim the ends off snow peas.

Heat the oil over a medium-high flame in a large skillet or wok. Add the gingerroot, garlic, and sesame seeds. Cook for about a minute, being careful not to burn. Add the snow peas and soy sauce. Cook until the snow peas are done to your desired tenderness, or just a couple of minutes. If the mixture starts to become very dark, add water a teaspoon at a time to prevent burning.

When you're ready to serve, add salt and pepper to taste (soy sauce is salty). Drizzle with sesame oil.

Steaming Times for Vegetables

To steam vegetables, heat $1^1/_2$ to 2 inches of water to a rapid boil over a high flame in a large pan. Place a folding metal steamer or a bamboo steamer in the pan, making sure that the bottom of the steamer is above the waterline. Add the vegetables and cover. You can also use an electric steamer, in which case you should follow the manufacturer's directions. The following times are approximate only. Tender veggies picked at the beginning of the season take less time to cook than tougher, older ones that have sat on the vine for a while. And of course, smaller pieces take less time to cook than larger ones.

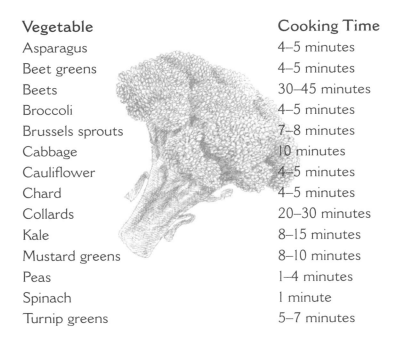

Vegetable	Cooking Time
Asparagus	4–5 minutes
Beet greens	4–5 minutes
Beets	30–45 minutes
Broccoli	4–5 minutes
Brussels sprouts	7–8 minutes
Cabbage	10 minutes
Cauliflower	4–5 minutes
Chard	4–5 minutes
Collards	20–30 minutes
Kale	8–15 minutes
Mustard greens	8–10 minutes
Peas	1–4 minutes
Spinach	1 minute
Turnip greens	5–7 minutes

Kale

unch, munch, munch those leaves, dude, and set that inner ape free. Leaves are a great way to taste the bounty of the land. Steaming produces bright green, tender kale. This dish adds a bit of freshness next to deeply flavored, heavy, or spicy dishes such as black beans and rice, Jerk Fish (page 186), or jambalaya.

 SERVES 3–4

1 large bunch kale

1 clove garlic, minced

Juice of $\frac{1}{2}$ lemon

2 teaspoons soy sauce

Olive oil, to taste

Salt, to taste

Clean the kale, pull the leaves from their tough stalks, and chop fine.

Heat about an inch of water in a large pot over a high flame. Steam the kale in a steaming rack or steamer until bright green and tender, about 8 to 10 minutes. If you prefer, use an electric steamer following the manufacturer's directions.

Toss the cooked kale in a large bowl with the garlic, lemon juice, and soy sauce. Taste, adding olive oil and a bit of salt if necessary.

Broccoli Sesame-Style

Broccoli is an everyday food that holds endless possibilities in its tiny stalks. Its good energy shines forth in its beautiful color and wonderful taste. With almost any cuisine, and with a slew of other flavors, broccoli just goes with the flow and loves whatever is around.

 SERVES 4

1 pound broccoli, chopped or diced

1 tablespoon sesame seeds

3 tablespoons olive oil, divided

2 cloves garlic, chopped

1 tablespoon vinegar of your choice

1 tablespoon soy sauce

1/4 cup raw brown sugar

1 red pepper, seeded and sliced
   into strips

Over a high flame, heat about an inch of water in a steamer or a pot with a steamer insert to a boil. Steam the broccoli until it's tender. Set aside.

Heat a small, dry pan over a medium-high flame. Add the sesame seeds and toast until fragrant. Remove from the heat and set aside.

Heat 2 tablespoons of the olive oil in a small pan over a medium-high flame. Add the garlic and cook until golden. Remove the garlic to drain on paper towels, discarding the oil.

Combine the remaining tablespoon of olive oil with the vinegar, soy sauce, and brown sugar in a saucepan and simmer until heated. Pour the sauce over the broccoli and toss. Garnish with the sesame seeds, garlic, and pepper strips.

Summer Squashes

Steaming food in the water used to cook another item is a great way to decrease your water consumption, not to mention cutting down on the time it takes to wash up. This dish showcases the beautiful squashes of summer.

 SERVES 4–6

8 red-skinned new potatoes, unpeeled, quartered

3 zucchinis, cut into $^1/_2$-inch-thick slices

5–6 small summer squashes, tips cut off, quartered

$^1/_2$ tablespoon butter

10 green onions, sliced

1 bunch fresh dill, stems removed, chopped fine (about $^1/_2$ cup)

3 tablespoons sour cream

Salt and pepper, to taste

Bring the potatoes and enough water to cover (3 cups, or more if necessary) to a boil in a large pan over high heat. Cover loosely and reduce the heat to medium low. Cook the potatoes until tender; remove them from the cooking water.

Increase the heat to high. When the water's boiling again, place the zucchinis and squashes in a steaming rack or steamer over the boiling water. Steam until tender.

In a skillet, heat the butter over a medium-high flame. Add the green onions and cook until bright green, just a minute or two. Set aside.

In a bowl, mix the potatoes, squashes, and zucchinis.

To the pan with the onions, add half the dill and all the sour cream. Mix well and pour over the vegetables. Stir. Season to taste with salt and pepper, garnishing with the remaining dill.

Ratatouille

On the show, Bruce prepared this poolside on the Italian coast. Even coming from a humble home kitchen, however, ratatouille is special. If you wish to make this a main dish, you could serve it with bread and cheese, over a grain or couscous, or even as a pasta sauce.

 SERVES 4–6

$^1/_4$ cup olive oil

6–8 cloves garlic, peeled and chopped

1 white or yellow onion, peeled and chopped

1 eggplant, sliced into large chunks

Dash of oregano

Salt and pepper, to taste

1 zucchini, chopped

1 red pepper, seeded and chopped

1 green pepper, seeded and chopped

2 cups seeded and chopped tomatoes, divided

$^1/_2$ cup chopped fresh basil, divided

1 cup chopped green beans

$^1/_4$ cup freshly grated Parmesan cheese (optional)

Heat a large pan over a medium-high flame. Add the olive oil and garlic and cook for a few seconds—just enough to take the edge off the garlic without really cooking it. Add the onion and eggplant. Stir. Add the oregano and a bit of salt and pepper. When eggplant has released its water and the pan begins to sizzle again—about 5 minutes—add the zucchini and peppers. Cook for another minute or two.

Add half the tomatoes and half the basil. Let the mixture cook until it's almost dry, about 5 minutes. Add the remaining tomatoes and cook for a minute or two. Add the green beans. Cook until slightly tender, about 3 or 4 minutes. Season to taste with more salt and pepper. Serve with the cheese (if desired) and the remaining basil.

Corn and Peppers

ove your neighbor; vegetables love theirs. When you are putting together new dishes, a good rule of thumb is to combine vegetable flavors from the same part of the world. Corn, peppers, and tomatoes all originated in Latin America, and they like to play together on the plate.

🍐 SERVES 4

4 ears corn

1 tablespoon neutral oil, such as soy
   or grapeseed

1 small yellow or white onion, peeled
   and chopped

2 cloves garlic, peeled and chopped

2 poblano peppers, seeded and chopped

1 medium tomato, seeded and chopped

2 tablespoons chopped fresh cilantro

Generous squeeze of lime juice

Salt and pepper, to taste

Remove the husks and silk from the corn. Working over a large bowl, cut off the kernels, then scrape the cobs with the knife to get the juices out.

Heat the oil in a large pan over a medium-high flame. Add the onion and cook until browned, about 5 minutes. Add the garlic and peppers. Cook until the peppers have softened, 3 to 4 minutes. Add the tomato and cook until most of the liquid is gone from the pan, about 5 minutes.

Add the corn. Cook until tender, about 3 to 5 minutes. Add the cilantro and lime juice and stir well. Cook until heated through, probably less than a minute.

Season to taste with salt and pepper. The dish will have quite a bit of liquid even when it's fully cooked. Go ahead and serve it, liquid and all; it's delicious.

Curried Cauliflower

A lot of people grew up eating soggy cauliflower drenched in gloopy cheese sauce, and as adults they think they hate cauliflower. Follow this recipe instead, and you'll see how bright and delicious it can be. For a more interesting flavor, substitute ghee (clarified butter, available at Asian markets or health food stores) for the oil.

 SERVES 6

1 medium head cauliflower

2 tablespoons neutral oil, such as soy
   or grapeseed

1 tablespoon grated gingerroot

1 jalapeño pepper, seeded and chopped

2 cloves garlic, peeled and chopped

2 teaspoons curry powder

Sprinkle of red pepper flakes

1/2 teaspoon ground cumin

1/3 cup water

1 tablespoon lemon juice

2 tablespoons chopped fresh cilantro

Salt and pepper, to taste

Cut out the core of the cauliflower and separate the head into florets.

Heat the oil over a medium-high flame. Add the gingerroot, pepper, and garlic to the pan. Cook until softened but not browned, about 1 minute. Add the curry powder, red pepper flakes, and cumin and stir well. Cook for a few seconds, or until fragrant. Add the cauliflower and stir to coat well.

Add the water and bring to a boil. Cover, reduce the heat to medium low, and cook until tender, between 7 and 10 minutes. When the cauliflower is tender, remove the lid and raise the heat to cook off the remaining liquid, about 2 minutes more. Stir in the lemon juice and cilantro. Season to taste with salt and pepper.

Asian Cabbage Delight

ast, easy, and super tasty! Cabbage is nutritious and still looks good in the dead of
winter, when other vegetables are long gone.
And when it's cooked with care, it has none
of the funky taste or odor of the boiled cabbage you hid in your napkin when you were a
child.

 SERVES 4

½ cup vegetable oil

1 cup thinly sliced yellow or white
   onions

1 tablespoon olive oil

4 cups shredded cabbage

1 cup thinly sliced celery

1 vegetable bouillon cube (or
   1 tablespoon vegetable bouillon
   powder)

½ cup hot water

2 tablespoons soy sauce

Heat the vegetable oil over a high flame in
a heavy wok or skillet. Be careful when you're
adding ingredients—the oil can splatter. Add
the onions and cook until dark brown.
Remove the slices to paper towels, discarding
the oil; wipe the pan clean.

In the cleaned pan, heat the olive oil over
a high flame. Add the cabbage and sliced
celery. Cook until slightly softened.

In a separate bowl, stir the bouillon cube
into the hot water and add the soy sauce.
When it's mixed, pour it over the vegetables.
Cook the mixture over high heat for about
5 to 6 minutes, until the veggies are tender
but still kind of crisp. Remove them from the
pan and place on a platter, sprinkling the
onions over the top.

Community Gardens

The land gives us life. We went from hunter-gatherers attuned to the slightest shift in the wind and budding of the leaves to farmers who coaxed life for our communities out of the soil. Throughout most of our history, we've lived close to, and off, the land. Even city dwellers kept kitchen gardens or lived within walking distance of real farms. Today, though, with most of our produce grown on factory farms and not in our own backyards, many of us don't have a relationship with the earth that nourishes us. In fact, there are people who don't know that potatoes and carrots grow in the ground.

Community gardens are a way for those of us who don't have our own piece of the earth to share in growing our food, to experience firsthand the wonder and joy of bringing life-giving nourishment from the soil. The idea is simple: Land that isn't being used is shared by community members who labor in the garden in exchange for some of the harvest. Hey, isn't a harvest of squash and tomatoes a whole lot better for all of us than a vacant lot full of rotting old tires and garbage?

It brings people together; nothing binds us so much as working side by side in the soil. It makes cities beautiful; instead of a sad old vacant lot, a glorious garden grows. It makes us healthier, by providing much-needed fruits and vegetables to communities that may not have adequate vegetable stands and fruit markets.

Community gardens are taking hold. Although no one knows the exact number, some estimates place the amount in the United States and Canada at more than eighteen thousand. Though starting a community garden isn't easy—especially if you want to grow on a vacant lot owned by absentee investors—it is possible, and thousands of others have done it. To find out about community gardens in your area, or about starting your own, a great resource is the American Community Gardening Association (www.communitygarden.org).

Summer Squash and Tomato Gratin

fter working in a community garden, you'll discover that summer squashes grow faster than you can harvest them. This recipe will help you and your neighbors finish some of those big boys, and it's perfect for a community potluck.

🍐 SERVES 4

2 medium or 4 small zucchinis, sliced
    thinly into circles or ovals
4 medium tomatoes, seeded and chopped
Salt, to taste
2 cloves garlic, peeled and chopped fine
1 tablespoon chopped fresh herbs—such
    as basil, marjoram, oregano, or sage—
    plus extra for garnish
2 tablespoons extra-virgin olive oil, plus
    extra to grease pan
$\frac{1}{4}$ cup grated Parmesan cheese

Preheat the oven to 350 degrees.

In a bowl, combine the zucchinis with the tomatoes. Stir in a bit of salt (remember that the cheese is salty).

In a small bowl, combine the garlic, herbs, and olive oil.

Grease the bottom of a gratin dish or a shallow baking dish with olive oil. Spoon the zucchini-tomato mixture into the pan, making sure it's even. Spoon the oil mixture over the zucchini mixture. Bake for about 45 minutes. When the mixture seems dry and is starting to brown, sprinkle with the cheese, then return to the oven until the cheese melts.

Slow-Cooked Green Beans

Hey, take it slow and easy, brother. Cooking vegetables quickly preserves their color and flavor, but allowing them to cook slowly coaxes out flavors you'd never know otherwise. What could be better than allowing yourself to experience all the different flavors of your food?

 SERVES 4

2 tablespoons extra-virgin olive oil

1 medium yellow or white onion, peeled and chopped

2 cloves garlic, peeled and chopped

4 cups chopped green beans

2 medium tomatoes, chopped

1 teaspoon dried oregano

1 tablespoon chopped fresh parsley

Salt and pepper, to taste

Heat the oil in a large pot over a medium-high flame. Cook the onion until translucent. Add the garlic. Cook a minute more. Add the beans, tomatoes, and oregano. Stir and heat until bubbling. Cover the pot and reduce the heat to medium low. Cook for about 15 minutes, stirring occasionally.

Remove the lid and increase the heat to medium high. Cook until the vegetable mixture is thick, about 5 to 8 minutes. Stir in the parsley and cook for a minute more. Season to taste with salt and pepper.

Starchy Vegetables

Starchy vegetables don't have the bright colors or showy appearance of their green or red cousins, but with a bit of care you can transform them into something warm, rich, and delicious. Hard sweet potatoes, covered in a thick, dull orange or red skin morph into bright orange and beautiful morsels. Squashes so hard you have to push the knife through with all the force you have become soft, delicate, and subtly sweet. And the humble potato, looking like a rock when you dig it out of the ground, becomes a bit of homey, starchy perfection. It shows how a little love can bring out the best in anything.

Herbed Potatoes

On the show, we served these with Orange Trout and Prickly Pear Cactus (page 188). Parboiling them allows the inside to cook thoroughly without burning the outside. Substitute your favorite herbs, and this dish can complement almost anything.

 SERVES 4

2 pounds potatoes (such as Yukon Gold)

3 tablespoons butter

2 cloves garlic, peeled and chopped

Pinch of rosemary, chopped

Salt and pepper, to taste

2 tablespoons chopped fresh parsley

Cut the potatoes into large chunks. Bring a large pan of water to boil over high heat and add the potatoes. When the water returns to a boil, reduce the heat to medium low, cover loosely, and cook for about 5 minutes. Drain the potatoes and lay them out on a flat surface to dry well.

Heat the butter in a skillet over a medium-high flame. Add the garlic and cook for a few seconds, until fragrant.

Add the potatoes, rosemary, and just a pinch of salt and pepper. Cook the potatoes, stirring occasionally, until golden. Add the parsley and continue cooking for a few seconds until bright green. Add more salt and pepper to taste.

Roasted Root Vegetables

If you see an interesting, unfamiliar root vegetable, experiment by adding it to this recipe. To vary the recipe, substitute another vegetable, toss with fresh herbs at the end, or add a bit of honey or maple syrup before serving for a sweeter flavor.

 SERVES 4

2 carrots, peeled and cut into large chunks

2 small turnips, peeled and cut into large chunks

2 parsnips, peeled and cut into large chunks

2 Yukon Gold or russet potatoes, peeled and cut into large chunks

1 medium sweet potato, peeled and cut into large chunks

2 tablespoons extra-virgin olive oil

Salt and pepper, to taste

1–2 teaspoons lemon juice (optional)

Preheat the oven to 425 degrees. In a large bowl, mix all the vegetables with the olive oil. Sprinkle with salt. Lay out the vegetables on one or two large baking sheets. You want them in a single layer, if possible, to help them brown. Roast for 45 minutes to an hour, or until tender. If any of the vegetables become too brown before the others are done, remove the culprits from the oven. Sprinkle with lemon juice, if desired, and season to taste with more salt and pepper.

Mashed Squash

Steaming, and then mashing, squash gives it a light texture while preserving all its natural flavor. There are dozens of varieties of winter squashes available, and farmers' markets have some really exotic types. Experiment to find your favorite.

 SERVES 4

1 large butternut squash, 2 large acorn
    squashes, or an equivalent amount
    of hard winter squashes
2 teaspoons brown sugar
1 tablespoon hazelnut oil or butter
Salt and pepper, to taste

Heat 1 to 2 inches of water over a high flame in a pan large enough to fit a steamer rack or steamer. If you'll be using an electric steamer, follow the manufacturer's directions.

While the water heats, cut the squash(es) in half and remove the strings and seeds. Peel and cut into large chunks. Add the squash chunks to a rack or steamer and steam for about 15 minutes, or until tender. Remove the squash chunks, reserving the cooking water.

In a large bowl, mash the chunks. Add the brown sugar, hazelnut oil or butter, and a pinch of salt. Add the cooking water, a couple of spoonfuls at a time, until the squash reaches your desired consistency. Season to taste with salt and pepper. If desired, reheat in a pan before serving.

Curried Sweet Potatoes

Sweet vegetables such as sweet potatoes and some squashes blend well with spicy flavors. Add some cooked chickpeas and serve with rice or couscous, and this becomes a one-dish meal.

 SERVES 4

1 tablespoon neutral oil, such as soy or grapeseed

1 medium yellow or white onion, peeled and chopped

2 cloves garlic, peeled and chopped

1 teaspoon grated gingerroot

2 teaspoons curry powder

$\frac{1}{2}$ teaspoon ground cumin

$\frac{1}{4}$ teaspoon ground cinnamon

2 large sweet potatoes, peeled and cut into chunks

About $\frac{1}{2}$ cup water

Salt and pepper, to taste

2 tablespoons cashews (or another nut)

Heat the oil in a pan over a medium-high flame. Add the onion and cook until translucent, about 4 minutes. Add the garlic and gingerroot. Cook for a few seconds more. Add the spices. Cook for a few seconds or until fragrant. Add the sweet potatoes and stir well. Add the water. Bring to a boil, cover, and reduce the heat to medium low. Cook until the sweet potatoes are tender, about 10 to 15 minutes. Then remove the lid, increase the heat, and cook until the potatoes are almost dry. Season to taste with salt and pepper. To serve, sprinkle with nuts.

Yucca and Plantains

Plantains look like large bananas, but they are far less sweet. Yucca, a Caribbean staple, looks like a tuber with pointed ends. It may also be called cassava. Both are available in Latin markets and some health food stores. Make sure that you cook yucca; it's inedible raw.

 SERVES 4

2 large yucca tubers

2 cups vegetable oil

2 large plantains, 1 fully ripened yellow,
    1 near-ripened green

$^1/_4$ teaspoon paprika

$^1/_4$ teaspoon garlic powder

$^1/_4$ teaspoon onion powder

Salt, to taste

Bring a large pot of water to a boil.

Meantime, cut the ends off the yucca and peel. Cut lengthwise into long, even slices. Drop these into the boiling water and cook for 20 to 30 minutes, or until tender.

While the yucca cooks, heat the oil in a large pot to 350 degrees. Peel both plantains and cut into slices. Using a wire mesh ladle, lower the unripe plantain slices into the oil. Cook until golden brown, about 3 to 4 minutes, stirring occasionally. When the sizzling subsides, the plantains are done; they'll be starchy and dry. Fish them out and dry them on a plate.

Repeat the procedure with the ripe plantain. Repeat procedure with yucca after patting dry (or the oil will spatter). Season all the vegetables with the paprika, garlic, onion, and salt to taste.

Sweet Potatoes à la Casserole

Sweet potato casserole the way it was meant to be. This could be the centerpiece of a vegetarian winter feast. This is sweet and rich without the sickly sweet overkill of marshmallows and maraschino cherries. Serve it any time of year for a comforting treat.

 SERVES 8

4 pounds sweet potatoes, peeled and quartered

1/2 cup (1 stick) butter, melted, divided

3/4 cup raw brown sugar, divided

6 tablespoons rum

1 teaspoon sea salt

8 tangerines

1/4 cup chopped pecans

Over a high flame, heat 1 to 2 inches of water in a steamer or a pot with a steamer attachment. Steam the sweet potatoes until tender, about 15 to 20 minutes. Reserve the water-juice to adjust consistency later.

Preheat the oven to 375 degrees.

In a bowl, mash the potatoes with about half the butter and 1/2 cup of the brown sugar. Add the rum and the salt. Continue stirring and mashing until smooth. Peel and seed the tangerines and add the sections to the mixture. Spoon it into a greased 15 × 11-inch casserole (or whatever size you have that will fit the mixture).

Top with the remaining butter, brown sugar, and the pecans. Bake for 30 minutes.

From the Vine to the Brine: The Art of Pickles

Pickling is one of the oldest methods of preserving food. Acid prevents the growth of bacteria, and so food stored in acid will last far longer than food left by itself. Some pickles are made by pouring an acidic liquid over them. Some are produced by fermentation; the fermenting food produces its own acid. Kimchee from Korea, sauerkraut from Europe, preserved lemons from North Africa, and Chinese thousand-year-old eggs are just a part of a worldwide pickle feast.

Why bother making your own pickles? For one thing, most stores have nothing but cucumber pickles, and as delicious as those can be, there's a whole world of preserved vegetables to explore. Okra, beans, onions, beets . . . the list of interesting vegetables you can make at home is almost endless.

More important, why you make your own pickles goes toward why we make anything at all. Why knit? Why make candles? Why do your own woodworking? It's about using your hands, not just your wallet, to create. It's about being mindful of the things around you, discovering the Zen of cooking, and appreciating the art in everything. Making your own pickles is creating and transforming your food. You'll never feel quite the same again about biting into the jarred version.

The recipes in this book are for simple refrigerated pickles. If you wish to keep them for a very long time, you'll need to learn the art of canning. We encourage you to go out and do it and experience another one of life's great cooking journeys.

Pickling Spice Blend

This simple spice blend can be varied to suit your taste; feel free to vary the amounts of any of the spices. Use it for the cucumber or bean pickles below, or for whatever you have an abundance of in your garden.

 MAKES SLIGHTLY MORE
THAN $^1/_2$ CUP

3 bay leaves
1 tablespoon dried chile peppers
1 tablespoon whole peppercorns
2 cinnamon sticks
1 tablespoon yellow mustard seeds

1 tablespoon dill seeds
1 tablespoon ground coriander
2 tablespoons coarse sea salt

Crumble the bay leaves. Measure out 1 tablespoon and reserve; save any remaining bay leaves for another use. Finely chop the dried chile peppers. Slightly crush the peppercorns with the side of a knife.

Break up the cinnamon sticks into small pieces. Measure out 1 tablespoon and reserve; save any remaining cinnamon for another use.

In a bowl, mix all the ingredients. Store in a cool, dry place in an airtight container, such as a jar.

Cucumber Pickles

lthough you can buy pickles in any grocery store, these are a lot more interesting tasting and fun to make. Watching the pickles transform in your refrigerator is wondrous. Substitute fresh dill for the basil for a more classic dill pickle flavor.

☙ MAKES 1 JAR

1 cayenne pepper

Small handful of peppercorns

1 tablespoon Pickling Spice Blend
(see page 242)

6 capers

3 cloves garlic, sliced

1 tablespoon salt

6 leaves fresh basil, chopped

6 cucumbers, each about 4 inches
long

Enough white vinegar to fill jar

Slice the cayenne pepper down the center, leaving the seeds intact. Slightly crush the peppercorns with the side of a large knife.

Place the Pickling Spice Blend, pepper, capers, garlic, salt, basil, and peppercorns in a large jar. Tightly pack the cucumbers into the same jar. Pour in enough vinegar to fill it, put on a lid, and shake vigorously. Refrigerate for at least 5 days, shaking the jar periodically.

Sweet Bean Pickles

These pickles use the same basic spice blend, but they have added sweetness. Unlike the cucumbers, the beans are cooked. This method would also be good with beets, carrots, tiny onions, or any other vegetable with sweet notes.

 MAKES 1 JAR

1 cup water

2 cups sugar

$^1/_4$ cup Pickling Spice Blend (see page 242), divided

$1^1/_2$ cups green string beans

$1^1/_2$ cups yellow string beans

$1^1/_2$ cups purple string beans

1 heaping tablespoon sea salt

$^1/_2$ cup white vinegar

Heat the water and sugar together in a pot over a medium-high flame. Stir well to dissolve the sugar. Bring to a boil, add 2 tablespoons of the Pickling Spice Blend, and turn off the heat.

In a large pan, heat about 1 inch of water over a high flame. Place the beans in a steamer rack or bamboo steamer, and set this over the water. Cover and steam the beans for about 5 to 7 minutes, or until tender.

Add the remaining 2 tablespoons of spice blend to a jar along with the sea salt. Add 1 cup of the syrup and mix well. Tightly pack the beans into the jar. Pour the vinegar over the beans; fill the jar to the top with any remaining syrup. Cover and store in the refrigerator for at least 5 days, shaking periodically.

Sauces and Condiments

Sauces and condiments are a staple for healthy eating and do their part to enliven the palate, making each bite something new and exciting to experience. Cuisine from India, for instance, is all about tangy, spicy, and creamy sauces and condiments that are meant to increase the flavor of each course, giving your taste buds a chance to have a real festival!

These sauces are simple, and if you learn a few of them you can make a meal of steamed vegetables and plain rice seem like a party. It's like the change from a simple beachside fire to a group of hippies dancing around a blazing bonfire, abandoned to the rhythms of a jam band. The flavors are pure, strong, and bright. The colors are vivid but all-natural. And they play alongside, rather than drown, the foods they're served with.

Yogurt Sauce

Yogurt sauce makes a dish of plain green vegetables extraordinary; try it with asparagus, green beans, or brussels sprouts. If you like, you can substitute other herbs. Made with mint and cilantro, this would be a great sauce to calm down the heat of spicy dishes.

 MAKES 1¼ CUPS

1 clove garlic, peeled
Salt
1 cup yogurt of your choice
¼ cup chopped fresh dill
1 teaspoon lemon juice

¼ teaspoon grated lemon peel
Salt and pepper, to taste

Roughly chop the garlic clove, then add a generous sprinkling of salt. The salt will act a bit like sandpaper, helping you to break down the garlic. Continue chopping, periodically smashing the smashed garlic with the side of your knife, until you have a fine paste.

In a bowl, mix this garlic paste with the yogurt, dill, lemon juice, and lemon peel. Refrigerate for about 10 to 15 minutes to allow the flavors to combine. Season to taste with salt and pepper.

Lemon Sauce

This is a thin but rich sauce that you can drizzle over cooked vegetables or fish. It would also be good to baste on grilling veggies. It could easily be made vegan by substituting extra-virgin olive oil or soy butter for the butter.

 MAKES ABOUT ½ CUP

2 tablespoons butter
2 shallots, sliced thin
1 tablespoon Dijon mustard
¾ cup dry white wine
1 teaspoon grated lemon peel
1 tablespoon fresh lemon juice
Salt and pepper, to taste

Heat the butter over a medium-high flame. Add the shallots and cook until softened and translucent, about 3 to 4 minutes. Add the Dijon, white wine, and lemon peel. Continue to cook, uncovered, until reduced by about a third, about 5 minutes. Stir in the lemon juice. Cook for a few seconds longer. Season to taste with salt and pepper.

Ginger Sauce for Vegetables

Try this sauce with steamed or raw vegetables, tofu, or fish. You could also use it as a salad dressing. If you use a blender, the sauce will be smooth and you won't get any large lumps of gingerroot, but you could also just chop everything by hand.

 MAKES ABOUT ⅓ CUP

About a 2-inch piece fresh gingerroot
¼ cup soy sauce
2 tablespoons rice vinegar
Pinch of sugar
Dash of toasted sesame oil
1 green onion, chopped, green part only
Pepper, to taste

Peel the gingerroot and cut it into large, rough pieces. In a blender or food processor, combine the chopped gingerroot with the soy sauce, rice vinegar, and a pinch of sugar. Process until smooth. Stir in the sesame oil and green onion. Refrigerate for 10 to 15 minutes to combine the flavors. Season to taste with additional soy sauce, if desired, and pepper.

Pesto

aste the beautiful green of summer. Pesto can be used in pasta, beans, fresh vegetables, soup—just about anything that needs a good shot of flavor. If you want to make a vegan pesto, leave out the cheese, adding a few more pine nuts and a touch more salt.

🍐 MAKES ABOUT 1³/₄ CUPS

12 cloves garlic (about 1 head of garlic), peeled

4 cups fresh basil

¹/₃ cup pine nuts, or ¹/₃ cup hulled hemp seeds

¹/₂ cup grated Parmesan cheese

¹/₂–³/₄ cup olive oil

Salt and pepper, to taste

Process the garlic in a blender or food processor, turning it off once or twice if necessary to scrape big pieces off the sides, until finely chopped.

Add the basil and pine nuts. Pulse on and off a few times until finely chopped. Add the cheese and process until it's incorporated. With the motor running, add the olive oil in a steady stream until the pesto reaches the texture you like. Add salt and pepper to taste. Keep in mind that the cheese is salty.

Place the pesto in a bowl and cover. Refrigerate until you're ready to use it. The oil may separate while the pesto sits. If it does, just stir it right back in.

Roasted Garlic

Roasting tames garlic's mighty bite and turns it into a soft, earthy bit of heaven. It's great straight on bread, or mixed into mashed vegetables, soups, and beans. If you want to make more, just increase the recipe and wrap each head individually.

 MAKES 1 HEAD

1 head garlic
2 teaspoons extra-virgin olive oil
Salt and pepper, to taste

Preheat the oven to 425 degrees.
Peel off the papery outer skin of the garlic, leaving the head intact.

With a sharp knife, chop off a small bit of the top portion of the garlic. This will expose the top of the large, outer cloves and most of the inner cloves. Place the garlic on a square of aluminum foil large enough to wrap it. If you have a small garlic roaster, you can use it instead. Drizzle the garlic with oil. Wrap up the foil or put the top on the garlic roaster.

Roast for 40 to 50 minutes, or until the head is soft. When it's cool enough to handle, separate the cloves and squeeze out garlic. Save the oil to drizzle atop. Season to taste with salt and pepper.

Spinach Chutney

This bright green chutney packs a surprising amount of taste. It's a big, bold wallop of flavor that can liven up neutral flavors such as beans, tofu, or grains, or can stand up against your biggest, most complex spicy dishes.

 MAKES ABOUT 1 CUP

1 quart (4 cups) fresh spinach, finely chopped

1 large jalapeño pepper

$1/2$ cup sesame seeds

$1/4$ cup pine nuts

2 tablespoons mustard seeds

$1/2$ tablespoon neutral oil, such as soy or grapeseed

1 teaspoon curry powder

1 teaspoon ground cumin

Bring about an inch of hot water to a boil in a pot large enough to fit a steamer rack or steamer. When the water is rapidly boiling, place the spinach on the steamer or rack. Steam for 1 or 2 minutes, or until tender. Remove the spinach from the pot and set aside.

Place the jalapeño directly on the iron grill of a gas stove and cook until fully charred. Use tongs to turn it while it cooks. If you don't have a gas stove, place the pepper under the broiler until it's charred—a couple of minutes per side. Split the pepper in half and scrape out its seeds. Set aside.

In a dry frying pan over high heat, cook the sesame seeds until tan, just a minute or two. Remove them from the pan and set aside.

In the same dry frying pan over high heat, cook the pine nuts until light brown, just a minute or two. Remove from the pan and set aside.

Again using the same dry frying pan over high heat, roast the mustard seeds until they begin to pop, a minute or two. Remove from the pan and set aside.

Add the oil, curry powder, and cumin to the hot pan. Stir, immediately remove from the heat, and set aside.

Put the spinach, pepper, sesame seeds, mustard seeds, and cumin-curry blend into a blender or food processor, along with half the pine nuts. Pulse a few times until well blended.

Place the chutney on plate, surrounded by the remaining pine nuts.

Apricot Chutney

This is a great recipe if you're learning the art of canning. It's both sweet and acidic, and very easy to preserve. Fresh or preserved, it makes a wonderful accompaniment to any hot or cold main dish.

 MAKES ABOUT 9 CUPS

2 teaspoons salt

1 quart (4 cups) water

3½ pounds (about 30) firm apricots (pitted)

½ cup diced gingerroot

3½ pounds (about 9 cups) raw brown sugar

1½ cups cider vinegar

¼ cup Worcestershire sauce

2 large cloves garlic, peeled and minced

1 cup chopped white onions

¾ cup lime juice

¾ teaspoon ground dried ginger

½ teaspoon cayenne pepper

½ cup white raisins

½ cup dried currants

Salt and pepper, to taste

Put the salt and water in a large bowl. Place the apricots in the salted water and refrigerate for 24 to 36 hours. Drain.

In a small saucepan, cover the gingerroot with water. Cook over medium heat until almost tender, or about an hour. Drain and reserve the water. Save the cooked gingerroot to throw in a stir-fry or another dish.

In a saucepan, add the sugar, ginger water, vinegar, Worcestershire, garlic, and onions. Bring to a boil over medium-high heat. Add the drained apricots and remaining ingredients. Cook slowly until the apricots are translucent, about half an hour. Then take the apricots out of the pot and let everything else cook down to a thick, syrupy consistency, about 15 minutes.

Pulse the apricots and sauce together in a food processor, or mince the apricots finely by hand with a knife, adding them to a large bowl along with the sauce. Season to taste with salt and pepper.

Relish Your Zucchinis

hen the zucchinis in your garden are creeping up on your house and scratching at your windows, this recipe will take care of a few of them. It makes a beautiful relish for any festive BBQ or family meal.

MAKES ABOUT 6 PINTS

10 cups finely chopped zucchinis

4 cups finely chopped white or yellow onions

2 red or yellow peppers, seeded and chopped fine

1/4 cup sea salt

2 1/2 cups cider vinegar

6 cups raw brown sugar

1 tablespoon dry mustard

2 tablespoons celery seeds

1 tablespoon ground nutmeg

1 tablespoon ground turmeric

1 1/2 tablespoons cornstarch

Salt and pepper, to taste

Combine the zucchinis, onions, and peppers in a large bowl. Sprinkle the salt over the mixture and let stand overnight. Drain, rinse thoroughly, and drain again.

Combine the cider vinegar, sugar, mustard, celery seeds, nutmeg, turmeric, and cornstarch on the stove in a large pot, cooking slowly over medium heat for approximately 10 minutes, or until thickened.

In a large bowl, mix the liquid with the vegetables, season to taste with salt and pepper, and place the relish in glass jars. Chill for at least 30 minutes before serving. This relish should keep for a couple of weeks if refrigerated.

Mango Papaya Chutney

n the show, we served this with Jerk Fish (page 186). It will cut the fire from your spiciest dishes, and the way its sweet, earthy, and slightly acidic flavor blends with spices is something not to be missed.

MAKES ABOUT 3 CUPS

2 medium mangoes, peeled and cut
    from large pit
1 large papaya, peeled and seeded
1/4 cup dried apricots
Juice of 1 lime
2 tablespoons honey
1 tablespoon fresh mint leaves
Peel of 1 lime

In a blender or food processor, add about one-third of the mango, one-third of the papaya, and all the apricots, lime juice, honey, and mint. Puree.

Dice the remaining two-thirds of the papaya and mango.

In a large bowl, mix the pureed fruit, chopped fruit, and lime peel. Refrigerate until you're ready to serve, preferably at least an hour. Remove the lime peel before serving.

Fun with Compost!

While we throw everything from banana peels to the kitchen sink (literally) in the trash, nature loves to recycle. The earth grows the squash, you peel it and stick the scraps in the compost bin, and a few months later you have rich compost to grow the squash in again. Perfect and easy.

Composting is simple, even in a small, urban garden. The only requirements are a bin or a pile, some organic matter, and a little time. You can make your own bin or buy one online or in many garden stores. Some come with nifty hatches allowing you to pull the compost from the bottom when it's ready.

Once you have a bin, add green matter (kitchen scraps) and brown matter (leaves, twigs, or biodegradable paper and cardboard), and let nature do its work. Other than checking that you aren't getting too much or too little water, all you need to do is make sure that the compost gets some air.

To find out more about getting started, there are lots of resources. A couple of simple books without a lot of technical mumbo-jumbo are *Let It Rot!* by Stu Campbell, and *Worms Eat My Garbage* by Mary Appelhof. Or just check out the Internet, your local library, or the gardener down the street.

9. Desserts

Share the love. Dessert isn't about getting rid of your hunger or about feeding your body. It's about feeding your soul with joy. Nobody's grouchy mother ever made them sit at the table until they finished dessert. Dessert is indulgence and fun, and it's welcomed by almost everyone. It's about lingering a little bit longer around a table crowded with your friends and family.

Sweets are the center of many of our happiest memories throughout the world. When the annual period of Muslim fasting, Ramadan, ends, it is often celebrated with beautiful sweets. During Rosh Hashanah, Jews dip apples into honey to wish for a sweet year. Most Christian Christmas celebrations around the world are bursting with sweet desserts and treats. Even Halloween

started as a Pagan celebration. No matter what our religion or culture, we share a love of good things to eat the world over. We're all brothers and sisters under the skin, after all.

People often view eating vegan and vegetarian cuisine as some kind of sacrifice. In fact, living the hippy way isn't a sacrifice at all. It's a celebration of doing good and living well. It's about finding your joy and being true to yourself. It's about letting yourself find pleasure in even the simplest things, and living in each moment of every day. Dessert is about pure pleasure, and you don't have to eat cream or eggs to find that.

Giving pleasure to others is how we show our love and appreciation. When Bruce wanted to pay tribute to the men and women of San Francisco's fire department, he made some awesome treats to bring to the fire station. He knew that nothing makes a person feel loved quite like fresh baked goods, so he baked up his Oatmeal Raisin Cookies and Chocolate Chip Cookies from all-organic ingredients and with care. Both sent warm, wonderful aromas wafting through the house and filled everything with positive energy. Forget psychotherapy—a good cookie cures all! Those firefighters knew how much we loved and appreciated them when they tasted these homemade treats.

Of course, hippy cooking is also about being healthy and environmentally responsible, so eating cheesecake every day, even one made at home from completely organic ingredients, isn't really the hippy way. A few pieces of fruit picked at their peak can give as much pleasure as something elaborate. You don't have to make some big, over-the-top presentation of four-layer cake with a filling and a frosting. Dessert can be a small glass of liqueur or a cheese plate. In fact, ending a meal with sweets isn't the norm

in most of the world. Even in Europe, where sweets after the meal are common, you're more likely to see something small after dinner than an elaborate concoction. Although if you're Bruce and you're at Il Lùcumane in Castello di Populonia, Italy, be careful about asking to "sample" the desserts, because they'll bring you five of each kind!

Still, if you love creating something grand, that's all good, too. Quiet concentration on making something that requires care is a way of practicing Zen. Baking takes precision, love, and concentration. When tackled with the right spirit, it can be as relaxing and centering an experience as any form of meditation.

This chapter includes the simple and the complex. While we don't recommend indulging every day—and when you do, we recommend using organic and natural ingredients whenever possible—we also say that you should let loose and enjoy yourself once in a while. Do what feels right for you. Most of all, have a good time.

Apple Fig Compote

his simple compote is brown, rich, and gooey. It's a cross between a sauce and a cooked fruit dish. You could serve this with ice cream or yogurt, pound cake, or all by itself.

SERVES 4–6

2 fresh apples (such as Granny Smith
  or Fuji)
2 tablespoons butter
12 dried figs, cut in half, stems removed
1 cup brown sugar
1 cup sherry

Peel and core the apples. Slice them into quarters (or eighths if you have large apples).

Heat the butter in a heavy pan over an outdoor grill or over a medium-high flame on an indoor stove. When it's melted, add the apples. Cook until they're thoroughly heated but still have a bit of firmness, about 5 to 7 minutes. Add the figs. Stir. Add the brown sugar and cook until it's melted and a caramel-like sauce has formed, about 3 minutes more. Add the sherry. Cook until the mixture is hot, thickened, and bubbly, a minute or two more. Keep warm until you're ready to serve.

Caramel Sauce

Caramel sauce is nothing more than sugar cooked until it is almost, but not quite, burned. Fire makes it good, man. For a chocolate caramel sauce, stir in a bit of bittersweet or semisweet chocolate after you add the cream and omit the butter. Serve this sauce over ice cream, yogurt, cake, fruit, or whatever tastes best to you.

MAKES ABOUT 1¼ CUPS

1 cup sugar
⅓ cup heavy cream
1 tablespoon butter

Heat the sugar in a dry saucepan over a low to medium-low flame. Stir until it's melted and gold, about 5 to 7 minutes. Stop stirring, but shake the pan occasionally, and cook until the caramel is a deep gold, about 3 minutes more.

Remove the pan from the heat and very carefully pour in the cream (don't let the spattering caramel ruin your party by burning you!). Return the pan to the burner and stir until the sauce is smooth, a minute or two longer. Stir in the butter. Remove from the heat and serve warm, or refrigerate for later.

If you'll be serving this later, reheat over a low flame, stirring while you do.

Fruit with Mint Syrup

The simplest, truest-to-nature dessert is fresh fruit, but everything is better with a little taste of herb. This recipe uses fruit ripe at the height of the summer. If you're making it at another time of year, go with the fruit that looks best to you.

SERVES 4

¹/₂ cup sugar

¹/₂ cup water

1 cup fresh mint leaves

1 cup fresh cherries, pitted and halved

2 peaches, pitted and cut into slices

2 red plums, pitted and cut into quarters

Heat sugar, water, and mint in a small pot over a medium flame. Stir often, pushing down on the mint with a spoon to bring out its oils, and cook until the sugar dissolves and syrup comes to a boil, about 5 minutes. Remove from the heat and cool for a few minutes.

Over a small bowl, pour the syrup through a sieve. Discard the solids. Chill the syrup until it's cold, then mix with the fresh fruit. Serve right away, or refrigerate for a couple of hours to allow the flavors to meld together.

Vegan Applesauce Cake

ndrew Field, pastry chef of Ravens Restaurant at the Stanford Inn in Mendocino, California, prepared this Applesauce Cake on our show. He served his cake with fresh, organic blackberries from his garden; serve yours with whatever looks best in your neighborhood.

🍒 MAKES 1 CAKE

Oil cooking spray
1 cup whole wheat pastry flour
1 cup unbleached white flour
1 teaspoon baking soda
1 teaspoon baking powder
$1/2$ cup evaporated cane juice
1 cup applesauce
$1/2$ cup canola oil
$1/2$ cup maple syrup
$1^1/2$ teaspoons vanilla extract
2 teaspoons orange zest
2 tablespoons orange juice
1 teaspoon ground cinnamon
$1/4$ teaspoon ground cardamom
$1/4$ teaspoon ground nutmeg
Powdered sugar, to dust cake

Preheat the oven to 350 degrees. Spray a 9-inch springform pan with cooking spray and line the bottom with parchment paper.

Over a large bowl, sift together the dry ingredients: whole wheat and white flours, baking soda, baking powder, and evaporated cane juice. If you don't have a sifter, use a fine-mesh strainer or a colander with small holes.

In another bowl, whisk together the applesauce, canola oil, maple syrup, vanilla extract, orange zest and juice, cinnamon, cardamom, and nutmeg.

Whisk the wet ingredients into the dry until combined. Pour the mixture into the prepared pan. Bake for 25 minutes or until the center springs back when you touch it. Cool and remove from pan. If desired, dust with powdered sugar.

Orange Crepes

Flame it, man! These impressive crepes are packed with orange flavor—a bit like a cocktail on a plate. To avoid a soggy dessert, make these moments before serving.

🍒 SERVES 6–8

1 recipe Buckwheat Crepes (see page 33)
2 tablespoons butter
2 tablespoons orange marmalade
$\frac{1}{4}$ cup orange liqueur (such as triple sec)
$\frac{1}{4}$ cup orange juice
$\frac{1}{4}$ cup brandy
Powdered sugar, to dust
Orange slices, for garnishing

Fold the crepes into quarters to form wedges, then lay the wedges on top of one another to form two long lines of crepes that fit into the skillet and that you can handle with a spatula.

Heat the butter in a large skillet over a medium-high flame. Add both stacks of crepes to the pan, and when they're thoroughly heated (about 2 minutes), flip over. Add the marmalade and orange liqueur. Work the marmalade a bit with spoon to break it up. Add the orange juice. Cook down until a nice sauce forms around the crepes, about 3 to 4 minutes. Add the brandy and light with either a match or the stove's flame.

Remove the crepes to individual serving plates, sprinkling with powdered sugar and garnishing with orange slices.

Picking Fresh Fruit

Apples crisp from the tree in weather just cool enough to leave your skin tingling; blueberries almost bursting with sweetness in the hot summer sun; tiny, moist strawberries that are too perfect to ever be seen on a grocer's shelves: if you want the very best fruit, sometimes the only way is to go out and pick it yourself. Fruit doesn't grow in plastic bins; it grows on trees . . . literally! Or on bushes and vines, of course.

Picking fresh fruit is a great way to meet your local farmers, to experience the growing process, to make sure that your food is the absolute freshest available. And at many farms, you can pick heirloom varieties that are delicious, unique, and sometimes just plain strange. These are the fruits that, like us hippies, don't like being shipped in a container truck across the country; they are best when they're near the soil. If you have children, it's a wonderful way to get a little exercise while teaching them about the food they eat and where it comes from.

If you don't know where to start in your own area, ask at your local farmers' markets (many of the vendors are happy to let someone else do a bit of the work for a change) or go to www.pickyourown.org.

Oatmeal Fruit Crisp

This crisp recipe will work with any fresh, ripe fruit that you might see in a pie: Try peaches, berries, apples, nectarines, or pears. Use less sugar for sweet fruits such as very ripe peaches, and more sugar if your fruit is tart, like tart blueberries. For variety, add nuts, citrus zest, or spices to the topping.

SERVES 6

3¹/₂ cups fresh fruit

¹/₄–¹/₂ cup sugar

1 tablespoon cornstarch

¹/₃ cup whole wheat flour

1 cup rolled oats

Dash of salt

¹/₄ cup brown sugar

¹/₂ cup (1 stick) butter

Preheat the oven to 350 degrees. Grease an 8 × 8-inch baking pan.

In a bowl, mix the fruit, sugar, and cornstarch. Place in the prepared pan.

In another bowl, mix the flour, oats, salt, and brown sugar. With your fingertips, work in the butter until the mixture is crumbly. Top the fruit with this flour-oat mixture. Bake for 40 to 50 minutes or until the topping is browned and the fruit is bubbling.

Crème Brûlée

Hey, man, who said hippy cooking couldn't include a little richness sometimes? All right, blame Bruce's training in French kitchens for this dish. When you want something that's creamy and decadent, turn to this recipe.

🍒 SERVES 12

Butter to grease 12 small ramekins
    (4–6 ounces each)—approximately
    2 tablespoons
1 quart (4 cups) half-and-half
4 ounces (about ½ cup) sugar, divided
6 eggs
1 teaspoon vanilla extract
Enough brown sugar to coat the top of
    each crème brûlée (about ¼–⅓ cup
    total)

Grease the ramekins with a light coating of butter.

Using a double boiler with about an inch of water on the bottom, heat water until it bubbles. If you don't have a double boiler, you can use a panful of water and a heatproof bowl that fits over it without touching the water. Place the half-and-half in the top of the double boiler. Cook, whisking, for a couple of minutes, until it's hot and foamy. Don't boil it.

Add half the sugar to the half-and-half and set aside. If you'll be using the same double boiler pan for the next step, wash the top.

In a large bowl or the top of the double boiler, add the remaining sugar. Add the eggs and whisk over boiling water in the double boiler until foamy, about 3 to 4 minutes. Slowly add the hot half-and-half mixture and whisk until thick, about 5 to 7 minutes. Add the vanilla. Keep whisking until the mixture is thick enough to coat the back of a wooden spoon, another couple of minutes.

Ladle the mixture into the prepared ramekins. Chill overnight or at least 12 hours. When chilled, sprinkle a light coating of brown sugar on top. Using a blowtorch set on low, brown the sugar slightly. Be careful not to blacken it.

Oatmeal Cookies

This is the sweetest whole grain treat you've ever tasted—a bit like a cookie, a bit like trail mix, and all good. The only warning: When you're mixing the batter, start slowly to make sure all your oats don't go flying all over the place!

MAKES ABOUT 5 DOZEN

2 cups unbleached white flour

1 teaspoon baking powder

$^1\!/_2$ cup (1 stick) butter, plus extra
    for buttering pans

$1^1\!/_2$ cups brown sugar

2 egg whites

$^1\!/_2$ cup honey

$^1\!/_2$ teaspoon salt

1 teaspoon ground cinnamon

2 cups rolled oats

$1^1\!/_4$ cups walnut pieces

$^1\!/_2$ cup dried dates, chopped

$^1\!/_2$ cup dried currants

$^1\!/_4$ cup dried cranberries

7 dried apricots, diced small

1 dried pineapple ring, diced small

1 large piece dried mango, diced small

Preheat the oven to 375 degrees.

Over a large bowl, sift together the flour and baking powder. If you don't have a sifter, use a fine-mesh strainer or a colander with small holes.

In another bowl, using a mixer or working by hand with a wooden spoon, mix the butter and brown sugar for about 1 minute. Add the egg whites and honey. Mix for a couple of minutes until well blended. Add the flour mixture, salt, cinnamon, and oats. Mix for 2 to 3 minutes, or until evenly blended. Add the walnuts and dried fruits and mix until evenly distributed, about a minute more.

Grease a cookie sheet well. Drop on the batter by tablespoonfuls. Bake for 8 to 10 minutes, or until the cookies look almost done. Remove them from the oven, putting them on a cooling rack.

Bake the remaining batter in same manner.

Chocolate Chip Pecan Cookies

These are simple, homey, honest-to-goodness chocolate chip cookies. While you shouldn't fool yourself that this is health food, at least they're a lot healthier, and taste far better, than anything that comes out of a box.

MAKES ABOUT 4 DOZEN

3$\frac{1}{2}$ cups unbleached white flour

1 teaspoon baking soda

1$\frac{1}{2}$ cups butter-flavored vegetable
     shortening (trans-fat-free)

2 cups dark brown sugar

$\frac{1}{2}$ cup light brown sugar

$\frac{1}{4}$ cup milk

2 teaspoons vanilla extract

2 large eggs

$\frac{1}{2}$ teaspoon salt

2 cups semisweet chocolate chips

1–2 cups pecan pieces (or walnuts or
     cashews)

Preheat the oven to 375 degrees.

Over a large bowl, sift together the flour and baking soda. If you don't have a sifter, use a fine-mesh strainer or a colander with small holes.

In another large bowl, with an electric mixer or working by hand with a wooden spoon, mix the shortening and sugars until creamy, about 3 minutes. Add the milk, vanilla, and eggs. Mix for about 2 minutes. Add the flour mixture and salt. Mix until the dough comes together, about 2 minutes. Add the chocolate chips and pecans. Mix until distributed evenly, about 1 minute.

Drop the dough by tablespoonfuls onto an ungreased cookie sheet. Bake for 8 to 10 minutes, or until the cookies look almost done. Remove the sheet from the oven and, with a spatula, place the cookies on a cooling rack.

Repeat this baking procedure with the remaining batter.

Mocha Mousse

This dessert tastes dark and strong, yet it's as soft and light as a cloud. Because it's very rich and makes a whole lot of servings, it's best for a very special occasion, such as New Year's Eve, Christmas, or a good case of the munchies. *Note:* Because this dessert contains raw eggs, it should be avoided by pregnant women and anyone with a compromised immune system. Alternatively, these individuals may substitute pasteurized eggs, available in health food stores and some supermarkets.

SERVES 12–16

12 ounces (about 1½–2 cups) semisweet chocolate chips
2–3 tablespoons strong brewed coffee
1 teaspoon instant coffee
6 eggs, separated
⅔ cup sugar, divided
1 pint (2 cups) whipping cream
1 tablespoon vanilla extract

Bring water to a rapid boil in the bottom of a double boiler. In the top of the boiler, melt the chocolate chips, coffee, and instant coffee, stirring occasionally. If you don't have a double boiler, use a large pan with a heat-proof bowl that fits into it without touching the boiling water. Pour the melted mixture into a bowl and beat in the egg yolks with a whisk. Refrigerate.

In another bowl, beat the egg whites and ⅓ cup of the sugar until it forms stiff peaks, about 3 minutes. Set aside.

Beat the cream with the remaining sugar and vanilla until it holds soft peaks, about 3 minutes. Stir a couple of spoonfuls of the egg mixture into the chocolate to lighten it a bit, then fold in the remaining whites thoroughly but gently. Fold in the cream. Refrigerate until chilled. Serve within a day or two.

Tiramisu

Everything's better with a bit of screech, that wild Newfoundland rum—or at least it seems so with enough of it in you. If you can't find screech, use any dark rum. This version of tiramisu is packed with flavor. *Note:* Because it contains raw eggs, this dessert should be avoided by pregnant women and anyone with a compromised immune system. Alternatively, these individuals may substitute pasteurized eggs, available in health food stores and some supermarkets.

SERVES 12–16

9 egg whites

1 cup sugar, divided

1½ pounds marscapone cheese, room temperature

1 teaspoon vanilla extract

2 cups brewed espresso

½ cup amaretto

¼ cup screech

48 ladyfingers

½ cup cocoa powder

½ cup espresso powder

In a large bowl, beat the egg whites with a bit of sugar, adding the rest of ½ cup sugar as you whip. Continue whipping until soft peaks form, about 3 to 4 minutes. Set aside.

In another bowl, beat the marscapone until it's fluffy, about 2 to 3 minutes. Fold into the egg whites. Add the vanilla and set aside.

In another bowl, mix the remaining ½ cup of sugar, brewed coffee, amaretto, and screech. Soak ladyfingers in this coffee mixture for about half a minute or less.

In a large pan (about 15 × 11 inches), spread a thin layer of the marscapone mixture. Lay half the ladyfingers in even rows atop the marscapone layer. Top with half the remaining marscapone mixture, spreading until smooth. Repeat with the remaining ladyfingers and marscapone mixture.

Using a small strainer, sprinkle with cocoa, then with espresso powder.

Insert small skewers into the tiramisu and cover with plastic wrap (the skewers are meant to keep the plastic from touching the tiramisu directly and ruining the surface). Refrigerate overnight and serve.

A Special Thanks

The Hippy Gourmet is dedicated to changing the world one plate at a time, but we depend upon countless others to help us work for good. These organizations create positive change every day. Please give your time and your money to the men and women who work to make this a better world for all of us.

American Community Garden Association. An organization dedicated to creating community greening. Find out more at www.communitygarden.org.

American Red Cross. The Red Cross is a humanitarian organization providing relief to victims of disasters and helping people prevent, prepare for, and respond to emergencies. Find out more at www.redcross.org.

America's Second Harvest. A network of food banks and food-rescue organizations (such as Community Harvest) collecting and distributing food to those in need. Find out more at www.secondharvest.org.

CARE. Working especially close with women, this organization helps families and communities throughout the world escape poverty. Find out more at www.care.org.

Co-op America. An organization working to harness economic power to achieve a socially just and environmentally sustainable society. Find out more at www.coopamerica.org.

Global Exchange. A human rights organization dedicated to achieving social, economic, and environmental justice around the world. Find out more at www.globalexchange.org.

Green Festivals. A joint project of Global Exchange and Co-op America, Green Festivals sponsors two-day events at which local and national socially responsible businesses and community organizations come together to create positive solutions for the community and the environment. Find out more at www.greenfestivals.org.

Institute for Solar Living. An organization promoting sustainable living through environmental education. Find out more at www.solarliving.org.

Monterey Bay Aquarium. A beautiful aquarium on Monterey Bay as well as an organization dedicated to conservation and research. Find out more at www.mbayaq.org.

Performing Animal Welfare Society (PAWS). Provides a place where abandoned or abused performing animals, as well as victims of the exotic animal trade, can live lives of peace and dignity. Find out more at www.pawsweb.org.

Slow Foods USA. An organization working toward a food system that is based on high quality and taste, environmental responsibility, and social justice. Find out more at www.slowfoodusa.org.

The South Yuba River Citizens League (SYRCL). An organization dedicated to preserving, protecting, and restoring the South Yuba River Watershed. Find out more at www.syrcl.org.

Index